A. E 'Bert' Smith

A.E. Smith worked in the Royal Docks from 1947 until their demise three decades later and he was an eye-witness to the last generation of dockers who used traditional dock working skills. He was also the last of three generations of dockers who together spanned the Royals at their most vigorous. A wealth of experience is contained within these pages. Bert Smith was born and grew up in East Ham where he, in his turn, raised his family, later moving to Wanstead. He spent his retirement years living near Cheltenham.

LONDON'S ROYAL DOCKS IN THE 1950s:
A Memory of the Docks at Work

This account introduces people, predicaments and cargo types as A. E. Smith knew them both as a tally clerk and later as a ship's clerk working for Royal Mail Lines. It is a personal recollection of the men he worked alongside and the conditions they had to face in the five holds of a working ship. Wide ranging yet detailed, this record describes techniques which in many areas, were little changed from Victorian times. This is a gentle, non-academic introduction to a harsh environment now long extinct.

docksatwork@hotmail.co.uk

First published 2008

ISBN: 978-1-4092-5956-5

Front cover: Detail of the General Arrangement Plan for RML *'Highland Chieftain'* by kind permission of the National Maritime Museum, Greenwich.

Back cover: Detail of the Capacity Plan for RML *'Highland Chieftain/ Highland Brigade'* by kind permission of the National Maritime Museum, Greenwich.

To the memory of my Father, Grandfather, Great grandfather and the generations of dockers who worked with them in the Royal Docks.

Contemporary record of Imports for the year 1958 showing the dominance of sugar, grain and meat cargoes. Incidentally the record also indicates the decline in bagged sugar (see main text).

Ex 32 R.M.L. Ships from West Indies

Ex 6 R.M.L. Ships from Brazil (General)

Ex 20 R.M.L. Ships from North Pacific
Ex 10 Ships H.A.L. from North Pacific

Ex 32 P.S.N. Ships from West Coast South America

Ex 35 R.M.L. Ships from River Plate & Brazil (Refrigerated)   Mea
                                                               Fru
                                                               Gen

———
135

Tons discharged ex 102 Ships during 1953 - 455,396
Tons discharged ex 116 Ships during 1954 - 525,825
Tons discharged ex 127 Ships during 1955 - 592,058
Tons discharged ex 127 Ships during 1956 - 599,478
Tons discharged ex 124 Ships during 1957 - 542,030

D E P A R T M E N T.

O HANDLED DURING 1958.

	Tons Weight	Tons Meast.	
	215,463	246,835	(Inc. 165,470 Tons Bulk Sugar)
	19,660	25,349	(Inc. 2,462 Tons Bulk Wheat)
	85,224	91,460	(Inc. 58,973 Tons Bulk Wheat)
	22,724	28,516	(Inc. 11,407 Tons Bulk Wheat)
	109,625	106,035	(Inc. 54,000 Tons Bulk Sugar and 2,004 " Bagged Sugar)
Meat	119,060)		
Fruit	11,143)	139,581	
General	9,378)		
	592,277	637,774	

398	Weight	542,820	Meast.
825	Weight	587,190	Meast.
058	Weight	664,344	Meast.
478	Weight	648,250	Meast.
030	Weight	606,595	Meast.

LONDON'S ROYAL DOCKS IN THE 1950s

A MEMORY OF THE DOCKS AT WORK

The Royal Group of Docks

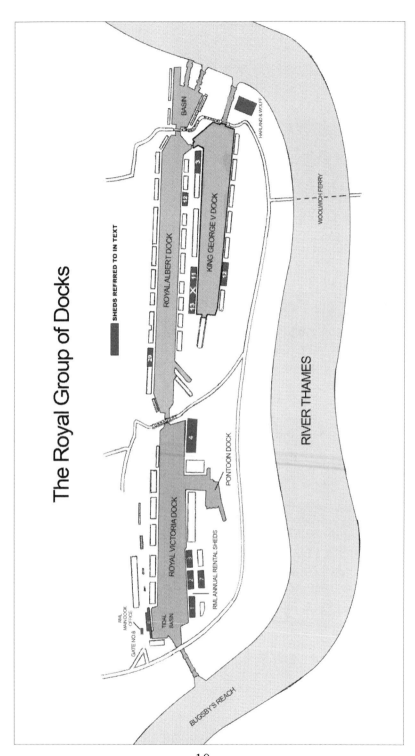

CONTENTS

CHAPTERS

END PIECES

ACKNOWLEDGEMENTS

Getting this record from being a scruffy collection of notes heaped in a cardboard box to its present form has taken the best efforts of various members of our family. First I must mention my late mother, Wendy, for her early typed versions then my wife, Jenny, and daughter, Tean for committing them in different forms to a computer. Next I should thank my son, Guy, for suggesting this method of production and pointing us in the right direction. Finally here I must thank Lucy Orgill for her assistance in producing the graphics.

Although actual research has been minimal I should like to thank, on my father's behalf, all those who responded by telephone or letter to his requests for clarification on a number of points. This was entirely his initiative and unfortunately he has not left a list of colleagues he consulted over the years. Our thanks to all those who helped. I must personally thank Jack Blackburn for lending me the minute book from his father's union meetings, it was very much appreciated.

Finally I should like to thank Graham Thompson at the National Maritime Museum for his advice and diligence in producing the ship's plans which decorate the front and back covers. My thanks also for letting me reproduce them.

MES

Finally, having seen for myself the opaque mask that the Royal Group of Docks now wears, it seem to me even more necessary to have this commentary on the life and people who once made today's pondscape relevant. My renewed thanks to Jenny and to Damian for helping me get this revised version up and running.

MES   August 2019

As I began helping my father with this record it became very clear how little I knew of this world. He became bored trying to explain points which to him were blindingly obvious and so there had to be a level of interpretation here with all the inherent scope for omission and distortion. Asking colleagues to confirm details, my father usually found that his own memory was the more solid and as time went on, it became disconcertingly evident that there was often no one left for him to ask. My father's memory alone had to suffice. Time was fast running out and in areas it became down to me to make what I could of these stories as I understood them.

This work is limited in another important way which must be mentioned. The process of 'turning a ship round' consisted of two distinct operations: discharging imports and re-loading exports. My father spent the majority of his time in the docks as an import clerk for Royal Mail Lines (RML). The equally important work of loading ships in consequence is not covered and we can only hope that other accounts have been recorded which will redress the balance. It is also the case that as a record of one man's memory it is necessarily partial; my father worked for Royal Mail Lines in the Royal Group of Docks. How things were done at Port Line or Blue Star or across the water at the Surrey Commercial Docks, as examples, are outside the scope of this work.

The time frame of this record deals mainly with the nineteen fifties but ranges across the two decades after the Second World War: incidents are included if they are thought informative rather than keeping the work to an exact time frame – my father found it easier to remember through cargo types and incidents rather than by year on year. This was a period of great transition as older men who had kept the docks functioning through the War and had learnt their disciplines in the earlier decades of the twentieth century, gave way to younger men who had no intention of grafting with the commitment of their elders. With minimal equipment, tightly knit gangs were essential to the docks in 1945 and the London docks themselves were essential to Britain's recovery. By 1965 containers, mechanisation, the transformation of Tilbury and a whole raft of innovations were altering the perception of what it meant to work in docks. Once mechanisation took over, old skills were lost and the new, efficient computer based business of dock work replaced physical toughness.

The older docks of London were becoming irrelevant. This account does not try to analyse these changes but simply introduces them as incidents demand. Our interest is with the older gangs and their traditional way of working which sets most events here within the period 1947-1960.

A further point needs making; my father was not a political man. He had no interest in the industrial relations of the time or in the transformations and ultimate demise of the docks beyond how they directly affected the work.

This record deals only with how things were done and as far as possible, with how things were done at their best. There was an excellence about the way the older men worked, especially those in the general cargo gangs, a definite series of skills which accumulated might constitute a craft in its own right. Others are better qualified to discuss industrial relations.

Finally it must be recognised that the incidents which stood out in my father's memory tended to be the exceptional. It might seem from this account that the docks were one long series of misadventures but the reality was of course that the country was fed, industry resurrected and the Nation rebuilt to a considerable extent on the flow of merchandise which passed through the docks day after day in a grinding monotony. By avoiding these ordinary successes we hope also to side step a deal of the monotony – but we should not forget it.

MES

Mrs Bryden used to say despairingly at her social gatherings that if your husband worked in the docks, he was a docker. Her husband, Capt. Ron Bryden, ran the ship surveying company of Edwin C. Waters and was a professional and well educated man but the stigma of working in the docks made him to the outside world, a docker. At least so Mrs Bryden believed. There was some truth in this surveyors had to acknowledge, for if one of their number were travelling home by train after a day spent down a hold assessing fishmeal, it would have been of little use for him to attempt to explain to his swooning fellow passengers that he was not, in fact, a docker but had simply acquired some of their more pungent attributes. More properly, 'docker' was a contraction of 'dockworker' but in order to maintain distinctions we felt it better to stay with the latter term when definitely not referring to stevedores, clerks, supervisors etc. The upshot for us here given the possible confusions, is that, rightly or wrongly, we have tended to use the word 'docker' sparingly.

Royal Mail Lines and its earlier incarnation, the Royal Mail Steam Packet Company, were universally known in the docks as 'Royal Mail'. Head Office in Leadenhall Street was called 'Royal Mail House' and the employee's society was the 'Royal Mail Association'. At that time post was delivered by the GPO – the General Post Office – an unrelated organisation which, as we remember it, only became 'Royal Mail' in common parlance when Royal Mail Lines as a shipping company had become all but extinct. The two services had nothing in common except that they both delivered mail, one on land the other by sea. To avoid any possible confusion in this work, we have referred throughout to Royal Mail Lines (RML) – but for authenticity you should drop the 'L' as you read.

Spelling has been a particular problem when referring to people; for years my father worked alongside men whose names he knew but rarely saw written down; then it didn't matter but here it is possibly a source of embarrassment. We apologise to families for errors which may have arisen in our interpretations of names.

One slightly sticky point must be mentioned. We have decided to refer only to Imperial measure, avoirdupois and £sd. It was the system which was ingrained into every aspect of dock work from stowage capacities to rates of pay. For some of us the idea of metrication sits uncomfortably in this post-War world: Messerschmitts were metric, Spitfires, feet and inches.

AES & MES

ROYAL MAIL LINES, LIMITED

TELEGRAMS:
INLAND: ROYMAILINE STOCK LONDON.
FROM ABROAD: ROYMAILINE LONDON.

TELEPHONE:
MANSION HOUSE 0522 (PRIVATE BRANCH EXCHANGE)

ALL COMMUNICATIONS TO BE
ADDRESSED TO THE COMPANY.

AGENTS FOR:
THE PACIFIC STEAM NAVIGATION C?

ROYAL MAIL HOUSE,
LEADENHALL STREET,

LONDON, E.C.3.

YOUR REFERENCE ....   OUR REFERENCE   SEC/S   25th September, 1953.

Dear Sir,

     We confirm our offer to you of an appointment in the
Company's service at our Victoria Dock Office, at a commencing
salary of £9.10/- per week, with effect from Monday, 5th October,
1953. Will you please, therefore, report to the London Marine
Superintendent on that date as arranged.

     In the event of your absence from duty through illness at
any time after you have completed one year's service with the
Company, you will be entitled to full pay (less National Insurance
benefit, if any) for a period not exceeding four weeks. If at the
end of such period you are still incapacitated from work, or if
you again become incapacitated within a period of six months, the
question of your future employment and an "ex gratia" grant of any
further payment in respect of wages will receive consideration
according to the circumstances of the case. Any payment made to
you by the Company during absence from any cause prior to the
completion of one year's service would be "ex gratia".

     This appointment, as customary, will be subject to
termination by one week's notice on either side.

     Please acknowledge receipt of this letter on the enclosed
copy of it.

                  Yours faithfully,
          ROYAL MAIL LINES, LIMITED,

                      Secretary.

Mr. A.E. Smith.

18

Before looking at how the docks moved cargoes back in 1947 it might be useful to mention a few, admittedly disparate, points which struck me quite forcibly when I first started working in the industry.

When he retired as first chairman of the Port of London Authority (PLA), Sir Hudson Kearley, one time MP for Devonport – Lord Devonport – famously declared in 1925 that if he had done nothing else as chairman at least he had starved the dockers into submission. My father would have worked under his chairmanship and his generation would have appreciated with some clarity what Lord Devonport meant. Unfortunately my father missed this unpleasant little boast for after having spent the War years loading ammunition ships down river he finally succumbed in 1920 to the consumption that he had lived with since childhood. The point though is that if he had lived he would have been one of that generation who, too old in 1939 for active service, had kept the docks going during the Blitz and through the early years of reconstruction that followed. His brother, my Uncle Ned, still worked there – by which time Devonport was just a nasty taste in the mouth – and had done so through the tough times of the inter-war years. This book is not about politics but it is about work and if we wonder why men worked as they did in the forties and early fifties in conditions that now beggar belief it is as well to remember the decades they had already spent in the docks before the Welfare State or the National Health Service. When I entered the docks, it was this older generation who continued to make the docks work and it was their way of working that this book is mostly concerned with: they could work with an intensity and discipline that had once been essential but which now, in those post-war years they realised, was becoming optional. Younger men a decade later expected an easier life.

One of my earliest recollections was a conversation I had with a crane driver. I had been standing all morning tallying the cargoes he was depositing on the quay – properly a 'landing clerk' – perhaps some three or four weeks after I started in the docks. The job was mind numbing and static with no way of escaping the sharp river wind but as it happened, things had been given a bit of zest by the quay foreman who was keen for me to let crates of fruit through to the black market. The crane driver up in his cabin saw what was going on and appeared to approve of my stance, in any case for some reason he seemed to take a shine to me. I was new and I liked to sleep at night so what came over on the end of the crane hook, I recorded. The foreman though, as he saw his backhanders evaporating got increasingly irate until by lunch time he was ready to physically lay into me. A year before I was still a physical training instructor in the Navy so he would have had to have taken his chances but before we actually got to trading blows, the crane driver who had also stopped for lunch came down from his cabin and ambled over to us. He was a large, solid man who had spent a lifetime in the docks, knew everyone, was a highly regarded operator and a member of one of the very best gangs – not someone to get on the wrong side of. He was known to everyone for another reason though; his most distinctive feature was a huge, misshapen, purple nose. Horrible it was. How the poor chap acquired it, accident, birth or disease I do not know and I never knew anyone brave enough to ask him. He was universally known as 'Blue Nose', though it was healthier not to call him it to his face. His misfortune was so wretchedly self-evident that it seemed to lend him increased stature among the work force –he was one of the pillars of the dock community. As he came across, the foreman broke off and left in a hurry. "Don't worry about 'im mate" said Blue Nose "I know 'im – and my father knew 'is father. Came in in 1912….." The significance became clear. He would have been one of the strike breakers brought in to undermine the dockers' struggle for an adequate living wage. Old enmities as well as old loyalties, I was learning, ran deep.

The well known description from the ship owners' journal 'Fairplay' dated 17th July 1891 that 'The simple docker alone, for whose purpose a turnip would answer for a head and a round of beef for brains, must have everything regulated for him….' Is not worthy of comment except to say that there were men still working in the docks who had been there in 1890's. Now in their seventies they were reduced to being needlemen and tally clerks but with their reputations still in tact amongst the gangers they were honoured survivors and forebears. These ancients had seen world wars come and go and had known seriously tough times; maybe the fledgling Welfare State would last but thank you, while they could they preferred to keep working. The community as well as the memory of these dockers went back a long way.

In those early days I was casually employed picking up work where I could. I worked for any number of different companies as a tally clerk but gradually I began to realise that there were patterns of engagement within the overall process of the labour force getting work. If someone at the Call liked the way you set about your job they looked out for you when they next needed a clerk, it was nothing official just a system of mutual confidences building up. Through this process I found myself increasingly being engaged to work on Royal Mail Lines' ships and I began to recognise faces, ships and gangs. The system was fluid and undergoing rapid change but for a while, and very useful for me, I discovered a consistency of engagement among the labour force. Ship gangs, I realised followed a shipworker. This will be covered more fully later but in essence, a stevedoring company, Furness, Withy, was contracted to off-load all the general cargoes on RML ships. Their representative on a working ship was the shipworker and it was he who engaged gangs at the Call to empty holds. Through good times and bad, particularly the bad, loyalties built up between gangs and shipworkers to such an extent that to see a shipworker on the top deck of a working ship meant to know, as often as not, the five gangs working the holds. The shipworker had confidence in the way the men worked, they knew their work was good enough for re-engagement and RML was happy that men who knew their ships and holds and had experience moving their cargoes were back on board. Gangs were only as good as their last engagement so maintaining standards was important and it was the skills of these men that so impressed me. This system was derided later and you can argue it which way you like, but for me the greatness of the docks was the way these tight, disciplined gangs worked.

'Ory Mantelow - his name was Horace but 'Ory' got you further – had one of the best 'White' gangs working exports – sometimes imports - in the docks. He had the prestigious No 2 holds and worked almost exclusively for Furness, Withy which meant that as a tally clerk on RML ships I got to see a good deal of him and his men. There was one man in 'Ory's gang, the time would have been the late forties, who was always miserable. As the new boy trying to establish links, I tried to be pleasant to him but he just didn't want to know, always seemed to have a chip on his shoulder. This distancing didn't seem to be personal for as far as I could see he was like this with everyone. He put in his share of work and if he wanted to live in a misanthropic world of his own, I decided, that was his business. Suddenly he stopped turning up for work, 'Ory found a replacement and I never saw him again.   Later I found out that he had become too ill to work and I understood that it was consumption. His health gradually declined and he died about a year later, I learnt. I wondered if he had always had the disease and that pulling his weight in a physically demanding job left no energy for pleasantries. He was not old, early thirties I would have said, about the same age that my father died twenty seven years earlier. The point though was this: when he was housebound and no longer able to be an effective member of his gang and when there was no possibility of him recovering, the rest of the gang did not desert him. The Welfare State might have been up and running but each week without fail there was a whip round for him and a couple of men from his gang would go round to see him, taking it in turns, keeping him up with the news and handing over a couple of oranges or grapefruit or whatever they could smuggle out during this time of strict rationing. In those days the toughness of a gang was not just physical.

RESPONSIBILITIES

The Royal Docks existed to move cargoes, not passengers. In the days before containers each commodity made its presence felt and gangs knew all too intimately what they were working, usually by the ton load. Import gangs which specialised on one particular commodity such as meat or grain had some idea of what each day might bring of course but the vagaries of the crossing might have thrown up a few surprises.

General cargo gangs by their very nature had less idea of what they might be facing and as a consequence, what they might earn. A ship which had encountered heavy weather might have scattered loads and smashed crates in their hundreds. A hundredweight bag stowed directly under a hatch was a different proposition to one squeezed down a narrow passage; and while oranges were a precious luxury after the war, rotting oranges in a hold were just refuse. Prior knowledge of what each shipment held went part of the way to understanding what the gangs would have to contend with but how the goods were stowed and the level of damage involved could significantly affect working conditions. A major factor was the way different goods in different countries might be stowed, how they were packaged or the level of mechanisation available to them; this of course bore no relationship to the modest, bomb damaged equipment on offer to gangs in London. (See the sections on 'sugar').

Damaged goods were a huge problem not only for gangs but also ship's clerks. Gangs were paid on piece-work rates, dealing with damaged items slowed them down and they expected compensation. The question naturally was by how much had they been slowed down and what level of compensation was appropriate?

Equally damaging financially for the shipping company was the response of importers. A broken crate of apples might leave most of the fruit sound and capable of repackaging but if an importer could claim the loss of a whole crate he stood to make a tidy profit. Surveyors were employed by importers to assess the state of a cargo and it was their function to find reasons why compensation needed to be paid by the shippers. Attributing responsibility required good memories and sound monitoring. And all this before goods had left the hold.

Once cargoes were on the move, responsibilities became more complex. Because of Britain's long maritime history different shipping companies had evolved along different lines. Blue Star for example was the shipping branch of a much larger organisation, carrying the cargoes the parent company needed and arranging their movements as an in house operation. Royal Mail Lines (RML) on the other hand had always concentrated on her fleet and trade routes – particularly the case after the War as her South American assets had been sold off by the Government. Thus RML had a large fleet capable of carrying a high percentage of the trade Britain's survival depended upon but had no means by itself, of loading or discharging ships. To cover this work RML used the services of three different stevedoring companies in the Royal Docks. So it was that the shipping company was responsible for the cargoes it carried while the ship was at sea but for general cargoes, for example, Furness, Withy (FW) was responsible for getting imported goods out of the holds safely. To further complicate matters shipments could either leave by road – very occasionally by train – or by lighterage, each importer making their own arrangements for their preferred means of transport. There was also the possibility for importers of storing goods in the docks' transit sheds where they became the responsibility of the Port of London Authority (PLA). It doesn't take much imagination to understand the vast scope that existed, if goods arrived finally at their importer's destination damaged or late, for creative buck passing. Records at every stage had to be meticulously maintained.

In older, simpler times merchants would hurry down to the docks to see their shipments off-loaded and the whole quayside would be alive with traders and merchants bargaining over the latest imports. Gradually quayside trading disappeared and by the post-War period most importers were never seen in the docks, they just 'phoned Head Office in the City to say what they expected to happen. In this Byzantine world it was essential that the shipping company had direct representation as each item was off-loaded from each hold. Tally clerks recorded goods out of a hold, others noted them onto the quay or in a lighter, while yet more would see them onto a lorry. The overall responsibility for producing water tight records for the shipping company and for being aware of situations where claims, genuine or creative, might be advanced was the lot of the ship's clerk. He worked outdoors on the top deck of a ship watching the developments in and out of all five holds.

One final responsibility needs to be mentioned, namely the ship as transport. While RML dock staff were responsible for discharging the range of commodities stowed in each hold – for them the vessel operated as a static storage unit - the ship was still a ship. Dock staff dealt with cargoes and holds while a relieving officer, usually a retired ship's captain, took up residence in and was responsible for protecting, the nautical aspects of the ship: bridge, engine rooms, accommodation and so on. These areas were strictly out of bounds to dockers as far as was practically possible. Most relieving officers did their best to disassociate themselves from the workings of the docks, and frequently from their RML dock colleagues. Prohibiting access was a major part of their brief.

As I spent most of my time in the docks as a ship's clerk for Royal Mail Lines much of this record, directly or indirectly, touches on aspects of the job. There are a few background points though that might be worth making at this early stage just to set the scene.

A general cargo vessel of RML would take roughly three months making the round trip between London and the Americas. During that period the ship would call at pre-arranged ports (typically around seven) according to her itinerary to off-load British exports then tour the region picking up local exports for the return journey. This was not a random operation. Patterns had developed according to which produce was in season and there were always staples such as sugar or grain to be carried. Occasionally there were surprises but on the whole an experienced ship's clerk could predict, knowing the ship, the time of year and its ports of call, what range of cargoes she would contain.

Beyond the safe storage and value of cargoes, the master, officers and crew had only modest interest in what was being carried, apart from the fact that it was paying them their wages. Once the ship berthed her master reported to Head Office then, like the rest of the crew, went off on shore leave. So long as the ship was transport, particularly if she was carrying passengers, the crew were gainfully involved. At berth she had effectively become a floating warehouse, had lost her glamour and senior officers wisely distanced themselves. This was reflected in the attitudes of many of the relieving officers in their minds their ship seemed more an extension of the City, only the holds belonged to the docks and those had become the responsibility of the ship's clerk.

For the dock staff this was a problem. In the nature of things, Head Office and the senior management tended to be retired ship's officers sympathetic to difficulties at sea such as heavy weather but they became testy over problems of working cargoes. On the whole Head Office staff wanted to get no closer to the docks than the end of a telephone; their preferred focus was the passenger liners out of Southampton.

Stevedoring companies had their own priorities: they had a responsibility to see that goods their men discharged deteriorated no more than the state they found them in in the ship's holds but their chief responsibility was to their gangs not RML. As part of their duty they would try to maximise their men's earnings at the expense, naturally, of the shipping company. Bill Saggers used to say and I don't know how frivolously he meant it that before the War you had to have been in prison to work for Furness, Withy. It was a way of reminding newer staff that the two representatives, shipper and stevedore, might be working alongside each other looking down into a ship's hold but their respective companies' interests were very different.

So different were the regimes of the three stevedoring companies RML dealt with that to ship's clerks they felt like different jobs, each had their own working methods, priorities and ambience. Some goods needed their own system of management: meat, rum, copper, and fruit for example all needed specific controls which were not always straightforward given the conditions. Add to this the need to work in different units, Imperial tons and American short tons for example, and it should be clear that some degree of mental agility was useful for a ship's clerk. In these days before calculators competent mental arithmetic was essential.

In retrospect one of our major handicaps was limited communication. The dock offices had a few 'phones but import ship's clerks had to go to where each ship berthed and this was, more often than not, nowhere near our bases. The whole organisation relied on a group of runners who constantly carried messages and paperwork around the docks and up to the City. It was the system the docks had got used to and had to work with but in difficult situations, and there were many, responses could be a long time coming.

We shouldn't overlook the fact that this was a dangerous environment; five working holds each with crane tackle weighed half a ton bearing a two ton set skimming the coamings left no scope for complaicency, these were not things you wanted to get in the way of. I was fortunate, the worst that happened to me was a crack on the leg: one afternoon late when we were trying to get a job finished, as the crane came over, the ball hit the top hatch coamings with some force. A large case of machinery six feet high, four feet deep and about eighteen inches wide had been placed away from the hatch ready to be re-stowed for an on-going port while the rest of the hold was being cleared. It was top heavy and the thump of the crane ball sent it toppling over. I had my back to it and leapt out of the way as people shouted but it caught my calf and ankle. Nothing was broken but it was bad enough for a trip to hospital. Inevitably there were other close shaves but as I said, I was lucky.

Uncle Ned was not so fortunate. Hatches were always dangerous places and the deeper gangs excavated into the holds the more serious the threat. Sometime between the wars he caught his foot on the coamings as he dodged a set in mid trajectory and he fell a long way into the hold. He was in a coma for thirteen weeks and never fully recovered; from then on he always had hunched shoulders and his face was somehow incapable of expression, set permanently in a rigid grimace. He was known in the docks as 'Smiler'.

*   *   *

CHARLTONS
Occasionally, as a tally clerk, I worked for Uncle Ned's firm of Charltons. To cut costs they never employed a Port Clerk which meant that while tallying goods onto Brocklebank Wells ships, a tally clerk had to measure cubic capacity, note type, destination, exporter's mark and quantity as delivery gangs were taking sets to the ship's side - and all this without delaying the gang's work. I only worked there a few times!

With the cargoes above it already removed, twenty feet down in a hold something like 1,500 – 2,000 tons of neatly stowed sugar in 2cwt bags would lay across the bottom of a ship's lower hold in rows and layers like rock strata. Because of the weight and scale of sugar shipments, the cargo was used both as ballast and as a structural reinforcement to brace more tender ships against hogging and warping in heavy seas. As a result quantities of sugar might vary considerably between the holds of each sugar ship but in large holds fifteen hundred tons was unexceptional. Pitted against this mass were twelve men: six downholders building the bags into sets, a crane driver working under the guidance of his top hand and finally, four men waiting on the barge to stow the sugar. The imperative with all manual work was to conserve strength by lifting as little as possible but initially, in order to break into the stratified layers, lifting was unavoidable. Before the men divided into teams they all worked in the hatchway lifting out five or six sets to create a 'well' into which all the other bags could be rolled as later sets were formed. The idea was that gravity should as far as possible, place the bags on top of each other but for this first stage the working had to be different and this is where we start to get technical: one end of three adjacent bags in the centre of the hatchway was lifted and a section of a rope loop slipped under all of them. The process was repeated at the opposite ends of the bags so that all three sat on two lengths of the rope with two long loops stretched out on either side. Three more bags were now lifted, one man at each end of the 2cwt load and placed on top of the first with yet another three more on top making a block of nine sitting on the rope lengths. The two loops of the rope could now be bought round the set, one threaded inside the other and attached to the waiting crane hook but in the best gangs a tenth bag was always placed on top to close the 'triangle' formed by the rope and crane hook:. With the tenth bag in place, as the crane pulled, the bags compacted more quickly to form a secure load and it also meant that the gang was moving one complete ton at a time. Incidentally, whether gangs sent over nine or ten bag sets depended upon their top hand but whatever the decision it was strictly adhered to so that each team did their quota of work. Barge hands knew what to expect and in consequence could establish their own pattern of working. As an aside this was one of the fundamental under-standings that broke down with deregulation in later years as strangers worked alongside each other. Uniformity disappeared, arguments began and work rates fell away.

After something like a quarter of an hour the well would be big enough for the gangs to separate out into three teams each with their own rope loop and at this stage the top hand would leave them to guide the crane hook accurately towards each team in turn. The priority for the teams was to work away from each other as quickly as possible, partly to give themselves more room to work but more particularly to avoid someone else's crane hook from coming down the back of their necks. Once the teams were all burrowing underneath the coamings out of sight of the top deck the need for accurate placement became less critical not least because the men now had some protection. While they were working close to the hatchway it was possible for them to reach out, grab the hook as it came down and pull it towards their set but gradually it became necessary to swing the half ton crane ball under the coamings to get enough length on the hook to reach where they were working. Eventually, other teams would have to leave their sets, clamber across the lower bags and force the ball under as the first team hauled the hook to their set. Obviously this slowed the work rate considerably while increasing the communal effort to discharge each set, a problem particularly acute in most ships' No.3 holds as we shall see later.

Often, with a morning start on sugar, this situation would occur around lunch time and men would do what they could until then to keep the bags moving. Over lunch the top hand would send away to the FW store for a 'leg' and at the one o'clock Call he would engage an extra man into his gang who took on the job of 'leg runner'. A leg was simply a length of rope with an eye at one end for slipping over the crane hook and a hook at the other for picking up the sets thus extending the reach of the crane and it became the job of a runner to collect the hook as it came down and clamber over to each completed set in turn. The runner was employed by the gang, his pay came out of their takings but his role was so vital in re-establishing a good work rate that everyone benefited. Even with an additional leg, much of the time the runner would be straining to pull the crane ball deep into the bowels of the hold and, in a good gang with a high work rate, sweat would be pouring off him just as much as the rest of the gang. Another option for the top hand was to employ a 'rope man' if he thought the gang's overall work rate would be improved. The rope man laid out the rope for each team to build their sets on, then attach them to the crane hook when the set was completed, first taking off the returned rope for him to lay out again for the next set. In this arrangement it was the rope man who ran the risk of losing a finger as the rope was grabbed by the hook.

All this time, of course, the crane driver, remote from the action, was working blind and could only position his crane hook from the signals of his top hand, a good understanding between them was essential. Out on the lighter by contrast the barge hands, in full view of the crane driver could do their own directing but, here again, in a well knit gang whose members drank together, efficiency was increased with a driver intent on helping his mates. Back in the hold the precise positioning of the hook became of secondary importance to the rate at which the crane driver released the hawser. Once the runner had taken off with the hook, suddenly letting out an extra length of line allowed the momentum of the descending ball to help swing it under the hatchway towards the waiting set; mistiming this might mean another team having to stop work to heave it under the coamings. Equally important was the rate at which the driver hauled in as the set needed to be dragged slowly at first so as not to spill it nor disturb the lower layers, then rapidly as the set swung clear and began to pendulum. This must all sound trivial to an outsider but to men discharging two thousand tons of sugar at the rate of three hundred and fifty tons daily this represented a week or more hard graft. Anything, however small, which consistently made the labour easier was to be welcomed and it was through incorporating these finer points that men had the energy to return the next day. It also goes some way to explaining why poorer gangs remained less effective.

Looking down into an empty hold was uncannily like looking up at a ceiling and so the floor of each deck was known, rather confusingly, as the ceiling. On the general cargo vessels of the nineteen forties and fifties when sugar still came in bags these surfaces were studied with posts and cleats strategically positioned for occasionally securing large loads such as tractors and combine harvesters. Unfortunately these protrusions would have disembowelled any bag dragged over them by the crane and so, as the teams worked, they left the lowest layer in place to act as a cushion for the sets to ride over. When only this last layer remained men worked from the outside inwards towards the hatch so that each set was still able to be cushioned by the untouched bags. Also the bottom bags of each set, as the rope loop was placed under them, were angled slightly against their neighbours so that as the crane pulled, the set was encouraged to ride up over the remaining bags rather than scatter them in a broadly gauged furrow. The final sets could be constructed from bags lying directly in the hatchway and so could be lifted straight out. All common sense perhaps once it had been explained but it was depressing to see in later years once bagged sugar had become a rarity, how many of the new scratch gangs failed to adopt this, or any, consistent methodology. The system wasn't foolproof, some bags always tore but the technique was basically sound and the older gangs knew the amount of time they had saved themselves clearing up at the end.

The great advantage of dispatching goods in unit packaging such as bags was that it could be handled in much the same way wherever they were placed in a hold, shed or lighter. The great disadvantage was that however good gangs were they were dependant upon the quality of the shipment, as we are about to discover.

*   *   *

CUSTOMS
All cargoes discharged had to be reported on a docket to Customs and Excise 24 hours before working or they couldn't be discharged. When a request for Sunday working went in it was specified 'between the hours of 8am and 5pm including the hours of Divine Service' otherwise Customs could require the cargoes not to be worked between 10am and noon.

Sugar was just one item amongst any number of commodities brought to Britain in bags: dried fruit, quasha chips, spices and beans all came from the West Indies and South America in manageable, predictable bags. A shipment of haricot beans arrived in the Royal Docks much as it had been loaded, as a collection of convenient bean bags. Sugar bags were heavy and came in huge numbers but so long as sugar stayed in its sacking it could be worked like all the other commodities, physically exhausting but benign. Unfortunately sugar tended to arrive in the docks in a different state to that in which it was stowed producing the side effect of bringing men directly into contact with raw brown sugar. Sugar was granular and sticky, a casual wipe across a forehead became a rasp with coarse sandpaper; it became sticky when sitting on sweaty skin, matting hair, clogging ears and working its way inside clothing to make every move an irritation.

Such was the huge demand for cane sugar in Britain that before the Second World War the commodity was worked by eight man gangs who specialised exclusively in it, the gangs being known in the docks as 'Sugar Eaters'. During and after the War dock labour was reorganised into twelve man gangs throughout and sugar became just another commodity to be handled by general cargo gangs. Working sugar every day had been a gruelling, energy draining discipline and only the very fittest could take it on – men were burnt out by the age of forty five and in pre-War days had to go over to the easier demands of general cargoes. In this new arrangement general gangs found themselves taking on the work of the disbanded sugar eaters and their new found status meant that they were competing with a legend. The old sugar gangs had built up an awesome reputation for themselves and the physical prowess of gangs such as 'Poskits' became a revered memory. In the City it was always assumed that it was piece-work that kept men working hard but down in the holds there were other personal, deep seated spurs: old men goaded, young men proved their manhood, sons freshly out of the Forces took on the experience of their fathers. There were points to be made, traditions to be upheld. Sugar itself was the challenge. Moving 350 to 400 tons of sugar a day was an enormous undertaking and one of the constants which carried over from the pre-War days was that sugar would only be worked from eight to five each day*, overtime was impossible if men were to continue the following morning. By establishing this strict regime gangs could work to a precise schedule pacing themselves to a set timetable.

Because of the huge demand, Tate and Lyle bought cane sugar from a number of different sources which Royal Mail Lines shipped in its war depleted fleet according to the allocations set down by the Government. Where the sugar came from markedly affected the gangs' day although outside the holds of the ship few would have been interested.

*Only handling cement bags, that I can remember, was also restricted to 8am to 5pm working.

Most sugar, mercifully, came from Jamaica and Barbados where there was a tradition for making good, strong jute sacks; both islands depended heavily upon bagged exports and sack making was seen as an important support industry to their sugar and spice trade. These bags were designed to hold two cwt and could be worked steadily, manoeuvred without forcing and so allow a comfortable work rhythm to be established – important in any physical labour but essential for the heaviest. These bags stood up well to the demands of a docker's hook and although some inevitably in each shipment would burst these were not normally enough to interrupt the basic work pattern.

Sometimes however the refiners bought their consignments from Cuba where a tradition for making strong jute bags also existed but here they had standardised upon three cwt units. To someone seated in his City office two or three hundredweight bags hardly signified but for the men who had to do the moving the differences were important. Three hundredweight was accept–ed world wide as the upper limit for cargoes needing manhandling but here gangs were not being asked to work at this punishing limit for an hour, this was the contents of a lower hold. The rule was to build only six bag sets as lifting these heavier bags up to a third layer was too hard – but they still managed to move 300 – 400tons a day. At the end of each working session the men were shattered. Gangs wanted the throughput just as much as the shippers and importers, their income was directly related to it after all, but the additional effort involved in moving those weights each time was too draining and work rates suffered. Perhaps the Cubans who stowed the bags already had fork lift trucks in the holds, or perhaps they were all Olympic boxers but for general gangs with only a hook and a crane the physical demands were excessive. Compounding these miseries was the fact that many more bags split on handling, torn literally between their own inertia and the docker's hook. After Castro when the US blacked any ship that traded with Cuba RM lost this trade and much of the sugar then went to East Germany.

By contrast, sugar imports sometimes arrived from Brazil in which country sugar seemed to have been an afterthought to the coffee industry. Here sugar was packed into thin, flimsy cotton sacks which might have been excellent for beans but which were incapable of supporting the hundredweight of sugar each was supposed to hold. Dockers' hooks sliced through the material with virtually no resistance making normal working impossible: each bag had to be lifted by hand or gingerly rolled, the extra bending got to the back and kidneys and was universally loathed. At the forefront of the men's minds of course was the fact that, to add insult to injury, each bag only held half the normal quantity meaning they would have to move them at twice the standard rate to achieve parity. Naturally bags burst in their hundreds: rolling them burst them, standing on them burst them and as the rope bit into sets as they were pulled clear of the hold, bags burst above the downholders' heads cascading hundredweights of cane sugar onto themselves and the remaining bags. Downholders were forced to grope amongst the increasing heaps of loose sugar to discover intact bags for constructing their set. Did the old sugar eaters handle it any better…?

Bags were an ancient means of transporting goods in quantity and had the great advantage of being easy to repair. In the docks dating from the age of sail presumably, RML took on 'needlemen' to sew up torn bags and re-bag spilt goods while men continued to work around them. Needlemen were invariably ex-cargo gangers, often ex-sugar eaters, men too old or infirm to be able to take their place in a gang but who knew their way around a hold and understood the conditions. With most bagged goods and with Jamaican and Barbadian sugar, the system worked pretty well, spillages were light and manageable but for other sugar imports with piles of loose sugar mounting everywhere, one aging needleman made no impact. At times it was necessary to enlist the services of RML's shore gang to take on the work of repair for the downholders to refill. It was a problem which needed to be picked up early and a ship's clerk studying the manifest before the vessel arrived would have warned the gangs of impending trouble and advised Furness, Withy to send a large supply of replacement sacks of the correct size – maintaining work rhythms was important – but of a stronger manufacture, to aid sanity. Unit quantity measured weight and by sending 'Cuban' 'Brazilian' or Jamaican' size bags the arithmetic also was kept easy for supervisors when rates were being calculated. By predicting the problems it also gave gangs advanced warning that at the end of the day, there would be an extra hour's work sweeping and shovelling sugar into spare bags alongside their needleman, a job they hated because it dramatically lowered their overall work rate. Had they known it, this last hour's work was the shape of things to come: by 1950 the age-old method of moving sugar was coming to an end.

Brazilian sugar was hard but there was worse. When a Peruvian shipment was expected, gangs armed themselves with crowbars as well as shovels and brooms. Sugar from any country could produce rogue shipments from time to time but these usually occurred as isolated patches amongst an otherwise workable load but Peruvian shipments for some reason always seemed to cause problems. The bags themselves incorporated the worst features of all types as they were made of thin cotton yet were expected to hold two cwts ensuring that even with perfect consistency bags would burst simply by looking at them. But, and this was the odd thing, the sugar refused to be contained by the bags even during the voyage. Somehow it invariably seemed to liquefy, bleed through the cotton and bond with neighbouring bags until the entire mass of several hundred tons became one conglomerate of granular toffee. In this form it tended to be stronger than the bags theoretically containing it and gangs were reduced to separating sections along the lines of least resistance. As men cleared a well, thick molasses oozed slowly over bags, ceilings, shoes and trousers. Needlemen stood no chance and everyone knew that there would be a dispiriting session at the end of the day when tired, dirty and sticky they would have to bag a material which glued itself to brooms, shovels and skin.

Sometimes Peruvian sugar played another trick – it set like concrete. Once again the contents oozed initially on the voyage then compacted and set hard fusing each bag to the next. Gangs would use pickaxes, crowbars and shovels to lever the bags apart and in this stone hard, flattened form these bags of sugar were known as 'tombstones', it was a good description. Dockers' hooks were useless, increasing the risk to back, toes and particularly, fingers; all the usual assumptions broke down, that bags would yield, that they could be rolled or that they would come together into a unit as the crane rope bit into them. Instead sets rose precariously above the men's heads, rocking and chafing against each other, shearing and slipping like so many chunks of fragmenting rock. Sudden collapses of these sets were common as one or more tombstones fractured and escaped the set. But there was another potential problem: the pressure of the upper layers during the voyage could increase the amount of sugar which bled through in the lower levels fusing the shipment into large, solid conglomerates. The removal of individual tombstones became harder as men themselves became more exhausted. Downholders had to be content to chew or prize away any shape or size so long as it could be bundled into a set and the bags became just shredded cotton rags. Eventually all hope of constructing sets was abandoned and boulders, pebbles and grains of sugar were tossed into a canvas spread together with their strips of matted material. The amount of sugar moved on paper, the only interest to the world at large, bore no relationship to the efforts put in by the gangs and pay rates were a constant source of trouble. Those who never saw what the gangs were faced with assumed that they were simply trying to conjure up extra bonuses and no attempt seems to have been made through all the generations of sugar imports to discover ways of preventing this fundamental problem.

Protective clothing was never considered in the early days and rather than put up with the irritation of working with handfuls of sugar rasping their way downwards inside shirts and trousers, men stripped to the waist, tightened their belts and hoped for the best, no matter what the weather. The men who suffered most from this practice were the barge hands out on the water who were permanently exposed to the winds blowing off the River. It was impossible to do that work on a full stomach and men got by on four or five pints of beer at lunch time; bouts of pneumonia were common. To make matters worse, when tombstones were being worked, barge hands were having to carry two cwt loads across a rocking, crumbling surface which got worse with each new layer in the lighter. Broken ankles were a constant threat.

Sugar was one of the great cargoes imported through the Royal Docks and even in the period of rationing large quantities were worked by the general cargo gangs. One of the results of the reorganisation of labour post-War was that older men now found themselves working sugar when before the War they would have had to quit the sugar eaters. A second outcome was that top hands had a greater flexibility to extend their gangs' working day and neither of these points necessarily worked in the gang's favour. Once, Fred Jackson's gang had worked sugar all day from the lower hold and at 5 o'clock were ordered to 'hatch up'. As they climbed up through the decks Fred saw the two hundred tons of molybdenite by-passed for some reason a couple of days earlier when they worked the rest of the cargoes. They were one of the very best gangs and always worked No 2 Hold which meant, in this case, that on the following morning as they worked the last of the sugar, a gang already finished in one of the smaller holds would be set to work on the molybdenum to get the ship cleared for loading. As Fred saw it, his gang would lose money for work that was rightly theirs and so set his exhausted men to work immediately. The light was failing and as everyone wanted to get home the effort was intense, unheard of after a full day working sugar, especially as the molybdenum drums weighed four cwt each and had to be run out to the hatchway. An added complication was that 'Stacky', the gang's regular crane driver had missed the Call that morning and they had had to take on someone new. When Stacky finally joined them at the 1 o'clock Call he became the top hand and Fred, like all good gang leaders lead by example down in the hold. Men came to know how their crane drivers worked, how the crane hook came over and where to stand in relative safety in the hatchway. One elderly man on this occasion, drained from the day's exertions and momentarily distracted was struck badly by the swinging hook. In the half light, Fred took one quick look at the wound pouring blood and shouted down "Don't worry about it, you can see a doctor later" and with that the gang returned to their task. But the injury was a bad one, the man never recovered, within a short time he became a needleman.

Countries exporting cane sugar produced a granular substance in manageable bags according to their own ideas of suitability while at the opposite end of the journey the refiners could cope with sugar in any condition as their first operation was to dissolve it in boiling water. Only the handling gangs had to face head on the caprices of those sugar shipments.

*   *   *

SUGAR – TATE & LYLE

If a RML sugar ship could berth at one of the annual rent sheds and the sugar barges were going to Lyles, they had a very comfortable journey going out at the top of the Victoria Dock and straight round to the refinery. If they were going to Tate's they had the less convenient route, through the congested lengths of both the Victoria and Royal Albert before going out onto the River and round to the refinery. Often though the Queen Victoria lock was closed through a build up of silt and barges destined for Lyle's refinery then had to pass through the two docks before doubling back up river to Lyles, a stone's throw from where they started.

The holds of cargo ships held certain features in common. Most ships had five holds numbered one to five, fore to aft, dropping vertically from the top deck down to the bilges. The outer perimeter of the hold was the shape of the hull so that No.1 Hold in the bows and No.5 in the stern were always oddly shaped, often relatively small. On older ships, designed when passengers were the priority, the internal hold space tended to be the void left over once accommodation needs had been determined, perhaps an extra state room seemed a good idea or extra crew cabins might be relocated to the bows. Whatever the inspiration it could mean that any of the holds might include unhelpful nooks and recesses though the oddest shapes were usually found at No. 1 & 5. For the gangers, Nos. 2 and 4 holds were preferred being large and capacious and formed from the main, straight sided stretch of the hull; they tended to be more cleanly shaped and gave the best financial rewards. No.3 hold was a problem for ship designers; amidships had to sit the accommodation block but this was confined only to the superstructure and top decks, beneath it lay the considerable volume of the lower decks. In spite of the intrusion of the engine housing, it still left a lot of space for cargo and this could not be ignored. Because of these constraints this central space which formed No.3 hold tended to be the most variable in design. The basic solution was to sink a vertical shaft through the central volume of the accommodation block to link with the lower hold. The precise shapes and proportions were left to designers balancing the need for hold access with the lifestyle needs of passengers. The most extreme form for a Royal Mail Lines ship was probably the *Loch Ryan* where a tall restricted hatchway suddenly opened out downwards into a wide cavernous hold, difficult to work with certain cargoes, for example grain, and where a gang's experience proved important. If a No.3 hatchway cut through a substantial accommodation block designed for a large number of passengers then the hatch itself would rise considerably higher than the ship's top deck. This could be an awkward space to fill and a still more awkward height to off-load through.

Each hold was divided from the next by vertical bulkheads slicing through the depth of the hull and each hold was divided horizontally by decks. There was no hard and fast rule here, different ships were built for different trade routes and there was considerable scope for innovation. All ships had a top hold and a lower hold usually with tween decks, upper and lower separating the two. Typically the top and tween decks would have a height of around eight feet each while the lower hold might be fifteen feet and it was here that bulk goods would be stored.

Entry into the hold spaces for cargoes was through hatches set into the top deck. These were large, rectangular holes, one for each hold and each with its own set of derricks, the onboard ship's purchase. When a ship was being worked, the areas around the hatches were always dangerous but in fact the whole space down to where the men were working was a potential hazard. Most ships had a manway set back from the hatches giving safe ladder access to anyone needing to visit the work areas but some ships like the '*Loch Ryan*' were built with huge hatches to accommodate large pieces of engineering –locomotives, combine harvesters, or even oil rig sections for the newly developing Venezuelan oil fields: those were the days when we still made things. These gaping hatches left no room for separate manways and if you had to go down into the holds it was by ladder set against the side of the open hatch. In order to avoid a potentially fatal side-swipe it was worth noting with some precision just how the crane driver was working the 2 ton sets before committing yourself to the descent.

As well as the top deck hatches, internal hatches lead down through the hold levels so that hatches were placed, for example, between the tween and the lower hold, so dividing each vertical space into a series of 'rooms' which varied, not only in size and shape with each ship but also differed in number depending upon the uses assumed for each vessel. Two examples may be worth looking at to give an idea of how conflicting pressures could result in discomfort for the down holders. Ships making the Argentinian meat run needed refrigerated compartments. Insulation technology was improving, but there were still limitations. In the upper holds where a carefully maintained 'chill' temperature was required decks were low and each hold was sub divided into smaller 'lockers' to better regulate the level of refrigeration. This compartmentalising through the upper holds necessarily limited the ship's usefulness for alternative cargoes. When meat imports were low, a common alternative was for ships' captains to switch to crates of fruit which neatly fitted the locker spaces but which were extremely awkward in practice for men to work. Carcasses were hung vertically and could be carried directly out to the hatchway, boxes of fruit were stowed and carried horizontally which through restricted locker doors required angling each box with yogic contortions to back and arms, a slight inconvenience for half a dozen boxes but potentially dangerous when counted in their thousands. Once again a trivial sounding point to anyone not actually doing the work

As a second example we need to look back at a piece of curious maritime history. The story as we learnt it was this: when the Suez Canal opened, merchant ships had to pay dues according to their cargoes and cargo carrying capacity. Considerable changes in ship technology were resulting in a wide range of vessels and some of these were at a distinct disadvantage if one system of measurement was used uniformly. In particular, sailing ships and sail assisted steamers needed and were allowed one deck, known as the spar or shelter deck, in which ropes, sails, spars, etc. could be stowed free from tax assessment as necessary spaces for the ship's maintenance. Some ships later had their sails removed and converted solely to steam but the exclusion rule applying to their shelter decks remained. Canny ship's masters, whether the ship still used sail or no, were able to stow additional cargoes in this deck space and so considerably enhance profitability. When the Panama Canal opened, although sailing ships by then really belonged to history, the same ruling applied but it remained in the interest of the shipping companies whose vessels were likely to use the Canal, to build into their ships 'spar'decks, however unlikely it was in reality that these twentieth century vessels would ever convert to sail. RML ships engaged on the River Plate meat run had no need for such modification, but for those trading at the Pacific Coast ports of North and South America, the inclusion of a shelter deck was a distinct advantage.

Whatever the truth behind all this, all the 'Loch' boats in the RML fleet, for example the '*Loch Avon*' and the '*Loch Garth*' both launched in 1947, had spar decks. The distinguishing feature of these decks was that they had to run the complete length of the vessel, presumably to accommodate the length of a spar, and this was achieved on these later boats by linking the space of the two fore holds themselves only divided by stanchions with those two aft by running two narrow corridors, one each side of the central accommodation block. It was a neat solution for the designers; No.3 hold remained isolated with a central shaft dropping vertically down through the accommodation block to the large lower decks which in turn were flanked horizontally by two long passages. These narrow passages had to earn their keep of course and became awkward extensions of the ship's hold space. It was a good solution for the architects and financiers but not so good for the gangs. Men had to carry bags, boxes and crates along narrow corridors squeezing past each other, all the way out to Nos.2 or 4 hatchways. The effort needed for each unit carried was considerable. To help them planners had equipped those ships with 'clusters', crude metal frames with perhaps a dozen low wattage light bulbs which the gang would hook up on any convenient spike near to the cargo they were working. These were plugged in to the ship's power supply, usually at the mast house but unfortunately it was rare, especially after the War, for all or even the majority of the lamps to be working. It was also the case that there were never enough onboard clusters to spread between the gangs and extra ones, rustier and equally deficient, had to be hired from the PLA to give the men some hope of reading marks and methodically working through the different consignments. Cracked ankles and scuffed knuckles went with the job but it was the deliberate awkwardness of those corridors that really rankled.

*   *   *

IN CHARGE
The outer perimeter walls of the Royal Docks were manned by the police.
Overseeing the quays and land within the docks was the province of the Port of London Authority and HM Customs and Excise.
Dock Masters were the uniformed administrators in charge of the quays, warehouses, fire regulations and railways within the docks.
Water was the responsibility of the Dock Superintendents under whom were the Traffic Officers controlling lock gates, floating cranes, pontoons etc.

Most lighterage firms were owned or contracted to specific wharfingers. For example, Thames Steam Tug worked with the Enfield Rolling Mills on contract, General Lighterage worked for the PLA for much of the inter dock movements (eg wool to the London Dock, rum to the Brandy Vaults). Humphery & Grey covered all the work for the Hays Wharf Group while Union Lighterage worked with Butler's Wharf either side of Tower Bridge. General cargoes like timber often went to private wharves to be stored for importers where contracts were more small scale.

Barges and lighters were everywhere in the docks, sometimes with a lighterman on board collecting individual cargoes, sometimes grouped in a large convoy, unattended, round a grain or sugar ship. Ship's clerks told importers when their cargo was likely to be worked leaving them to arrange transport but it was never an exact science and flexibility had to be built into the system. If there was no pressure for barges, a lighterman might go off for a cup of tea and wait for a summons from a runner or the shout of the ship's clerk to get his craft up. There was no single, systemized pattern of working because cargoes and companies were so varied. What was not in question though was the fact that each lighterman was the master of his barge; he was responsible for the river worthiness of his vessel and that meant supervising how the craft was stowed. If the work of barge hands was not up to standard then fairly forceful exchanges with the shipworker or ship's clerk stressing this fundamental point echoed down the docks but for the most part barges were called up without incident. With the consignment completed receipts were signed to mark the transfer of responsibility of the goods and the lighter was on its way. Lightermen usually came and went without significant discussion. Often the smooth transfer of cargoes would have been assisted by the work of Royal Mail Lines runners who, under the direction of a ship's clerk, would spend time making contact with lightermen to make sure everyone knew the sequencing of cargoes out of each hold. They were effectively messenger boys, keeping the wheels oiled but with minimal status.

If a lighterage company employed a runner though, he was key to the success of their whole operation and really deserved a better title particularly for a company engaged upon general cargoes. Large companies like Thames Steam Tug or General Lighterage with a range of different types of lighters needed serious organisation to maximise their usefulness. The runner acted as chargehand deploying both barges and lightermen throughout the docks and waterways according to the contracts the company had undertaken. He would need to discuss times with different ship's clerks to estimate when lighters were needed and if he was any good, look at the commitments himself to form his own judgements. He would set this against the workings and movements of other ships they were contracted to and balance both against the state of the tide. As a result I had considerable contact with, and respect for, these runners two of the best being Fred Hardy for Thames Steam Tug and Charlie Hanley for General Lighterage. Charlie had a brother who was a runner for Humphery & Grey, he too was good, bit of a loud mouth but good, but for me at any rate, Charlie was outstanding. When he knew his company was involved with a ship he would make sure he got hold of a copy of the ship's plans to study, finding out where each cargo his company was to deliver was positioned and from this, knowing when the ship was due to berth and the likely off-loading times, he would make his arrangements. Sometimes things would look tight and questions would be asked but it was clear that Charlie always had things under control. Barges may have been promised for the following morning and at eight o'clock when work started, it began to look as if there would be delays. "I thought you said you were going to have a couple up for us this morning, Charlie?" "Yes, well they will be up on the ten o'clock lock. You won't need them till then, will you?" Sure enough, by the time the hatches were opened and the more accessible cargoes removed, it would be coming up to ten o'clock and there, making their way down the dock would be two General Lighterage barges. His timing was immaculate. There was a great deal of unwritten, careful planning in the successful deployment of a company's craft and an important factor was the careful distribution of the fleet the night before. Equally important incidentally was for him to find out what overtime was available for his lightermen who were governed more by the state of the tides than by regular dock sessions. Good runners not only carried all this information in their heads, they could also cope with sudden rescheduling as circumstances altered. Now I suppose middle management would reach for the computer.

The Port of London Authority insisted that each barge had to be manned as it passed through the locks but once inside the docks forty lighters for Tate and Lyle could be brought up and left clustered around a ship sitting idle until the work needed them.

There was in fact a considerable variety in types of dumb barge and no doubt there were a good many subtleties that I didn't pick up from the top deck of a working ship. I only noticed broad differences, associating barge types more with the cargoes we were loading into them than specifics of design. Silvertown Services, Tate & Lyles' lighterage company, generally used wide, gaping barges, easy to fill and easy to off-load. Once empty, we were told, they were steam hosed –not so much to clean them as to extract every last morsel of sugar. These craft were well suited to their function of carrying non-precious, bulk cargoes which needed no more than a tarpaulin thrown over them to keep out the rain and much polluted river spray for their short journey round to the refineries.

At the other extreme were barges that needed to be enclosed and secure. Some for example could be refrigerated to carry occasional consignments of meat, others moved valuable and easily portable items which needed protection from the black marketeers. Narrow barges carried copper, zinc and lead to the myriad small factories lining the Lea and its creeks and canals. Most secure, I suppose, were the barges which carried rum and other dutiable goods. It might just be worth looking a little more closely at an older design of barge to illustrate the sort of incident which might occur post-War. These more ancient craft achieved security by laying a series of boards down the length of the barge which had their bottom ends sitting on the coamings and their top ends resting against a fixed central ridge to form a pitched 'roof'. With these boards in place an additional bar could be locked over the top to secure them and their contents. For a commodity like rum a Customs Officer added a second lock to the lighterman's which could only be released at the final destination by another Customs Officer.

Lighterage companies which carried a range of cargoes would necessarily need a range of barges to cover all their contracts but this wasn't without problems. To take just one entry in the Minute Book of the National Amalgamated Stevedores and Dock Union for April 9th 1948:
* "Br. Mott could Br. Rutter tell him when and were was it agreed by the Two Unions that men should work Perkins and Homer Barges with Fixed Beams on Butter. Firm Port Line No.4 hatch.

Bro. Rutter said that agreement was a Gentleman agreement. Resolution in future. No firm should work any Barge with a fixed Beam this referred to all firm Moved by bro. Fadden Second by Bro. Rutter. Put to Vote Carried."

If I'm interpreting this correctly Perkins and Homer probably had over-stretched their resources and in order not to hold up discharging, had asked the ship worker's permission to bring up an older, less convenient barge. It would have been this fixed central beam which prevented sets being delivered efficiently to the hold and for a poorly paid item like butter this would have given inadequate returns for a frustrating session's work. In fact the last of these fixed beam barges were soon replaced after the War by more flexible craft and I suppose whole orders of barge types came and went without the attention given to more fashionable craft. This little incident does hint at the belt and braces approach that was needed for much dock work given its depleted state during the 1940s and early '50s and it is not surprising to find men whose livelihoods depended on piece work, remonstrating.

One other barge type might be worth mentioning not because it was a problem but simply because when it was needed it was something of an event and the class may no longer exist. We occasionally had dealings with the lighterage firm of Woodward Fisher, a big organisation specialising in timber over at Surrey Commercial Docks. Mr Woodward was a lighterman, Mrs Fisher his wife ran the office and they had craft capable of dealing with any size or shaped lengths. From time to time RML ships carried on their top decks very large baulks of timber brought in from North America some

*My thanks to Jack Blackman for this inclusion.

of which could be simply floated out but for others the ship's clerk would need to send across for one of the firm's improbably long barges to accommodate them, a rarity in the Royal Group.

Away from high tide, ship movements, for example changes of berth, were rare so that it was easy enough for large lighterage companies to park their barges in the Royal Docks until they were needed. Lighters stretching the width of a dock were rarely a problem as most movement then was the jostling of craft up to or away from working positions alongside each ship. To have a dock fully clogged with barges had its advantages for us ship's clerks: if I were supervising two ships on opposite berths – and this was not uncommon during the 1950's – I could clamber across the local barges to the centre of the dock and by just swinging my outer barge round bring it against the outermost barge of the neighbouring group to act as a bridge to them. This saved a deal of leg work walking round the quays and made a pleasant little diversion away from the clamour of working holds.

Out on the river a working barge had to have a lighterman in control of it but not necessarily on it. Smaller lighterage companies who did not have their own company tugs would have to progress by whatever means the lighterman could achieve. Normally this did not matter as journeys were short and speed unimportant but if there were a passing tug from one of the larger companies – eg General Lighterage, Mercantile Lighterage, Norskins or Woodward Fisher - perhaps taking a collection of empty barges back to base, a lighterman might hitch a lift to cut his journey time. With his craft powered by a tug the lighterman often joined the skipper for a cup of tea, five shillings might change hands but the lightermen formed a close knit community and the custom was always to help each other out.

It was not only the trade unions that had to be tolerant of the smaller lighterage companies; if shippers and stevedores hadn't made allowances a number of them would not have survived. Morgan and Scanlon seemed to survive with just a few lighters working the North Pacific borax trade but probably the smallest was Mrs Brown whose husband had been a lighterman until she was widowed. Her company had only two barges and firms this small seemed to stay in business less through the efficient deployment of their craft than through the consent of the rest of the docks. The problem for shipping companies like Royal Mail Lines was the lack of flexibility within these small concerns for if Mrs. Brown had her allotted barge delayed it was likely that she had no alternative to offer. A runner from the RML office would bring a message with a request to delay the working of her cargo and the ship's clerk would have to get the gang to change to a different, maybe less accessible, item in order to keep the men earning. This of course was only possible so long as other lighterage companies had their barges standing by, small companies might have been quaint but the world was changing and sentiment was losing out to economics.

Ships entered or left the docks around high tide, towed up to their berth or out to the lock by tugs and during this period a clear passage had to be made for them although for most of the working day barges took over the water routes, sometimes few in number and able to work their way in comfort but often so many that there was near total grid lock. Occasionally this dominance was disrupted when a ship had to change berths or when one was taken off to a dry dock, those in the Royal Albert were particularly awkward because it was often the case that lightermen used the water by 26/28 or 29/33 sheds to park a mass of waiting lighters and these would need to be jostled out of the way by their none too happy wards to let the ship through. Typically though for most of the day it was the barges which were active on the water.

It was the responsibility of the lightermen to get each company barge up to the hold when it was needed and ship's clerks spent a good deal of time down the holds monitoring the rate of working so they could advise lightermen with a shout to get ready. Ultimately though it was part of a lighterman's responsibility to assess when his craft would be needed and to be on hand to make it available; to do this he had to know and accept the order of discharge worked out by the ship's clerk, the top hand and the ship worker.

This need for co-operation varied in intensity depending upon the cargo. For example a large flotilla of lighters round a ship discharging grain or sugar would probably be all from one lighterage company and the order of filling them was of little significance. The lighterman could fill his craft as it suited him. For rum, on the other hand where an equally large collection of barges were stood ready, each would be separately engaged by an importer using his preferred lighterage company. Rum shipments would be a mixture of qualities all destined for different importers with each barge only taking a few barrels but they had to be specific to the importers' instructions so that the Customs Officer and ship's clerk had to be very clear who was taking what. Getting each barge up to collect its consignment or part consignment, needed a lot of manoeuvring – and considerable patience. In general though, whatever the cargo and no matter how quickly barges were wanted, with the water thick with craft, it could take up to two hours to get one to a working position, even with the full co-operation of everyone. For ship gangs, these change-overs could be a welcome respite although too long a delay meant a serious loss of earnings, disruption to the working rhythm and muscles cooling down dangerously. Sometimes there were delays because the work went quicker than expected and a runner would have to call a lighterman away from his cup of tea to get his lighter up. It was another area which was finely balanced because it was also a possibility that his company had made the misjudgement and sent him away up the dock to work another of their lighters. Tracking him down and getting him back might prove difficult as men searched among the masses of craft – delays, costs and congestion would be mounting. In theory, if a barge and lighterman were not available at the agreed time, the shipping company could charge 'demurrage' from the transporters but this was rarely done in practice. Clerks and shipworkers tried to move the gang onto another accessible cargo, one which did have a barge standing by, there had to be give and take. In an industry of interlocking responsibilities keeping negotiations flexible and at a personal level was important for the more legalistic the system became, the more it ground to a halt. Lighterage companies, for example, could respond to heavy handed interpretations of the rules by demanding reimbursement for keeping their barges standing by for an unacceptable length of time. Too much officiousness would have been highly unproductive and in the interests of something approaching harmony, alternative solutions were always sought. The worst that could happen, and this is where things got really serious, was if a cargo *had* to be moved and it was known that no barge was in prospect. If 'phone calls and runners produced no results, the decision might have to be made to discharge onto the quay and leave the lighterage company to sort out the loading of its barge. This would have been hugely expensive for them both in time and manpower and was ever only done as a last resort by shippers, but it was an ultimate threat which helped keep minds concentrated. The opposite situation could occur when loading a ship, of course. It was possible for a loading ship to run into insuperable problems and for a barge full of cargo to be standing by for hours on end. This time, with the added insult of having a desperate shipworker and clerk watching, the lighterman could order a gang to off-load the goods onto the quay and send the shipping company the bill. Whether loading or discharging there had to be a schedule, everyone had to know it and work to stay within it; each ship's plans had to be studied together with the manifest before work began so that a pattern could be constructed. Everybody had to know where they fitted in and that had to be the basis from which any rescheduling was approached. Each shipment was unique and working it required its own conjunction of personnel, it was a situation where acrimony and misunderstandings were never far away but experience taught older and wiser heads that vendettas got them nowhere.

When a ship was surrounded by a large number of barges, the marshalling was constant and in order to reduce delays, extra hands were made available. The docks employed their own lightermen whose job it was to assist the overall flow of traffic. These men however would not necessarily hold the Freeman of the River Certificate which was required for fully qualified lightermen to take barges anywhere on the waterways serving London. As a consequence, they were restricted to working only within the dock group. River lightermen had served long apprenticeships learning the dangers inherent in navigating the Thames and they were a respected breed. Dock lightermen lacked this expertise, their role within the docks was important but they did not have the status of Freeman. They were dockers, Freemen were not.

A particularly awkward situation that might be worth mentioning was when the docks were thick with lighters and a ship had to change berth or head for the River, dock tugs would have to clear a path through to let her through. The lightermen might have gone off for a cup of tea and the tug master wouldn't have been fussy about which barges he moved or where he towed them. If the ship's clerk on a working ship at a nearby berth was not aware of this situation, men would expect to start work on a new consignment and find that all the barges had disappeared. If the downholders couldn't be switched to a different cargo – one with lighters available - the ship gang would be losing money and it was up to the ship's clerk, the shipworker and anyone else handy to scour the docks to try and track the craft down – and they could be a long way from where the lighterman had left them. It was even necessary at times for RML to have to hire a dock tug to collect and return the barges to their rightful ship.

It was not inevitable that ships had a large jostle of barges round them. Some cargoes left by road or rail, some cargoes were slow to deliver thus stretching out the time to fill a barge and knowing this, other lighters would only be sent at a rate to keep pace with the off-loading. When there was a large fleet of lighters though gangs and supervisors seemed to step up the working intensity a notch. There was something threatening about a full ship surrounded by forty gaping craft all wanting to be filled yesterday. For the gangs, the money was there for the taking, all they had to do was bend their backs, while permanent staff knew that across the dock a shed was full of exports waiting to be loaded. Shortcomings could not be blamed upon machines – there weren't any – it was down to the best efforts of the men working within the limitations of the system. When barges were crowding round a ship, often jostling with others serving neighbouring ships, everyone might be needed to make sense of the chaos. Ship workers, clerks, runners, anyone who was on hand, would jump into the barges to lend their muscles to help clear a route through for a lighterman to get his craft up.

There were men specifically employed by RML to help even with this work and they would spend their time at crucial points manoeuvring lighters so that the main business of the docks could continue. These men were known as 'pokers' whose distinguishing attribute was the tool of their trade, a coil of rope with a hook on one end slung over a shoulder. Some of these men were ex-gangers, men who had perhaps suffered an accident but who were still fit and agile enough to take on this heavy work while others simply preferred working on their own rather than in a gang. Their days were spent clambering amongst a shifting mass of craft, some empty, some full to the gunwales with 300 tons of cargo, pushing and pulling them into some sort of order under instructions from both the ship and lightermen.

It was possible for a lighterman to insist that only he move his barge and if he chose, he could take his time bringing his barge up, or more probably in moving away with a full load after having had a bit of needle with the barge hands. If insults had been exchanged, it would be one way a lighterman could get back at a gang, or rather the barge hands, particularly if he was not satisfied with their work; normally though such an isolated position was not in his best interests. As a rule good gangs made a point of stowing to his standards while he got his craft up and away as efficiently as possible, mutual cooperation helped maintain the pay rates. Later, as life got easier, scratch gangs got away with what they could and acrimony became standard.

When a barge was full, it was the lighterman's job to clear it from the working area and take it up to one of the locks to await high tide. Lighters, sometimes up to a hundred and fifty at a time could pass through the locks closing the road above for long periods and if this happened during the homeward rush hour, caused the frustrating delay known to dockers as a 'bridger'. Once away from the congestions around a ship, a lighterman might find clear water and unencumbered travelling. The figure of eight scull was the regular method learnt as part of his apprenticeship and large cargoes could be ferried along the waterways simply by working a single oar. Where possible though, lightermen would save themselves the effort and take advantage of any favourable winds. With some skill a lighterman would note the wind direction decide where he wanted to go and place himself accordingly on the craft using himself as a mast. By simply opening his coat and holding it at the right angle to the wind he could gain enough power to sail the barge along the dock. It may seem unlikely that three hundred tons of cargo could be moved and controlled from such a modest jury rig but such was the case.

At other times the experienced lighterman would look around, judge the direction of the wind and the position of other craft and just raise an end of his covering tarpaulin. He placed a piece of dunnage under it to keep it propped up like one end of a small ridge tent and by letting the wind catch the raised cover the barge gently powered itself down the dock. This was a particularly useful solution in situations where the lighter needed to be got away yet the lighterman was needed to stay near the ship, perhaps to bring up the next barge. The full lighter could be sent on its way across the dock and he would walk round or ride down on a later barge to collect it ready for locking out. There was more than a touch of bravura about this as he casually lit up while watching three hundred tons of someone else's goods sail itself down the dock, but it impressed the onlookers.

This method of travelling, though, was strictly reserved for the docks; once outside on the Thames, the lighterman had to stay with his barge, unless he could hitch a lift from a passing tug and join the skipper in his cabin for a cup of tea.

If a lighterman had not been contacted by his runner, he would telephone his office around 4 o'clock each day to see if he was working overtime. This had to be a basic requirement of organisation. With men and barges scattered all over the waterways and new situations developing on ships throughout the day, getting craft into the best positions to pick up work on the following morning was a major factor in the success of a company. Planning was essential but that had to include a level of flexibility on the part of the lightermen, particularly the hours they worked, when the only fixed parameter was the state of the tides. To the envy of many in the docks, overtime was frequent as lightermen marshalled their craft very early or very late while the docks themselves were silent.

*   *   *

FERRY

There used to be a flat bottomed, punt ferry which crossed the Royal Albert Dock. There was an ancient right of way which had to be kept open and this allowed members of the public to enter the Royal Albert Dock through Savage Gardens to Central Gate (by Central Station). By crossing the railway lines to this water-jet ferry at 21/17 Sheds passengers could cross the dock to 22 Shed, South Side RAD allowing them to walk by the Pontoon Dock, and the Dry Dock and out by the Wicket Gate (Gate 16) into Silvertown. There were restricted times of opening, approximately 7-9am, 12-2pm and 5-7pm, it was for pedestrians only and the access was policed. Dockers could use this ferry and were thus spared a long walk round the Royal Albert to get to their next ship, gratefully tossing a copper or two into the pilot's hat.

Unfortunately there was an incident around 1960 when a ship before heading out to sea turned her engines over just as the ferry crossed her stern. The craft was overturned and sank while three passengers and the pilot had to be rescued. Safety issues were just beginning to be taken seriously and as having a small ferry dodging in between ocean steam ships was deemed too dangerous, the service was suspended. By this time though many dockers had cars and the ferry had begun to decline in popularity. People who lived in Savage Gardens and who worked in Silvertown might have been inconvenienced but, in future, they would be safely inconvenienced. That right of way was largely forgotten and as it now crosses a STOL runway, presumably it has just passed into forgotten history.

Thousands of tons of sugar passed through the docks annually and it would be easy to assume that dropping bags into a waiting barge would have been such a straightforward operation that no further comment was necessary. Nevertheless there were a number of factors which highlight just how complex a working environment the docks were and bearing in mind that problems usually equated with a loss of earnings, how effective men had to be at resolving their own difficulties. The best gangs were better than the facilities they were offered and ultimately better than dock work required them to be. Once again sugar is used here as the most demanding example of a whole range of bagged goods.

With a quay crane loading barges from a ship, the most necessary additional piece of kit was a 'dummy' or pontoon. Dummies were floating rafts hired from the PLA which were placed between the quay and the centre of the ship to keep it at a fixed distance from the quay. Dummies were the width of two barges sitting side by side giving the supervisors and downholders some flexibility in the sequence of discharging – different barges could take on different consignments. It also allowed a full barge to be taken away and a new one to be brought up while the gang continued working into the adjacent barge. This enabled the lightermen to work their craft round to 1, 2, 4 or 5 holds so that quay cranes could lift sets out of a hold and lower them into the barges in full view of the crane driver. No 3 hold in the centre of the ship and situated across from where the dummy was placed, could not be discharged by a quay crane; typically No 3 hold usually worked 'overside', into a lighter on the far side of the ship using derricks. If everything meshed, five holds could be working continuously with only occasional and predictable breaks being made as full barges were replaced by empty.

Tate and Lyle's own fleet of lighters, Silvertown Services, was formed to suit their own inclinations and not necessarily those of shippers or handlers. The standard size for a dumb barge was 295 tons and most Silvertown Services' barges were of this capacity, except that whoever made them for Tate and Lyle built them slightly wider than the other lighters I encountered so that, using a standard dummy, as these lighters took on sugar and settled lower in the water, they wedged fast to each other and between ship and quay, locking two barges together. This problem only occurred at No. 2 and 4 holds where the line of the hull reduced the water space to no more than the width of the dummy; so to free the barges, mooring ropes had to be slackened at the corresponding end of the ship allowing her to swing out slightly into the dock. This little manoeuvre potentially disrupted the work of three gangs: if No.2 barges were jammed and the bow ropes eased, No.3 barge working overside would be jostled out of alignment with its derricks and, commonly, No1 crane would not then have sufficient reach to make

No.1 hold. On many ships, using a dummy only allowed the crane hook at best to just scrape down into the hold because of the restricted arm length of most cranes and swinging the vessel out into the dock a few feet brought work to a standstill. If this were happening at No.2 hold it would only be a matter of time before No. 4 and 5 holds were similarly affected. The net result was that three gangs at a time, through no fault of their own, would be standing idle losing money while lightermen and ship's clerk tried to organise something. The trouble was that once these circumstances had been set up the problems were built into the system; every barge at No.2 and 4 hold would cause the same problems.

There was a solution however. All dummies were nominally the same size but they were not made with engineering precision leaving some wider than others. A canny ship's clerk, knowing the ship, the berth and the cargo would make sure that the PLA sent the widest dummy they had and prayed it was wide enough to permit uninterrupted barge movements.

At one time Tate and Lyle took the initiative to accelerate off-loading by introducing two 500 ton lighters. The assumption was that fewer lighters meant fewer change-overs; a neat solution from behind a desk perhaps but the thinking did not allow for the practicalities of the Royal Docks. Because of their size they were unable to come round by the dummy and so could only be worked overside which in turn meant that the crane had to be stood down in favour of derricks. This was at the time when both bagged and bulk sugar were possibilities and being forced to use the sticks for bulk sugar prohibited the one ton grab from being used (see later). Instead downholders had to shovel sugar into canvas 'spreads'. Now a crane working into a standard size barge was able to deliver its set almost anywhere with little manoeuvring of the craft but derricks with their more limited compass loading a 500 tonner could barely cover a corner. The lighter would list as the first sets arrived and the down holders would be trying to carry bags or shovelfuls of sugar uphill to stabilise it. The alternative was to continually shift the position of the barge; space in the dock water was very limited for such a large vessel and because it was a dumb barge without any power of its own, as it filled, just moving such a mass was a struggle. The net result was endless delays and frustrations, particularly for the downholders who cut off visually from what was happening on the water, could only fume while barge hands and lightermen juggled as best they could. There was a line of thought which suggested half filling one end of these barges, changing position so as to completely fill the opposite end then re-manoeuvre it back to complete the loading. Clearly this was not a suggestion offered by someone who had tried to jostle a 500 ton barge, three quarters full of sugar. It was quicker to replace one smaller barge with another and to fill both than load a 500 tonner. As this fact became obvious to even their greatest advocates, in time they were quietly jettisoned.

Traditionally sugar arrived in bags and by the time a sugar ship reached her berth, regular Furness, Withy gangs would have been engaged, a wide dummy would be in place and all the equipment necessary for the likely state of the cargo together with suitable lifting gear would have been organised. Tate and Lyle, for their part, would have arranged for twenty or so 295 ton barges under the supervision of a lighterman to have been taken by tug along the dock to the working ship where they would stand off as general cargoes were removed from the upper holds. As each gang cleared their space and prepared for the sugar, the ship's clerk ordered up the first sugar barge. On some shipments only two or three holds might contain sugar leaving the other gangs, usually those working the smaller No. 1 and 5 holds, to continue with general cargoes.

Barges were under the control of their lightermen as it was their responsibility to make sure their barges were stowed securely for the journey onto the Thames. A regular lighterman who knew the barge hands and was happy with the way they worked might only stay to watch the first layer of bags set out, content that his craft would be properly stowed then estimate how long it would take and go off for a cup of tea. Immediately lines of communication became stretched and it was important in such circumstances to have a competent runner working with the ship's clerk to help defuse potential problems. For example, if a barge were fully loaded and the lighterman had not returned, the barge hands might move it away themselves bringing up the next one so that the gang could continue earning money. Strictly against the rules but this needn't have been a problem if the lighterman and barge hands got on well. On the other hand, if there had been some argy it was imperative for the runner to recognise the situation and track down the lighterman before war broke out. What barge hands could get away with might vary from gang to gang down the length of a working ship and a good runner helped his ship's clerk not only by anticipating areas of conflict but also by knowing the personalities involved. Today I suppose we'd call it trouble shooting and only employ graduates to attempt it.

The working environment for barge hands was very different of course from that of the downholders who worked in a stable environment protected to some extent from the elements. By the time they were working sugar deep in the lower holds downholders were often working in a considerable gloom but they were at least protected from the wind off the River. Barge hands worked out in all weathers with the cold seizing up backs and numbing muscles during enforced stoppages, dislocations to their working rhythm were dangerous as well as unprofitable. Dumb barges when empty sat high in the water, clambering from one to another while dodging swinging sets meant that there was a real and constant risk of toppling into the filthy dock water. As barges were filled they settled lower becoming more stable to work on while the ship relieved of much of her cargo rose higher making the discrepancy in heights more pronounced. In itself this was never a problem except that at the end of an exhausting day barge hands had that bit further to climb up the rope ladder to rejoin their gang on the top deck. Gangs always left their ship as a unit.

It might be worth mentioning here that dockworkers and stevedores, as barge hands, worked differently. The four barge hands of a 'White' gang all worked together to lay out the bags across the ceiling while their 'Blue' counterparts adopted a strict division of labour: with a ten bag set two would carry two or four of the bags to the coamings and tuck them in tightly while the remaining two men would 'throw away' the other six or eight bags near where the set was put down. All barge hands though, Blues and Whites, arranged the work so that they began amidships working down one side of the barge to the prow. As they worked back down the opposite side towards the stern, 'Blue' gangs reversed roles so that carrying 2cwt bags across to the coamings was shared equally. However awkward Silvertown Services barges were at fitting the dummy space, internally bags of sugar seemed to fit comfortably across the ceiling forming a good tight surface for men to work the next layer from. You could have gone ballroom dancing on that surface. If the lighterman required them to work 'out the window'* with such an orderly stowing regime it was a simple matter to build it into their pattern. This disciplined manner of working had the additional advantage for the ship's clerk calculating pay rates in being able to readily calculate the tonnage worked by counting one layer and just multiplying up.

As a lighterman had ultimate responsibility for his craft's River worthiness it was an important aspect of the barge hands' job in efficient gangs to build a good relationship with him. Although there was no necessity for this, the better gangs did not change individuals between downholders and barge hands, each settled into their respective patterns of work allowing the same men to regularly communicate with the lightermen; familiarity with people, environments and working methods always seemed to help push the job along.

Barge hands wanted each set put down tight against the previous row so that the lowest bags of each set did not need moving, and if the reach of the crane was insufficient this might mean the crane driver (or winchman at No 3 hold) just holding the set a foot or two above the surface while the men swung it over the spot they wanted filling, then signalling for the set to be quickly dropped. This took some nice timing from a capable and co-operative crane driver and needed everyone to be wide awake.

When the older, established gangs (branded as 'blue-eyed gangs') were broken up and scratch gangs took their place memories of the standards set by the sugar eaters gave way to each individual getting away with what he could. The downholders, owing no allegiance to the barge hands, would send over sets of varying sizes according simply to what was convenient to them, making it impossible for the barge hands to establish a pattern. There were times when barge hands sent sets back and work stopped until the gang thrashed out a basic working order with the top hand passing insults between hold and lighter and all strangers to each other. It was a sad and demeaning spectacle for those who had known the pride and tradition associated with the sugar trade. Just as the down holders took to careless set construction,

*See 'Wool and Trans-shipment'.

49

barge hands began to simply unhook the sets and let them scatter across the ceiling with only the smallest effort to straighten a few bags up. Lightermen were at first appalled with what they were being offered but over time, as it was only a short journey round to Tate and Lyle's refineries eventually they had to accept these declining standards as sufficient. Ships' clerks having to assess the quantities worked could only look at the heap and make informed guesses. The changes did not happen overnight and many battles raged between those who knew how to work and those who had no intention of over exerting themselves. Mechanisation, ultimately, would more than compensate for these shortcomings in handling but a way of working and the pride associated with it was being lost. It is worth remembering that at their best men were working up to four hundred tons each day.

Not only were the old gangs fast but they were organised and tidy, it was all part of the assumed intensity. Cranes were fast but derricks were faster for as soon as a set was released, the forty gallon drums were hauling the hook and rope loop back across to the hold. Cranes had the reach, derricks the speed, it was a nice balance.

Finishing up a sugar shipment needed some careful judgement on the part of the ship's clerk. Obviously it made no sense to tie up five barges each only partially filled with sugar to be taken to Tate and Lyle, nor did gangs want to be kept waiting while one barge made its way from hold to hold collecting the last sets or sweepings. Gangs were paid to work and once they were finished they could make themselves available for another vessel; joining some polite queue was not part of a docker's psyche. What normally happened was that at some point towards the end of the work one partially filled barge would be told to stand off in the certain knowledge that what was still left in the hold would fill another barge. As this second barge was filled the first could be brought up to other holds to collect their remnants as they approached finishing. If everything worked out this one lighter could complete the off-loading at each hold then make its way to Silvertown with all the other barges full. Sometimes a second lighter would need to be stood off, it was all a game of chess and one at which a new ship's clerk immediately needed to prove his competence for the gang's earnings depended upon it, and they would remember ineptness.

*   *   *

When the change to bulk sugar became a regular fact of life (of which, more later), new headaches arose for the clerk who had as a primary task to monitor the quantities of sugar taken out of the hold. One frequent oddity which was never solved was the constant loss of sixty tons of sugar from each hold on each shipment; manifests were read, plimsoll lines on ships and barges were scrutinized and cubic capacities were estimated but the figures regularly failed to add up. For men who took some pride in their mathematical capabilities, it was awkward. At the RML dock office the only solution they could conjecture was to push the blame back to the West Indies where it was assumed that sugar weighed before it was delivered into the hold was partly sticking to the conveyer belt and so returning back to shore. It was pure supposition but it was a convenient way of getting round the embarrassment that they were no longer capable of maintaining their own strict control over the quantities of sugar being off-loaded.

Another problem estimating loads was related, oddly, to where PLA ordered each ship to berth. On the south side of King George V Dock fixed pontoons removed the need for dummies and each 'T' shaped pier stretching the length of a ship was equipped with cranes to which one ton grabs could be attached for working bulk sugar. Lighters could swing round the end of the ship, position themselves between pontoon and quay and be reached comfortably by their cranes. It was a good solution and when it worked, it worked well. The problem was that for some reason never overcome by the scientists, the Thames insisted upon depositing vast quantities of silt precisely here so that there was often only a seven foot draught for a barge to work with. As a result one of two possibilities existed: first, a lighter could be half filled in its proper position using a crane and grab, work would then stop while it was taken outside the ship to deeper water where derricks and a spread would have to finish the job as the crane arm could not stretch across the width of the ship. Using this method the same gang completed the loading of each lighter. Second, the barge could be filled as much as the draught allowed then sent round to No. 3 hold where the gang was experienced in working overside from derricks to complete the loading. The first option meant that the stevedores were hiring a crane which for much of the time was standing unused while the gang had to waste time setting up derricks for the overside work, then return back to using their crane with each new lighter. The second option, and the preferred choice, in which No.3 gang completed filling all the barges from the other holds was an elegant and praiseworthy solution to an awkward situation – until it came to calculating each gang's pay when for each lighter, two gangs would both know for certain that each had loaded two thirds.

*   *   *

WEST INDIA DOCKS
The West India Docks were built to handle imports from the West Indies so in theory, and very occasionally in practice, the PLA could order a sugar ship round to these docks to be worked by their own PLA gangs. In practice though RML maintained a continuous berthing facility in the Royal Victoria Dock and this commitment was very important to the PLA. Royal Mail Lines needed this to pay for itself and the PLA needed the revenue, so the vast majority of sugar ships were discharged in the Royal Group using Furness, Withy gangs near where exports were being collected for the outward voyages.

51

Innovations were being tried in other countries, notably the United States and closer to home in Rotterdam, to move cargoes faster and more efficiently. British docks could not ignore the trends – the pre-War days were not going to return – and for an industry so steeped in tradition it meant an uncomfortable period of readjustment. The move from bagged to bulk sugar imports showed how ungainly the process could be.

At some time during the early fifties Tate and Lyle decided that bagging up sugar in the West Indies for stowing in holds then, in London, manhandling it into barges was inefficient and taking their lead from grain imports, decided that it ought to be possible to get sugar in and out of holds without the encumbrance of bags. This was decidedly unknown territory as far as we knew and although RML was apprehensive, as Tate and Lyle were prepared to underwrite the operation, they agreed.

The gangs too were not happy. The skills that they had inherited from the sugar eaters allowed them to empty holds, earn a respectable wage and have enough energy left for starting again the next day. For men whose tradition and livelihood were based on piece work, uncertainty risked both safety and income, the unions were heavily involved, the matter still unresolved as the first shipment arrived. In addition there was the implied criticism, the men assumed, that the way they had worked and the effort they had put in all their working lives wasn't good enough; to add further insult to injury, the intention seemed to be that in future work would move closer in style to that of the cornporters for whom they had scant regard. Their experience of loose sugar was the niggling commitment to sweeping and shovelling the contents of burst bags at the end of work, usually an hour's impediment before moving onto their next ship. To downholders it looked as if they were in for one and a half thousand tons of clearing up and with no idea how to pace themselves.

On the other hand bagged sugar itself was physically demanding and if a system had been invented which meant less lifting and a quicker throughput, there would be sound reasons for change. The trouble was that there was no suction machine (see GRAIN) capable of raising sugar. Instead the PLA made a one ton grab available set on a three ton crane. Suddenly the exercise appeared less like moving grain and more like quarrying rock or sand. It was an ominous sign.

Nothing daunted Tate and Lyle arranged for their first bulk shipment on a Royal Mail Lines ship. The officers monitoring the situation in the West Indies were bemused to witness how bulk loading was being introduced where no previous infra-structure existed. What normally happened was that sugar already bagged was taken out in shallow-draught bum boats to the ship moored in deep water off-shore. Set boards were lowered by derricks and the sugar bags loaded two tons at time straight into the hold for distribution across the ceiling. This process was similarly followed for bulk sugar but with the additional action of cutting each bag open and pouring the sugar out, a technique known as 'cut and start'. It didn't seem at the time to have much of a future.

Perceptive minds at Royal Mail House were equally disturbed for they knew that the holds the sugar was being poured into were unsuited to such a task. Ships such as the *'Araby'*, *'Brittany'*, *'Esequibo'* and *'Ebro'* were built as general cargo vessels following age old trade routes and picking up goods as they became available or in season. Their holds were designed to give a flexibility of purpose from crates, barrels to heavy machinery which could be lashed down to cleats or stowed between stanchions. If the bulk sugar experiment were to prove successful it would need a different sort of ship with cleaner, less cluttered holds and it would mean that ships already under construction as part of the post-War rebuilding programme would already be obsolete. As sugar had formed such a large item in the commercial viability of the West Indies trade its removal to better designed ships would be grievous indeed to Royal Mail Lines.

The *'Gascony'* had the dubious honour of bringing the first bulk sugar shipment into the Royal Docks in 1952 or '53, one and a half thousand tons in No.2 hold with around five to six hundred tons in each of the others. Once the general cargoes had been cleared away and the sugar exposed, the hypothesising had to give way to practicalities and it was down to the gangs to improvise while Royal Mail Lines, FW and PLA staff, Union and Tate and Lyle representatives together with health and safety officers made helpful suggestions to men who had been off- loading sugar all their working lives. Centre stage was the one ton grab, which working on a three ton crane, limited each load to two tons. The trouble was that no one knew what two tons of bulk sugar looked like in a grab and tests went on all day to satisfy the concerns of safety officers.

Once the hatchway was cleared, the downholders were able to jump down into the sugar and scramble under the coamings out of the way of the swinging grab. The massiveness of the sugar was the main impediment: men sank deep enough to make all movements laborious and when they tried the cornporters' technique of running sugar downhill into a well excavated by the grab they found that sugar wouldn't flow, gravity was no help. They had been equipped with cornporters' shovels, you could see where the theorising had come from, but one shovelful was found to weigh over half a hundredweight. During that long first day the men managed to move around a hundred tons and the general opinion from the top deck counted it a success. The gang, had they been asked, might have been less enthusiastic.

Over the next few days smaller shovels were introduced, gangs got used to the movements of the grab and began to measure their levels of endurance against this new way of working. Safety officers relaxed when they found the grabs were not overloaded; in time the holds were cleared, the representatives and advisers around the hatchway melted away and the gangs were left to make of it what they could.

In one way the gangs were lucky with that first consignment. At least the sugar moved. Advisers could watch the grab ploughing into the mass and taking out its catch, they went away contented. Unfortunately with later consignments bulk sugar was found to have the same tendency to solidify as earlier, bagged shipments, requiring days of arm juddering effort as downholders chewed, chipped and gouged the rock face with picks and chisels. To help lighten the effort if no one was watching more informal uses for the grab were found: if the sugar had solidified in the hatchway, the one ton mass could be dropped by the crane driver to pulverise it ready for shovelling but if it caked into a vertical wall possibly fifteen feet high and if it could be reached by the grab, three or four men would take hold of it as it came down then running over the broken surface, smash it into the block. Strictly forbidden, of course, but the men who set up the conditions were never the men who had to operate them. Of more concern to Royal Mail Lines was the expense of hiring a PLA grab, if it was returned damaged the cost of repair could wipe out the cargo's profits. For the gangs though, given the situation that was thrust upon them, the temptation was too great and if no one was watching, the grab became a battering ram.

If the sugar caked, it did so unpredictably some areas would remain loose and could be moved by shovel and grab others would set rock hard and had to be hacked away. This solidification could be no more than boulder size or as big as a room. At one stage Furness, Withy considered using pneumatic drills but finally decided the fire risks were too great. When a solid block was discovered, the decision had to be made by the top hand when to dismantle the grab and go over to using the spread and pick axes knowing that a wrong decision would add considerably to the men's frustrations. Changing the crane's tackle was time consuming and couldn't be lightly decided upon. As far as possible the downholders would excavate around solid masses keeping one eye on them as they worked in case they toppled or in case overhangs suddenly broke free above them – encouraging walls of sugar to collapse under their own weight became part of the new found technique but not with men standing underneath them. It needed nice intuitive judgement. Often the sugar was semi solid: too hard for shovels to make much impression while chisels were too mincing. There was one chap, Harry Something, six feet four tall and built like an ox who could get his shovel half into a congealing mass while his fellow downholders were just nibbling. He was proud to show off his strength and none of the others wanted to let him, or themselves, down. Sweat poured off them. Once again, it was Peruvian shipments which caused the greatest problems and there were times when the dark brown mass turned white from the myriad score marks slashed across the surface as men tried to get their shovels and pick axes to bite into it.

Once the grab had become ineffective the discharge gang would send the shore gang across to the FW store for spreads and these would be introduced during a break, over lunch or while the barges were being changed. Once the decision to use spreads had been made, the gang usually tried to work straight downwards in order that they might be able to lay them out flat on the ceiling to break off lumps into it. Initially there was only space for one spread but as the excavations progressed the men were able to split up into three two-man teams each with their own spread working according to the state of the sugar they encountered. The further away from the hatchway the gang worked, the further the crane hook had to reach to pull the set out and while catching and bumping over the ceiling's cleats and bars the spread could easily lose half its load: it was frustrating work. As bulk sugar became the rule, in the West India Dock the PLA gangs were given small bulldozers but FW in the Royals never did. They believed that a machine bouncing across the uneven surface so close to where downholders were working was too dangerous but the PLA gangs seemed to find a way. Nevertheless it was one further pointer, if one were needed, that mechanisation had arrived and the old ways were becoming just a memory.

For a few uncertain years gangs continued to work bulk sugar from general cargo vessels in pretty appalling conditions. In the West Indies conveyor belts were introduced to take sugar directly to the ships' holds but no parallel equipment was found for FW gangs to get the sugar out. Newer ships tended to have cleaner holds which helped reduce sugar caking round protrusions but it didn't solve the fundamental issue of mass extraction. For the refiners this remained an experimental period culminating ultimately in Tate and Lyle forming their own purpose built fleet which effectively ended RML's long association with cane sugar and the West Indies trade.

The worst bulk sugar shipment was in about 1955 when the 'Damaska' had all five holds caked solid with Peruvian sugar. All dock work was based upon the fundamental economy that gangs were taken on to completely clear a hold and that in doing so they would earn a living wage but in the case of this consignment men would have been reduced to absolute destitution if normal rates had applied. It took gangs a month of unremitting toil, hacking, scraping and pounding at the rock surface with hand tools, and it is worth noting again that men were not provided with special clothing, stripping to the waist being the least uncomfortable option. Everyone could see the magnitude of this problem of course and special agreements had to be hammered out between the shippers, stevedores and unions, while Head Office looked to Tate and Lyle for re-imbursement.

*   *   *

MORTUARY
The mortuary had stretchers on wheels for conveying corpses along the quays and it was an unpleasant and sobering sight to see them being wheeled passed.

There will be people who are much more competent than I am to discuss the distinctions between stevedores and dockworkers but I must make some reference to them, trusting that what I write will not be too wide of the mark.

As I understood it, there used to be a simple distinction between these two branches of manual labour in the docks, stevedores moved cargoes on and off the ships, dockworkers moved them on the quays. Stevedores worked in holds, removed hatch covers, rigged tackle and used derricks, they understood ships. Even if members of a stevedore gang had never been to sea, like my father, their working experience was ship based, learning from older members the priorities and equipment on each vessel. It was an understanding built into the gangs through their traditions since the days of sail and many, perhaps most, would have known from first hand experience the importance of a properly stowed cargo in rough seas.

Dockworkers were landsmen. If they had not served their time at sea, working in the docks would not have increased their knowledge of ships. They were essentially tough, competent warehousemen and porters; goods for them were stacked, stored or segregated, never stowed. They needed no maritime understanding, receiving goods as they came over onto the quay or, for exports, bringing them up to the ship's side for stevedores to load. To the shipping and stevedoring companies they were less skilled and therefore less valuable.

Of supreme importance to the shipping lines since the days of sail was the ability of stevedores to load a ship fast yet maintain her sea worthiness in all weathers. When cargoes came in all sorts of packaging or none at all and when ship technology was less sophisticated, accurate stowage was crucial to a ship's safety; to have the thirty years experience of someone like Ted Smith organising the loading was a great reassurance for the ships' masters. Ted Smith, family tradition had it, used to overload his Brocklebank Wells boats because he knew that once they were in salt water they would ride higher at their maximum loading. Perhaps this was general practice or perhaps just a matter of reading the Plimsoll Line but it took fine judgement and we were told that safety officers would look very closely at Wells ships as they left the docks. Loading was the chief skill among ship gangs, indeed among the whole mass of labour and it was a jealously guarded preserve of the stevedores, off-loading by comparison was always considered the poorer stevedoring relation.

The reorganisation of labour during the War radically disrupted these niceties and no one seemed clear to what extent they could be re-imposed during the post-War period. All stevedores belonged to the National Amalgamated Stevedores and Dockers Union while most dockworkers belonged to the much bigger Transport and General Workers Union. The NASDU was a small specialist union dealing specifically with dock work and although the title suggests a broad base, in practice very few dockworkers belonged to it, it was an elite. The TGWU on the other hand covered most types of work from tally clerks, gearers and coopers to dockworkers, but never stevedores. NASDU men were known as 'The Blues', TGWU members 'The Whites' and the distinctions as separate unions were carefully maintained. The return to peace did not signal a return to pre-War distinctions fully and although the two unions were revived generalising initiatives like the National Dock Labour Scheme reduced their effectiveness over the longer term. In the immediate post-War period the balance of work between stevedores and dockers – nearly, but not quite, a balance between the two unions – was as follows: stevedores alone loaded Company ships, RML and FW would only entrust the work to them thus keeping the prestige jobs and pay with them. Some branches of the TGWU originally all quay gangs remember, had taken on ship work during the War and a number of the more ambitious formed themselves into White gangs to rival the stevedores at off-loading. Inter-union competition was intense, the Blues believing that the Whites were basically unskilled, the dockworkers keen to prove that they were just as effective as the stevedores; as the Blues used to say to the dockworkers "We got it in, now let's see you get it out". Within the day to day working though, this rivalry was kept in check by the Blues and Whites not working alongside each other; ships were either discharged by Blue or White gangs, never both together. This was no ingenious management ploy but arose naturally from the way casual gangs were taken on at their place of 'Call'.

Even after the War, stevedores insisted on having their Call outside the dock gates by the Connaught Pub and also at Custom House. A FW shipworker who 'called them off' would himself have had to have been a 'Blue', to have known the men and been part of their tradition. Fundamental to the stevedores' ethos was the insistence that they formed their own gangs; when they were engaged, companies took on complete gangs and when they walked through the dock gates they went as a team with their gang leader at their head. This would have had greater significance before the War when different commodities and companies used different sized gangs but the later re-organisations to a generalised twelve man gang throughout the dock system meant that the composition of gangs varied only through sickness or internal re-adjustments. For ten or fifteen years after the War, I knew pretty well every man who would be working a RML ship just by recognising the shipworker, this was true of White gangs as well as Blue.

Stevedores had another distinctive custom: no matter how long it took a gang to load or off-load a ship they insisted upon being re-engaged each day. Although in reality they were contracted to complete the working of a hold once they had agreed to start it, (known as 'continuity with the job'), they required to be met by their shipworker at the Call each morning to be offered another day's work with the implication that they had a choice to accept or refuse employment.

Dockworkers on the other hand met inside the docks, coming in, in ones and twos and forming gangs only at their places of Call around the docks but substantially 'on the stones' inside Gate 9, Royal Albert or at the NDLB Offices in Victoria Dock. As with the stevedores, only a member of the White union could call off dockworkers so that a stevedoring company had to employ both Blue and White shipworkers to have the full range of casual labour available to them. In theory, White gangs which were men short could have a shipworker choose from the unattached card holders who he wanted to complete the gang but in practice, through contacts and friendships these organisational arrangements resolved themselves. In 1947 most young men were still in the forces, labour was in short supply and everyone who wanted work could get it. If there was ever a good time to be part of the Call system, this was it. There were times, post-War when it was unpleasant and ignominious with men running to try and catch an engager's eye but mercifully, during this period the system had lost its raw savagery. Built into it still was the demeaning, cattle market aspect but it had lost the struggle for survival which I ever only heard about, generally my experience of the Call was relatively benign; shipworkers who were ex-gangers engaging gangs or ship's clerks who, like me, were ex-tally clerks engaging tally clerks. They had all experienced casual labouring for themselves, many would still have been casually employed, they all held their union cards, as I did, in case they wanted to give up administration. Labour was scarce, destitution, praise be, was not a threat and the Call could afford to be relatively matey. Nevertheless loyalties were very much in place; shipworkers went to their regular place in the road and would expect to see their gangs waiting for them. There was a Royal Mail Lines/Furness, Withy pitch with P&O further down the road, Scruttons beyond them and so on – perhaps forty shipworkers would be stretched along the road looking for specific gangs and they, formed up behind their top hand, would gravitate to the area where the shipworker they knew would be waiting. As loyalties broke down under the new systems, dockers and stevedores became mixed, men and gangs from other docks started to appear and employment became less a matter of comradeship and trust. When old loyalties were still in place, top hands and shipworkers knowing each other well over a long period of time (often working originally in the same gangs) made the process of engagement relatively straightforward. Top hands taken on at the Call might engage men themselves if they needed an additional gang member, perhaps a leg-runner or winchman. The system was not quite as clear cut as the traditional view of brutal employers exploiting defenceless labourers might suggest - not in my experience, anyway, but if my father had been alive he might have had a different story to tell.

It was up to Furness, Withy to decide which shipworker they allocated to each new RML ship coming in. They had three permanent shipworkers in the Royal Docks, one Blue, two White but would take on others as they needed them, as far as possible, men they knew and who knew RML loadings. Each of the regular shipworkers had his five gangs continually employed on Royal Mail Lines vessels, the two White gangs usually discharging, the Blue at an annual rent berth loading. The system was fluid though, with Blue gangs sometimes off-loading or even, during very slack periods, settling for quay work. If Royal Mail Lines had no ships in, FW sought to pick up any other work available, but this was rarely a feature of the forties and fifties. Usually, a gang would be 'called off' the day before the ship was due to berth and the top hand and some of his men would be paid a day's wages by FW to get the equipment they might need to empty their hold – they would know the cargoes of course from the ship's manifest. They would also know what berth the ship had been allocated and whether they had the use of a crane. With this knowledge they would select their equipment from the Furness, Withy stores and put it in the transit shed at the door opposite their hold ready for work the next morning. During the periods of greatest pressure though, when berths were hard to come by, as a ship was allocated a berth gangs might be engaged at the Call, given an hour or two to get their equipment together then start work mid-morning.

What did not vary was the position of the gangs. Each gang was taken to work a particular hold so that a gang which worked No.1 hold always worked that hold whatever the ship. Remember Nos.1&5 holds were odd shaped often with the least savoury cargoes and they took a bit of knowing while No.3 hold often started high, had a deep hatch shaft then opened out widely beneath the accommodation block. It was also usually the case as we have seen that No.3 gangs had to work from derricks overside because of the hold's central position. Experience in working these holds was considered a big asset. The plum holds though were the capacious Nos. 2 & 4 with their higher financial rewards and it was the very best gangs who worked these. There was a degree of 'promotion' about changes of hold and although it was rare for an entire gang to move, say from 1 to 2, men might be invited to more lucrative holds if the top hand there needed replacements and had been impressed with a chap's work or stature in another gang.

Back in the late 1940s before I joined RML, an irritating legacy of the War still caused tension between gangs and the shippers. When ships made it to the Docks in spite of the best efforts of the U Boats, getting supplies out of the holds as quickly as possible was an obvious priority and whatever men were available were set to work. Neat distinctions disappeared and men worked when they could, where they could just to get the holds emptied. After the War gangs went back to working specific holds but when the gang working one of the more valuable 2 or 4 Holds had a lunch break, downholders from the less productive holds might move in, remove a few of the more valuable consignments and claim the financial rewards before the allocated gang returned. The complaints were about money, of course, but also about the chaotic state the interlopers had left the holds in. That had to be Furness, Withy's problem – Royal Mail wanted the limited number of ships they then possessed turned round as quickly as possible during this time of rationing and were happy to turn a blind eye. By the time I was a ship's clerk, this matter had been resolved.

One of the FW shipworkers I worked with regularly, for example, was Bill Holland – a Blue – so that when he was discharging a ship all the gangs were Blue: Teddy Gould worked No 1, 'Knocker' White, 2, 'Bluey' Jones, 3, Charley Goldstone, 4, and Bert Fenton, 5. 'Knocker' must have been born sometime before 1890, he had been in the docks well before the First World War and before the King George V was constructed: his views on the Call would have been interesting. He retired in the early 1950s and Fred Jackson took over his gang, another excellent top hand demanding the highest standard from his men. To give some idea of the daily intricacies and working standards during those early post-War days, consider this:

One day Fred's gang were working the large No. 2 hold of a RML sugar ship, one of the 'E' boats. They had been working all day clearing the upper hold of its general cargo so as to get at the two thousand tons of sugar in the lower hold but as they got to it, it started to rain heavily. The gang was ordered to 'Hatch up'. There was a fall back pay allowance called 'rain money' to compensate for this early end to work but it was only a fraction of what they could have expected to earn. It was after 3 o'clock and most gangs would have settled for two hours at the lower rate and enjoyed the respite, but that was not Fred's style. They hung on. Suddenly there was a new complication: the gang working the smaller No.1 hold would be finished by 5 o'clock and in order to get the ship turned round quickly, RML wanted and could require them to join Fred's gang in No. 2 on the following day. If two gangs worked one hold they remained separate both using a section of the hatchway to serve as the marker determining one gang's sugar from the next. Now hatches were never placed centrally over the hold so that there was a lot more sugar, and a lot more money, on one side of the divide than on the other. Unfortunately for Fred, the last consignment from the upper hold that his gang was going to have to move first thing next day lay forward over the smaller quantity of sugar. Having taken that side, he was committed to it for the rest of the hold so that the No. 1 gang not only had the benefit of having the upper hold cleared for them but also had the lion's share of the lucrative sugar. This was more than Fred could stomach so he ordered his men back down again using the manway and with the hatches still on and with the minimal light from a hastily rigged set of old 'clusters', started work. All we could hear from the top deck was a constant low rumble. When they were ready, Fred came back on deck and as soon as the rain eased, just before 4.30, he ordered the hatch covers off and there set neatly in the centre of the hatchway was the consignment of bitumen contained in its fifty odd huge barrels. The crane rushed the barrels to the quay with the men working at a punishing pace, clearing the upper hold by 5pm. With not a little satisfaction, the men hatched up once more secure in the knowledge that on the following day, as the resident gang they could nominate which section of sugar they wanted.

Of course, money was the spur, but knowing the personalities I'm sure it was pride which was the prime mover. The weather was poor, the daylight fading fast, the men had already worked hard all day and whatever happened, they would not starve. There was no great imperative requiring them to take on this challenge – except the determination to prove that they were not the No. 2 gang for nothing.

Good gang leaders did not simply goad their men to extra money, although this was important, but they were also concerned with their gang's welfare and safety, remember the consumptive in 'Ory Mantelow's gang. Always at the start of work, leaders like Fred would spend the first half hour or so down among the downholders organising the teams and looking out for problems. During this time he would put another man to act as top hand and only when he was sure that everyone knew what they were doing would he go back on deck. It was important for the gang leader to be the top hand for most of the work because he could keep in touch with all his men including the barge or pitch hands. He could see how barges were being brought up, he could liaise with his shipworker for extra equipment, consider the engagement of a leg runner or winchman and arrange possible work for the shore gang. He would also be keeping a look out for 'Charley Hatches', watching the weather, and finding out what new work was coming up the Channel. A wise leader would also be keeping a close eye on what the other gangs were up to.

With deregulation, as scratch gangs were becoming more common in the Royal Group, some sort of juggling by the ship's clerk became necessary to maintain the quality of off-loading. For example, if the older, loyal gangs were working Nos. 2 & 4 Holds where work was still in progress but the smaller holds had finished discharging, it was worth RML's working regime to switch the five gangs to the next ship arriving at berth especially if the new cargoes were sensitive. In the lower holds tended to be stowed less important items often acting as ballast – scrap metal was a common choice – and if this were the case here, these could be given over to scratch gangs without fear of damage. This left 'Ory, and Bill to set their teams to work on the incoming vessel. In this situation it might be worth waiting half a day for the good gangs to finish shifting particular cargoes in the discharging ship before offering them the next ship. The old idea of each gang emptying their contracted hold began to lose ground. By the very early 1960s both Fred Jackson and 'Ory had retired, increasingly the new gangs had access to scooters and fork lift trucks and the container revolution was getting into its stride. These more mechanised gangs were to occupy the Royal Docks for a relatively short period in the declining years of the industry's history.

*   *   *

I have mentioned elsewhere the little custom of barge hands clambering up to rejoin their gang on the top deck at the end of each day to leave the ship as a unit to hand in their tokens but perhaps I haven't done it justice.

Cornporters had the advantage of a grain machine which sucked the grain out of the hold and into the barge – more on this later – so that at the end of the day they were able to use the ladders on the machine itself to get back on board. On the older machines these were heavy, wooden ladders worked by pulleys which could be laid against the side of the ship and gave a reassuring sense of solidity but newer machines introduced lightweight, whippy aluminium ladders which were a technical innovation not appreciated by the cornporters as they wobbled and bounced their way up to the top deck

But the general cargo gangs had a worse possibility: working at the extreme ends of the ship by No.1 and No.5 holds barge hands sometimes found that craft couldn't moor parallel to the ship and had to moor at an angle 'between the ropes'. Frequently this was because lighters at 2 and 4 holds needed extra space to squeeze round, occasionally it was because a sailing barge could not get its mast under the mooring ropes. In any case, the result was that a lighter lay inelegantly under the bow or stern. At the end of a day or with the holds emptied barge hands somehow had to get back to the top deck from this odd positioning of their craft. At the other holds it was easier because the vertical sides of the vessel and the close alignment of barge and ship meant that metal ladders could be scaled but at the bows and stern the curvature of the hull meant that rope ladders had to be lowered. Barge hands, Blue or White, would do anything to avoid using them. Often it meant clambering over other lighters until they gained the quay and then ascended the gang plank but if their barge was completely isolated under the ship's bows, then they had no alternative but to become very reluctant trapeze artists wobbling their way up to the top deck – much to the amusement and jeers of the rest of the gang gathered there.

*   *   *

SPREADS, BROTHERS AND CHANDELIERS

Spreads were octagonal or hexagonal canvas sheets with rope loops at their corners for attaching to a crane hook. They would be used for collecting loose items such as spilt sugar or cowhides.

'Brothers' consisted of a pair of wires or ropes each with a hook at one end and joined together at the other by a single metal ring. The ring would be placed on a crane hook and the two smaller hooks could be used, for example, to bite into the opposite ends of a barrel or drum. Typically, two sets of brothers were used together on one crane to slot into the four corners of a set board when discharging, for example, a set of metal bars.

Chandeliers were an alternative to two sets of brothers: a square metal frame had four ropes or wires meeting on a metal ring which attached to a crane hook with four wires descending from the frame, each with its own hook. Thus four hooks were again available for lifting sets or set boards.

To recap: Royal Mail Lines had contracts with stevedoring companies (notably here Furness, Withy) to work their cargoes but the handling gangs themselves were, traditionally, casual labour. To bridge this administrative gap, stevedoring companies employed local representatives to balance the duties of import ship's clerks and these men were called 'shipworkers'. Shipworkers were always ex-gangers, and although employed as supervisors, always held onto their union cards in case they decided that paper work wasn't for them.

Furness, Withy employed three permanent shipworkers and hired additional casual shipworkers from among the labour force as work demanded. It was the unstated job of shipworkers to build up a rapport with the gangs they employed. The reputation of a stevedoring company ultimately relied upon the ability of shipworkers to get hold of good gangs. Equally, it was the job of gang leaders to get regular employment for their men and so very strong loyalties between gangs and shipworkers developed. Each shipworker would have his five gangs, one for each hold, following him and the import clerk for Royal Mail Lines would know when he saw the shipworker he was to work along side, which gangs would be off-loading the next ship. This was the fundamental organisational device. Stevedoring companies employed shipworkers who in turn organised the labour work on each ship they supervised. Above them were permanent staff, superintendents like Mr Darby or his assistant Mr Harvey while below them the casual gangs who were employed only for as long as it took to empty their hold. In practice such an open-ended method of engagement lead to men looking for people they knew, shipworkers and gang leaders, building up mutual trust and reliance in each other in the same way that gangs formed into definite teams of men who had confidence in each other's work rate. As a ship was finishing a shipworker was told the next ship he would be supervising, maybe already coming up the Thames, perhaps a day or two away. The shipworker would then tell his gangs when he would be next at the Call to take on men, the assumption being that work would be there for them if they wanted it. Once the National Dock Labour Scheme began to bite this practice was seen as favouritism and, I suppose, it was in its way but it was to a purpose. The experience of these older men was that in order to earn a decent wage the work would be hard and unrelenting; survival meant having faith in each other's commitment, knowing the holds and cargoes of the Royal Mail Lines fleet helped. The demand for everyone to have an equal opportunity of employment, Blue or White, irrespective of experience or dock base sounds fairer but in practice, in my experience, it had a depressing effect on working standards. Perhaps this is just another way of saying that by the 1960's younger men were no longer prepared to become slave labour.

Traditionally, permanent employees of RML and the various companies they had contracts with worked along side each other in all weathers and conditions so the small team of import clerks got to know their shipworkers very well and the gangs who followed them.

Fred Waterman was an example of a typically larger than life Blue shipworker, able to carry the responsibility for discharging a ship yet always wanting to be in on the action. We shall see elsewhere how different sheds altered the way cargoes could be worked but a Fred Waterman incident can introduce this idea. A RML ship was loading export cargo from an unusual berth, one situated on the south side of the Basin. The reason might have been because the quarantine sheds were there, for among the cargoes was a pedigree bull on its way to Argentina to improve blood stock. The apron round the sheds here was very narrow and it proved impossible for the lorry carrying the bull to get up onto the quay. Instead, the plan was changed to unload the animal behind the shed on the railway tracks then lead it up the ramp and on to the quay where a horse box was waiting to lift it into the ship's hold.

Knowing the animal was coming, Fred had been telling all the gangs that bulls didn't scare him, that he was a 'natural' with animals, should have been a farmer, and so on. He sensed a general air of disbelief and decided to take a look at the creature before it came aboard. While he was casting his eye over the bull he reasoned that he might just as well lead it up onto the quay himself, it would impress the natives. He untied it but unfortunately for him no one had told the bull how good Fred was with animals, with a sudden lunge the bull broke free chasing a seriously startled Fred up the tracks. One of the qualities shipworkers were noted for was thinking on their feet and with a ton of prime beef breathing down his neck, Fred had the presence of mind to slip in between two stationary railway wagons too narrow for the bull to follow. The bull came to a halt, confused, while Fred from his ignominious safety point shouted for the handlers. Once they had re-established calm and taken him onto the quay a very shame faced Fred crept out to confront the general derision – not for long though, he wasn't the sort to be kept down.

Fred was also a keen follower of all-in wrestling and used to go regularly to East Ham Bath's wrestling matches. One evening he went straight from the pub after work rather the worse for drink and was mortified to see the athlete he supported getting thrown all over the ring, eventually losing by a knock out. Unable to contain himself Fred let out a roar, climbed into the ring and made for the winner, 'Black Butcher Johnson', with his docker's hook. The wrestler rushed out of the ring closely followed by Fred and just managed to lock himself in his dressing room with Fred clawing at the door. The promoter, smelling money, invited Fred, a fifteen and a half stone labourer to resolve his little difficulty at the same time the following week but from inside the ring. Fred, beer in and wits out readily agreed and it was only as he sobered up that he realised that he may not have acted altogether wisely. Unfortunately, most of the spectators were dockers so he couldn't back out. As he said on the day following the encounter, his feet didn't touch the canvas – he spent his one and only time in the ring either in the air or on his back. But he was man enough to tell the tale and tell it with a grin. He was a widower with a house in Bonny Downs Road where the gypsies lived; he was a rougher diamond than most, but a diamond none the less.

Even a shipworker as alert and experienced as Bill Holland could sometimes get things wrong. He was helping a winchman change a runner one day when his attention was distracted to something that was happening on one of the lighters they were working into. As he was looking over the side, his ankle caught in a squirming hawser loop and he was snatched onto the barrel. The winch of course was a seriously powerful instrument and turning all the time to lay the runner; as he was dragged onto it his pelvis was crushed and he was confined to hospital for seven months.

*   *   *

FLYNN

There was a flamboyant, manic Irish top hand by the name of Flynn who worked No. 2 hold. He and his gang belonged to the 'Blue' union and the whole team were excellent workers, the trouble was he went his own way and you never knew what he might do next. Usually a ship's clerk discussed options with the shipworker and top hand so that everyone knew how work would proceed but Flynn just did things; as a supervisor you couldn't relax if he was working on your ship. For example, fogs were a huge problem for working ships: if top hands couldn't see what was happening to the men in the hold or out on the lighters he was unable to assess potentially dangerous situations and if the crane driver couldn't see the signals from his top hand, hazards were very quickly multiplied. If a real 'pea souper' came down there was no alternative but to stop work and lose pay. Except at Flynn's hold. When everyone else had bowed to the inevitable, he would be scraping around for old newspapers, oil cloth or hessian sacks to set alight and by waving these flaming torches above his head as signals he would keep his men working. Sets would loom suddenly out of the fog compounding dangers in a situation which was intrinsically hazardous even in perfect weather - but so long as the cargo Flynn was working allowed, he kept his men off-loading. He was a natural motivator. You could urge caution but he just brushed you aside and carried on shouting to his men, it wasn't comfortable having him around but, we had to admit, he was effective.

When work was slack he would do painting jobs for the Council. He painted at night by the light of street lamps or by an extension lead he had rigged up to one, the results next morning by the full light of day were horrendous but he was paid for quantity not quality. After a couple of hours sleep he would be back in the docks dressed still in pyjamas with a pair of trousers and a jacket thrown over the top, always filthy and stinking, ready for the new day. He had a brother who also worked in the docks and was the complete opposite, mild mannered, self-effacing, quiet.

To complete the picture of stevedoring involvement we should just look at the work of the superintendents. Furness, Withy as an organisation was based on the other side of the river over at Finland Yard in the Surrey Docks. The Company's stevedoring commitments to the Royal Group though meant that it was necessary to have someone permanently based there with overall authority, and in my early years in the docks this was Mr 'crude-as-hell' Darby. He had spent all his working life in the docks starting off as a tally clerk before the War and through sheer ability ultimately became docks superintendent for all Furness, Withy's interests there. On a day to day basis he was responsible for the loading of all the ships his company had contracts with, including, of course, Royal Mail Lines. Off-loading he left to his second in command. Through a lifetime spent in the docks he knew everything there was to know about the ships, the holds and cargoes but remained throughout an uncouth bruiser. He could look at piles of export items stacked in their bays in a shed and immediately say what volume they would take up and where they would fit in the overall loading of each ship. Officially the estimators used a 4ft rule but he never seemed to need one, he would look at a jumble of garden implements for example and say "That's 45 cubic feet, isn't it?" and nobody disagreed. Like the Blue gangs and shipworkers under him, he would pride himself on tight, efficient and stable loadings and he was the ultimate authority on what was possible. Gangs and shipworkers alike respected his judgement as he proved daily but if he did get into arguments his technique was simply out-swear the opposition.

It was proper that the dock superintendent for a stevedoring company should take on the exacting task of supervising loading but there was also a distinct advantage for him in that the rates of pay for these gangs were the best available. The men taken on for loading a ship were in consequence good, conscientious, hardworking and smart. Blue loading gangs were paid by volume while off-loading (usually Whites) were paid by weight which always worked in the stevedores' favour; a car weighing one ton would be discharged at that weight but it could occupy the space of a theoretical eight to ten cubic tons and would be loaded as such. In this custom lay the recognition that the safe, efficient stowage of a ship needed a skill unmatched by the off-loading gangs. There were times when careful measurement and placement were necessary from the loading gangs and a simple piece work formula of pay-by-weight-moved would have been counter-productive. It will come as no surprise that, compared with off-loading, the working relationships between permanent staff and gangs engaged upon exports were more consistently harmonious.

Four and a half ton concrete mixers were being loaded by union purchase into No. 4 Lower Hold onto the *Tweed* one day around 1950 destined for Brazil. I was still a tally clerk recording their stowage and Mr Darby came late in the afternoon to watch the last ones on. The work was coming to an end around 4 o'clock and you couldn't get a sixpence between the crates they were so tightly packed – with the exception of the last one which needed clearance to withdraw the chains once set in position. Immediately Mr Darby picked up on the fact that one of the blocks at the top of the sticks was seizing and he told the shipworker he wasn't happy. The space had been nicely judged by the men measuring, as they usually did, with their feet or a piece of string, the gangs never used rulers, and the last mixer was hovering over the hold space. Men were beginning to relax and a few of them were sitting on the crates playing the newly introduced card game of American crap. Almost as Darby was speaking, the block froze and the wire snapped. There was a loud crack as the wire whipped across the deck cutting Jimmy Old, the top hand's, head open and flicking off his cap. Down in the hold, the card players who had been waiting for the last mixer to come over found that it arrived a bit quicker than expected – fortunately the wire had shuddered and screeched a warning as it was breaking and the men just had time to dive out of the way. The four and a half ton set crashed into the hold tilting as it fell and smashed into the neighbouring crates where the men had scampered. It sat diagonally across its intended niche supported on either side by the shattered woodwork the downholders were still standing on. For a moment there was absolute silence while everyone took in what had happened, felt themselves to see if anything was missing then took a quick head count to see if anyone had been under it. Very fortunately no one was injured. My most immediate concern was the realisation that the derrick holding the mixer had, itself, come down and landed within three feet of where I was standing. The weary downholders just stood rooted to the spot as crates disintegrated beneath them. Whoever had rigged the derrick, either the loading gang or a shore gang, had made a poor job of it and its shortcomings had been overlooked but it meant that a rigged system that was theoretically designed to lift 10 tons had finally collapsed under the weight of the last mixer. It was at times like this that the full power of the forces dockers daily worked with came home to them and everybody suddenly felt very vulnerable.

Mr. Darby's vocabulary was tailor made precisely for this sort of moment. He issued a string of fairly unsubtle expletives, colourful, even by his standards to the effect that in his estimation someone must have erred and that on a practical point tomorrow would be soon enough to sort out the mess. The language may have been elemental but the decision was dead right; men with tired limbs already shaken by something so traumatic were in no condition to work their way out of this mess safely. The gang hatched up. Darby was boorish but he knew his job.

Under Mr. Darby was his assistant Mr. Harvey. How the two managed to work together I will never know for Mr Harvey was a very different character. He had a superior bearing befitting someone who had been a First World War cavalry officer and his manner in dealing with casual labour was always as an officer reprimanded squaddies. He had been a physical training instructor also and was happy to let everyone know what poor specimens the Second World War turned out. Singapore would never have surrendered if his men had been there and as I had been a physical training instructor in the Second World War the comments were not aimed at establishing good relations. For some reason I never knew, Harvey disliked Ned Smith, perhaps he had disliked Ted Smith before him, so he had no intention of looking favourably on a World War II Smith. Nothing vindictive, more contemptuously aloof but then most people in the docks seemed to come into that category with him. He was a strict Methodist and perhaps it was just as well that his working day only marginally overlapped with Darby's for Mr. Harvey's responsibilities were devoted to off-loading. He was highly respected as a man of authority and even the gangers treated him with some awe but the nature of his job guaranteed that arguments were frequent. Discharge gangs knew their rates were inferior to those of the loaders and looked for any allowances to increase their earnings. A shipworker might have agreed an hour's stand-by allowance as lighters had to be manoeuvred, and Harvey on a visit later might challenge him reckoning the time to be closer to ten minutes. It was his job in effect to get the gangs to do the work with minimal add-ons and gangs backed up by their shipworker not unnaturally fought this. Whatever the circumstances of their altercation, Mr. Harvey insisted that there must be no swearing. Down a hold embattled with a group of aggressive gangers he would quickly establish the rules of combat: "If that's the sort of language you want to use, I have nothing to say to you, you may stand over there. Now is there anyone else who can discuss this with me without swearing?" Burly dockers were suddenly back at school or in front of their CO but men obeyed him perhaps because not many years before their very employment would have depended on his good auspices and old habits died hard. He was equally critical of drunkenness so if men wanted to work with Furness, Withy they had to maintain high personal standards. Nevertheless the pressure of his job was unremitting and arguments with ship and quay gangs incessant. Eventually, while sorting out a ship berthed over in the Basin he died of a heart attack down in a hold arguing with gangers.

*   *   *

TRAINS vs SHIPS

Where railway lines bridged over locks the rule was that trains had the right of way through the Cut at the Connaught Road as this was between docks (ie internal to the Royal Group) but ships had the right of way out onto the River and into the docks as ships could not be stranded between tides. The passenger terminal at Gallions Reach was bombed in 1940 so this priority system became less an issue after the War. Passengers boarding ships then did so at Tilbury or occasionally in the Royal Docks.

Only Head Office in Fenchurch Street needed the complete knowledge of the RML fleet. They would know which ships were working, not only in the Royal Group but also in any other of the docks of London. They would know which ships were heading up the Channel, which were queuing at Gravesend and broadly where their ships were in the Caribbean and the Americas. Much of this we in the Royals would also know but our focus was closer: we had to concentrate on the vessels in front of us. Head Office would also be dealing with the cruise liners out of Southampton such as the *'Andes'* or the *'Asturias'* (both around 20,000 tons), ships which never came into London and with the Pacific Steam Navigation Company fleet (PSNC) which worked out of Liverpool but which did also berth in the Royals. They would be concerned with cargoes and traders but also with passengers and crews, both of which were outside our regard. Head Office had pictures of RML ships adorning their walls, ships out on the oceans or in exotic locations, I don't remember seeing any images there of vessels off-loading cargoes in the Royals. They had ships' plans and cabin options and they had beautifully detailed models of ships in their windows but they didn't work on ships; specifically, they didn't see goods out of holds. That was also true of some employees in the docks who got no further through Gate No. 6 than the main dock office. Only the Marine Superintendent who had a roving and formidable brief would have been as well acquainted with the overall state of the fleet as with the reality of working cargoes.

This is not a serious survey of RML ships but just an opportunity to introduce a few points as they affected dock work. Royal Mail Lines had lost twenty ships during the War and had had the infrastructure it had built up in South America sold off by the Government as part of the War effort. These events had come hard on the heals of a radical reorganisation of the Company (then the Royal Mail Steam Packet Company) in the wake of the Depression during which smaller businesses like the Ben and Nelson Lines had been absorbed into a new parent Company (Royal Mail Lines). After the War by way of compensation the Government handed over a number of US ships to bolster its fleet, not necessarily the ships the Company would have preferred but all that were available at the time. With this unplanned accumulation of vessels it set about transporting the imports and exports the Country so desperately needed, and it was through these ships' holds that dockers had to manhandle disparate cargoes.

For the dock staff of Royal Mail Lines, however modest our roles within the Company, the ships were always more than five working holds. Most of us had no experience of them as ocean transport but their appearance mattered; a ship designed with passengers in mind always sat well amongst freighters however unlikely a resurgence of mass passenger traffic might have been. Although the elite ships of RML's fleet, the ocean liners, worked out of Southampton by way of compensation we did have the 'Highland' boats (around 14000 tons). Ships like the *'Highland Monarch'* and *'Highland Princess'* had been acquired from the venerable Nelson Line and gave not a little status to us Company employees who worked on them. They were beautiful, well formed ships with more than a touch of opulence designed for their assumed two or three hundred passengers, with wood panelled 'Jacobean' and 'Tudor' state rooms. These were solid, broad beamed and stable ships making decisions about loading relatively straightforward but it was their appearance which made us proud to be associated with them. Deficiencies in their hold spaces could almost be seen as part of their charm.

Probably the oldest ship in the RML fleet was the *'Lochmonar'* (9400 tons) a medium sized general cargo vessel which joined the Company in 1924. It was said, probably apocryphally, that the reason she survived the War was that she was too slow to keep up with the convoys and so escaped 'U' boat attention.

Although known as a general cargo vessel, during the inter-war years when air travel was in its infancy, competition for passengers was fierce amongst the shipping lines and the *Lochmonar* in consequence had been equipped with quite impressive accommodation facilities. My time in the docks only overlapped with her by a couple of years, but one incident is memorable.

All working ships had a room made available for the ship's clerk to use as an office, often no more than a cubby hole or locker by No2 hold, a space just large enough for a couple of men to squeeze in and with a shelf long enough to set out the relevant paper work. On the *Lochmonar* I felt privileged to be offered the state room as it had no function, passengers had long since deserted the ship. It was an imposing room richly gilded and decorated in stark contrast to my usual working environment but one which had seen better days. Nevertheless, it was away from the elements and after wiping the dirt off one of the tables it did handsomely as an office, especially for someone new to the docks. The ship's plans were laid out and in due course my boss, Bill Saggars, arrived and we set to work organising the off-loading. This was not straightforward, especially for a novice, given the range of cargoes, importers and hauliers involved. As we worked specks of dust kept dropping off the decorative mouldings. We just brushed them aside and didn't give them a second thought, in an atmosphere determined by pea soup fogs and Becton Gas Works, motes were common enough.

It was only on the following morning that these other occupants of *Lochmonar's* state room made their presence felt, my skin was covered with angry, itching bites of various hues. The question was whether this was a personal hygiene issue or something I could blame on the docks and it was with considerable relief that, creeping back to work, I discovered Bill too was similarly afflicted: those motes were mites. On the whole we decided cramped outdoor lockers were preferable.

The Liberty boats built by the United States from prefabricated units were something of a revelation to RML, being simply holds, engine and crew's quarters. There was no status attached to them, passengers would have been an encumbrance, nothing to admire, just plain utilitarian. What was more, they were made of welded sections, not riveted, and the fear amongst the crews, we learnt, was that the lack of 'give' would cause them to break their backs in rough seas or crack like an egg under torpedo attack. Just nautical superstition as it turned out but in the docks, gangs working the holds found the smooth surfaces and good proportions very much to their liking. The nature of shipping was changing; these ships – RML called them their 'B' boats with names such as '*Berbice*' and '*Barranca*' (7,000 tons) – were pointing to a future in which freight, not passengers, were the priority. The '*Loch Ryan*' purchased in 1946 by Royal Mail Lines adopted some of these modernisations using welded sections and well-proportioned holds. We have already made mention of her large hatches.

Among the last ships to be built for Royal Mail Lines were the new 'A' boats (around 20,000 tons) launched in the late nineteen fifties and early sixties. They were something of a compromise with clean, open holds but still looking back to the days of passenger liners. The hope seemed to be that by introducing enough chrome plating and Formica, together with genuine innovations like escalators between decks and AC electricity, passengers would be tempted back from the new airline services, to trans-Atlantic shipping. Not only was the thinking questionable but the execution seemed skimpy; in order to create good hold spaces without stanchions it appeared as if the whole accommodation block had to be made lightweight. The impression given was that they were insubstantial when set alongside the old Highland boats and for many of us were something of an embarrassment. From a practical viewpoint, being physically lightweight these ships were 'tender' and as they were built for the River Plate meat trade, loading and off-loading could cause problems. (See 'Meat')

A couple of well intentioned innovations were associated with the winches of these newer ships and caused no end of trouble:

The design and placement of derricks around a ship's hold varied but each one needed a winch to raise and lower sets when cranes were not available. Each winch was a drum powered by a motor with a runner wrapped round it which could be played out or reeled in as the sets were worked. When a gang used derricks they used them in pairs and for each derrick there needed to be a winchman. One and two ton sets needed to be worked carefully requiring very good communication between winchmen and their top hand. In the past winches were noisy, diesel driven instruments but on the A boats someone decided to install nearly silent electric motors. This might have seemed a civilising step forward but in practice vibrations in the diesel motors 'spoke' to their operators just as a car engine tells you when to change gear. The inscrutability of the electric winches gave no indication of the strain they were under, until they broke. There was no warning, no sense of effort, just a smooth electric hum, or collapse. They had more trouble with those electric winches than all those on the rest of the fleet, much to the frustration of the gangs.

A second innovation was the introduction of cabins. Probably more to protect the winch than the winchman, each winch had been sheltered within its own housing and the winchman could only operate it by being inside. Unfortunately the designers had no idea, it seems, of the level of communication necessary in working cargoes from the 'sticks' and when each winchman was in his housing he was completely cut off from what was going on outside: teamwork became impossible. The first solution, in the Victorian tradition of dock work, was to hire an extra man whose job it was to run between the two cabins and the top hand passing orders. He was known as a 'crow' and in practice, was not particularly effective – responses needed to be more immediate, more integrated. The later solution, more in keeping with the sixties perhaps, was to smash away the metal bars at the tiny windows of each cabin. With half his head squeezed out the window a winchman might then just catch what was going on with sufficient understanding to clear a hold safely and not explode the winch.

There were innovations which caused mismatches between hold and handling and these could have very unpleasant side effects. There was a period of incongruities when older ships with rivets and stanchions, loaded with cargoes in the traditional way were being worked by gangs with newly available forklift trucks. These aids were scarce but if a gang were offered one, in spite of their lack of experience they would happily accept it in the knowledge that a lot of physical effort would be spared them and that their work rate would increase dramatically. Any tread built into the tyres quickly became shredded as they came into contact with the older riveted surfaces and when they were working on top of cargoes, eight feet by four feet metal sheets had to be laid to provide a surface to drive over. The wheels would spin uncontrollably as the tyres failed to grip to the metal then suddenly shooting the sheets out from under them to clatter against the sides of the hold or ricochet off stanchions. Men quickly learnt to keep clear of the area behind a fork lift, though as the machine skidded and bucked to get each load this was often easier said than done. One downholder I remember had both his legs broken by a flying sheet but in one sense he was fortunate: on this occasion sheets of plywood had been laid to form the surface, a metal sheet would have taken both his legs off. In another incident a poor man did in fact lose a leg as the fork lift slithering across this uneven surface suddenly bounced sideways to where he was standing. Within a few months he was back in the docks as a tally clerk. American observers were unimpressed by the way our dockers were using these machines but at the time there doesn't seem to have been any instruction or safety advice, nor were the ships constructed or the cargoes stowed necessarily with fork lifts in mind. In the United States they had probably been in general use for a generation, integrating the whole process of cargo movements into one mechanised system. Here shortcomings were put down to 'docker incompetence'.

72

In 1839 the young Queen Victoria granted the title 'Royal' to a new shipping company and an Act of Parliament established its duties and field of operations. The Royal Mail Steam Packet Company had been the brainchild of a much travelled Scot named James MacQueen who had had the perspicacity to see a commercial link between the rapid rise in trans-Atlantic mail and the new reliability offered by steam powered ships. His proposal was for an 'ocean stage coach' with the official duty of carrying Her Majesty's mail and thereby allowing him to operate a regular trading fleet with the added status and revenues from its semi-Governmental duties.

Because of this official function as a Government mail carrier the Company was put under the wing of the Admiralty who until 1902 insisted in appointing its Chairman. This turned out to be a mixed blessing for the Company but with the Admiralty's attention to discipline and cleanliness the Royal Mail Steam Packet Company at least gained a self belief in its own superiority over other mercantile fleets. Even after the Second World War, successive Marine Superintendents saw it as a major duty to demand that ships leaving the docks were well appointed to Admiralty standards. Unfortunately this period also coincided with a fashion for shorter funnels to give ships a sleeker appearance with the result that, particularly when steaming into the trade winds to the West Indies, thick deposits of diesel fumes were inevitably deposited on passenger decks and walkways. Whether or not passengers were expected, Marine Superintendents insisted that each ship left the docks worthy of the tradition of Royal Mail Lines. This meant work for shore gangs.

Shore gangs were employed by the Port of London Authority to clean and tidy the sheds and quays. Over the course of time the term became more associated with 'cleaning' than 'shore' so that the teams of men RML employed to maintain standards of cleanliness were known as 'shore gangs although they worked almost entirely on board Company ships. Cargo handling gangs cleared a hold then, as part of their overall function, the shore gang moved in to clean it. Each hold was inspected by a Health Officer and until it had been issued with a certificate of cleanliness a shipping company could not start re-loading.

For much of the time shore gangs and cargo gangs worked different parts of the ship but when they both worked in holds their duties were entirely different: stevedores and dockworkers handled commodities, shore gangs refuse. Ship gangs dealt with merchandise, shore gangs, hygiene. So long as a shipment remained sound, it belonged to an importer and discharging it from the hold was the first step towards getting it to its owner. Once a cargo had been condemned by the Port Health Authorities, it was spoilage to be off loaded by the shore gangs into refuse barges – most lighterage companies kept one or two – to be taken down River to a dumping ground. If, say, crates of oranges had collapsed, the fruit squashed and decaying, discharge gangs would not touch it. Under more typical circumstances, sound and damaged fruit would exist together in the same shipment and the handlers would toss the bad stuff aside to get at the cargoes, leaving the refuse for the shore gangs to clear up later. On a bad shipment there might be a substantial quantity for shore gangs to move and all of it, by definition, in a pretty unsavoury state. On the other hand with a good shipment of bulk sugar once the discharge gang had removed with broom, shovel and pick axe all they practically could, the shore gang arrived to hose down what was not now 'sugar' but 'contamination', in this case a relatively light task.

There was no overlap between the work done by handlers and shore gangs and in consequence no rivalry for only when it had been agreed generally that everything sound had been discharged, did shore gangs move in to remove the waste. Shore gangs handled what everyone else wouldn't – or as they said in the docks, 'shore gangs only handled cargoes to steal them'.

Under normal circumstances, for each RML ship berthed with five holds working, there would be one resident shore gang – there was rarely enough work for more. While the cargo gangs cleared the holds the shore gang would be cleaning the cabins and accommodation block, generally getting the ship fit to receive its de-ratting certificate which each ship had to produce before it was issued with a Bill of Clearance for each outward voyage. Usually shore gangs only took over a hold once its cargo was discharged.

There were frequent times though during the working of each hold when the shore gang might be called in to clear up particular messes which hampered the ship gang's work and it was often the downholders themselves who summonsed the shore gang while they took a 'breather'. Cargoes might be spoilt, barrels might be leaking badly, there might be timber to dismantle or separation paper to be taken away; for any number of reasons shore gangs might join a cargo gang down a hold for short periods. Because it made sense to get shore gangs in to tidy up as a hold was worked, lunch breaks were arranged differently, stevedores and dockworkers from twelve to one, shore gangs one to two, giving them an hour each day to get round the five holds re-establishing order for the afternoon session.

Although their work was unskilled and relatively poorly paid some shore gangs were permanently employed by RML and these formed experienced teams capable of taking on more than basic cleaning duties. Shore gangs came under the direct responsibility of the Marine Superintendent and were a branch of ship maintenance rather than cargo handling. On board a working ship there was no confusion of roles downholders were Furness, Withy, shore gangs Royal Mail Lines, and they saw the ship differently.

'Preparing the ship' was an official phrase for something like an hour's work getting each ship ready for the discharge gangs and might include, for example, clearing the decks of clutter, rigging and topping the derricks, under supervision and, on the newer vessels, removing the McGregor hatches for each hold. It was the direct responsibility of the shipping company to make cargoes available to the handling gangs.

Competent shore gangs would also be put to work improving the general state of each ship doing jobs unrelated to the work stevedores and dockworkers were doing. Major engineering work was beyond them but they might be told to oil pulleys, grease exposed pieces of metal. (Portholes however were outside their brief as by union agreements porthole repairs required two specialists, a fitter to undo the bolts holding a pane in place and a glazier to replace the glass). They would chip off rust and flaking paint, repaint decks and holds and generally get the ship spruced up to RML standards. This sort of maintenance work created the only time I can recall of friction between shore gang and discharge gangs. If a ship was on a strict time-table, for example if she was booked into dry dock or due to pick up passengers, the work of the shore gang might sit uncomfortably close to cargo gangs. On this one occasion a war nearly broke out when the shore gang had been told to repaint the hull of a ship where paint had blistered. There were twelve men suspended on platforms outside the hull chip, chip, chipping away at the rust while the discharge gangs on the inside found as holds emptied and, consequently, the sound less and less absorbed, that they were working on the inside of a gigantic metal drum. The supervisors on deck could of course hear the noise but were blissfully unaware how bad it had become deep in the hold until the demented downholders could stand it no more and appeared on deck with murder in their eyes. As the penny finally dropped the shipping clerk and shore gang beat a hasty retreat to re-assess options.

Many shore gangs were not permanent Company employees. Gangs might be needed at any time of the day or night, depending upon the ship's circumstances and the state of the tide rather than upon regular office hours so a shore gang 'leader' would be asked to get a 'scratch' team together. He would tour the pups and clubs to see who wanted some ready cash. Such gangs had no loyalty or commitment to the dock system, had no cohesion and were formed from anyone who needed beer money. They had no reference to Blue and White rivalries and no interest in making a career in the docks they were casual labour at its most casual. They belonged to any union or none and even if they were members of the TGWU they would not have been in the same branches as the dockworkers. This was an advantage in practice for whenever a strike was called it did not affect the work of these shore gangs and they were able to continue tidying a ship or making it safe.

Shore gangs had no status but neither did they seek it, their work could be done anywhere and these scratch gangs existed right on the periphery of dock life. What fixed the lowliness of their standing in the eyes of all the other workers was the tasks they had to perform clearing out the cabins. Merchant seamen, particularly those taken on for the long haul voyages to the West Coast of South America could be a pretty low form of maritime life and the last few days of a voyage would be spent in perpetual drinking. The shore gangs would arrive to find the cabins ankle deep in vomit.

The following incident might help illustrate how things changed during my thirty years in the Royal Docks:

Shouts, yells, bellows, raised voices were a constant in the docks competing with the noise of machinery or across open spaces but when you heard sustained shouting from a number of voices with plenty of swearing going on you knew there was trouble and you had to take note. I was in King George V Dock when this particular confrontation took place and I was relieved to discover that the exchange was happening away from our top deck on a ship at the next berth. Situations could get ugly fast and when you realised you were not directly involved, you offered up a blessing and got on with your job. At this time I had enough to deal with, with all five holds working – the trouble was not happening on a RML ship – and my attention returned to our cargoes. The altercation continued, it was obviously something out of the ordinary but it was not until much later in the day that I discovered what the problem was.

The ship had been off-loading a large shipment of timber into a lighter and occasionally there was a loud clatter as planks were tossed onto the ceiling. It was the late sixties and cargo handling gangs were already well past their peak. Voluntary redundancy had allowed disillusioned members of the better gangs to bow out gracefully while the National Dock Labour Scheme encouraged the formation of generalised scratch gangs with no loyalties and little cohesion. Now, acrimonious exchanges had replaced the rattle of timber and as they got louder and more insistent, work ground to a halt. A scratch gang had been making life as easy as it could for itself working the timber, downholders were 'snatching' the sets while the barge hands scattered the timber across the ceiling. 'Snatching' meant not building up sets but placing a rope around the end of some planks and letting the crane pull them out. Whatever it got hold of was carried across into the lighter where the hands released one end of the rope strap and as the crane hook rose, the timber was scattered across the ceiling. No serious attempt was made to stow the cargo, basically the lads were just playing around. The men were being paid to get the timber out and that is what they were doing, pride didn't come in to it. Unfortunately the lighterman on this barge was Dick Thomas of General Lighterage who had spent all his working life in the docks and he knew how timber ought to be stowed on his barges, he was responsible to the importers for the safe conveyance of their timber and beyond that he was responsible for this barge's river worthiness. He took pride in his work and had no intention of seeing his craft put in jeopardy by a bunch of idlers. He told these barge hands, youngsters with no sense of purpose, that their work wasn't good enough and instructed them to stow the timber properly. The old boy was duly ignored and they continued to scatter the wood around as the crane delivered it. Dick however knew his job and his rights and after a number of warnings ordered the hands off his barge, they had no alternative and had to clamber back onto the ship, that's when the serious shouting began. In theory it was the lighterman who loaded his barge, the barge hands simply aided him although most often in practice it was they who did all the stowing. In his eyes these 'helpers' were not up to the task and quite properly, he had ordered them to leave. Once he had his barge to himself he stood it off into the middle of the dock and set about carefully laying out all the timber which had so far been shot on the ceiling. Slowly and methodically he built up a cargo which was even, level and safely stowed.

The downholders and barge hands were all but strangers and owed each other no favours: the downholders had delivered arbitrary bunches of planks and the barge hands had no intention of organising them into anything cleverer than a rough heap. Now the entire gang was left on board with nothing to do except get to know each other better. Meanwhile Dick set about his task. He would only deal with the top hand and shipworker and he told them that when he had finished, the gang could continue but he would order them off again if their work didn't improve. It took him until lunch time to arrange the timber as he wanted it which left the gang inactive and loosing money. In the afternoon work improved marginally and an uncomfortable compromise was reached. In the overall scheme of things though, it was a losing battle, by this time it was perhaps only individuals like coopers or lightermen who would still take a pride in their work and not many of those were big enough to impose standards on others. It was a memorable incident because by bucking the trend it forcibly highlighted the general decline.

The Royal Docks handled little timber and Royal Mail Lines rarely had large consignments. When a vessel did occasionally carry a large load the general goods would be off-loaded first then the ship sent round to Surrey Commercial Docks where the gangs were specialists in timber handling. Moderate quantities though passed through the Royals requiring ships' clerks to familiarise themselves with yet another set of priorities, classifications and units of measurement. Narrow boats would take 75 tons of timber up the canals to the many timber yards on their banks while larger barges went to Rainham timber works. The basic distinction between hardwoods and softwoods as far as the docks were concerned was that all gangs were paid by weight for hardwoods and by volume for soft, though why this should be remained another custom lost in the mists of time.

RML ships coming in from the West Coast of North America would pick up softwoods at Victoria or Vancouver, mostly pine or Douglas fir destined for the building trade. Softwoods were measured in Standards – properly called the Peterborough Standard – and a 'measure' equalled 165 cubic feet. Discharging gangs were paid by the Standard and importers' consignments of softwoods, known as 'parcels', would typically range from twelve and a half to twenty Standards. The gangs in the Surrey Docks could achieve one hundred to one hundred and twenty standards a day, whereas FW general cargo gangs at the Royal Docks would average about thirty-five to forty-five. The problem with softwood was that the sizes of the pieces were never uniform and a wide range of lengths and thicknesses was possible, which not only made for an inefficient use of hold space but also made the construction of and particularly the lifting of sets awkward and hazardous.

What the scratch gangs of the sixties and seventies didn't know was how timber was worked in earlier decades by good gangs. Generally speaking each downholder working alone made up his own set, making sure that the pieces were all for the same importer and only if planks were very long would two men work together. This meant that scattered throughout a hold at varying distances from the hatchway, six or eight sets would be under construction at the same time. Each man would set down a piece of 3 x 3 timber and lay the wood of his set on it so that it leant uphill towards the hatchway and there was space underneath to pass the lifting rope. As far as the odd shapes allowed, each downholder would make up a set of about one to one and a half tons as neatly and as near square cross sectioned as possible. When complete he would unhook the snotter from the descending crane hook, wrap it once or twice around the centre of the timber set, hook the eye back on the crane and watch the set out on its trajectory. If the set was made up some way from the hatchway he might have to hold the end down, or even sit on it to prevent the bouncing timber crashing into other sets or men. The hope was that the rope of the snotter would bite into the wood and hold it in a compact bundle but it was far from foolproof; not infrequently, if one or two pieces slipped out, or if the set hit an obstacle, the entire load might collapse and the timber cascade back into the hold. Accidents were mercifully rare as spillages were a known risk and men knew that as they worked they had to be aware of the other moving sets, a far more common hazard was lost finger tips. As a crane pulled a set out, the tightening rope risked catching a downholder's finger while he held the rope in place. All it needed was a moment's inattention.

Snotters I should explain were, in this case, lengths of rope with two unequal sized eyes, one at each end. After the rope had been put round the bundle the small eye was passed through the large one and put on the crane hook or, if the downholder was working away from the hatchway, on to the hook of an extension leg. In the Surrey Docks incidentally they used a chain with an eye on one end and a hook on the other. The eye remained permanently on its crane hook, the chain passed under the set with the hook fastened into one of the links back on the chain itself. This saved the little job of unhooking the snotter and re-attaching it which did in fact save time appreciably but for some reason Furness, Withy never used them in the Royal Docks. Chains would also have bitten into the timber more effectively reducing collapsing sets. Maybe this little change in equipment was a factor in why the Surrey Docks were so much more efficient at working timber.

If particularly long lengths were being discharged then two snotters would be used, the one nearest the hatchway being given an extra turn round the set to shorten its length to the crane hook and thereby holding the timber at an angle to clear any clutter on its journey to the hatchway. Obviously it was in everyone's interest to get completed sets out successfully and the best insurance for achieving this was to make up sets as compactly as possible to avoid spewing or slipping. However, snotter ropes did have a tendency to form loops in themselves – known as 'half crowns'- as the rope squirmed under the rapid tightening pull of the crane and at any time as it was being raised this loop could unravel and cause the load to shed.

Out in the barge, good gangs would set up 'goal posts' for the team to work off and this was standard practice at the Surrey Docks. Two uprights and a cross bar about three feet off the ceiling of the lighter ensured that the crane driver could lower the entire set so that it was resting on the crossbar. This made it much easier for the barge hands to select and arrange the timber to sit well in the barge. As the lighter filled the crossbar was raised to maintain the gradient.

When a ship came from Latin America carrying timber it was usually parana pine from Brazil. These woods always arrived in uniform sizes and were hence much easier to make up into sets and even easier still to unload in the lighter. Goal posts were unnecessary, the set could be dropped onto a couple of pieces of dunnage to allow the snotters to be released and the timber left where the crane driver had accurately positioned it.

Problems could arise however. Hardwoods, brought into the UK carried substantial import dues, while softwoods, desperately needed for rebuilding programmes, didn't so in the post-War years manufacturers were keen to get their consignments imported under the 'softwood' heading. Chilean oak, rauli, and laurel were brought across and labelled 'softwoods' with nobody experienced enough to contest the description. The first time this happened the ship's itinerary said 'softwoods' and with no one any the wiser the gang off-loaded them in the usual way. It was only when the returning lighterman looked at his barge and saw water lapping round the gunwales, that we realised there was an important distinction that needed to be addressed between 'Chilean softwood' and 'softwood'. The gangs had been loading the barge assuming the timber weighed two and a half to three tons per standard when four to four and a half was nearer the truth; the difference in densities had suddenly become very evident. There was a fairly frantic half hour spent tossing timber on to the quay where it was weighed as a matter of course to confirm this as a bit of sharp practice. Had the lighter sunk the litigation might have proved interesting. From then on the ships' clerks learnt to ignore import classifications and instead examined the type of wood being sent.

Looking back, it is extraordinary how uncoordinated the process of getting the right imports to the correct customers sometimes seemed to be. South American hardwoods, Chilean mainly, were a case in point. We were told that the reason the timber was so shiny and covered in mould was because it was imported from a region where it rained three hundred and sixty days a year, the timber never dried and in the close confines of a hold during the journey back mounds of mould built up across the exposed surfaces, particularly at the ends. This was unpleasant, the slipperiness increasing the accident risk for men working it but the insurmountable problems were saved for ship's clerks who had to read the marks. Each exporter specified his customers' consignments by a series of paint daubs placed on the end of each plank, two red dots and a green perhaps or orange and blue. The code was perfectly clear to the exporter and in Britain each importer knew what to expect but down in the holds the clerk was faced with an uneven wall of grey green mould streaked with a confused, intermingling array of paint daubs. As the marks had grown out of the timber with the fungus, wiping the mould off just produced a vague slimy rainbow – useless for ascribing it to an importer. Either the exporters used water soluble paints or the paint simply didn't dry but whatever the cause it was impossible for a ship's clerk to interpret with any accuracy the importers' scumbled codes. You would have thought that a single telephone call to the exporters would have been all that was necessary but that was not the way things happened: Head Office kept its distance while blasting the dock staff for their incompetence and irate importers continued to get the wrong consignments. Commercially it just seemed plain suicidal. Whether this was a new trade just starting or one trying to re-establish itself after the traumas of war I do not know but the net result was that within a few years the trade for RML died away.

I was relieved on one such occasion to discover that a strike had been called; this at least gave me time to quietly attempt to match marks against the ship's itinerary. It was nice to have some quiet time to attempt a some Holmesian deduction. There would be time, I thought, to work methodically through the cargo and by a process of elimination do the colour coding some justice. In fact things turned out even better than I could have hoped, for the strike became serious and as days turned into weeks, the Government decided to call in the Army to discharge essential items, timber fortunately being one of them. The squaddies were not too committed to the process of matching marks with importers' listings so in this instance the wrath of the importers was deflected onto the military. Nevertheless it no doubt contributed to importers reconsidering their longer term strategies.

Sometimes the problems were not caused by the timber directly but by what was stowed alongside it. There was a time when the *'Teviot'* came in with all five holds half filled with timber and half filled with Brazilian sugar. The sugar sacks were of the thin cotton type and the timber all in 20 ft lengths. As the sugar was being lifted out of the hatchway the set would scuff against the wall of timber and tear, spilling sugar all over the rest of the cargo. When men tried reversing the procedure and take the timber out first, the swaying one ton sets would gouge into the sugar. This was particularly true as men tried to work cargoes away from the hatchway and the sets, whether of timber or sugar, necessarily careering into each other reducing bagged sugar to bulk and rags and clean timber into sticky, oversized lolly sticks. The only solution was for each gang in each hold to get out a hundred tons of sugar then a parcel of wood by turns, working their way down gradually to the ceiling, while out on the water, different lighters had to jostle continually up to and away from each hold. Downholders wasted time changing from one routine to another while barge hands slowed off-loading still more by constantly having to transfer from one lighter to another. In no time there was loose sugar everywhere, making the whole operation an unpleasant, frustrating affair, with an energetic session for the needlemen trying to keep up with the disintegrating bags.

One little journey made by some timber barges was round to Prince Tar at Silvertown. Their main products were oil, creosote and tar and as a sideline, they pickled railway sleepers. These would arrive already the correct size and were placed in a series of vats – holes in the ground – where they would sit, steeped in creosote, before going to the railways. While recording these one day a tally clerk friend, Reg Edwards, had the misfortune to stumble into a vat full of creosote and as a result it seems, became a diabetic for the rest of his life – conversations naturally and regularly turned to the new miracle of insulin and self-administered injections.

Our largest timbers didn't use lighters at all. From both the Royal and Surrey Docks large baulks – perhaps 16" x 16" x 60 ft would be off-loaded directly into the water. These timbers – Douglas fir from Vancouver, usually on the 'Loch Ryan' – were carried on the top deck and were relatively easy to discharge by ship's purchase overside one at a time. Specialist gangs from the Surrey Docks would build these floating baulks into rafts by driving big, sharp-spiked staples, into the logs to bind them together into a raft. When each raft set was completed, a tug would tow it out of the docks and round to Nine Elms Goods Depot where they were dismantled for individual baulks to be crane lifted onto flat wagons. Each one weighed a ton and would be destined for the Admiralty at Portsmouth where, I believe, they were left in the sea to season before being used to construct piers and jetties.

One of the timber oddities for lightermen and discharging gangs alike was balsa wood. For the gangs, being a hardwood, it ought to have been charged by dead weight which would have left the men destitute, so it had to be reckoned as a softwood. For lightermen, the weight of balsa in the barges was insignificant and the cargo would rise up eight to ten feet above the gunwales. With balsa wood, winds were the menace. Because he was responsible for each cargo he carried, a lighterman would always tie the tarpaulins himself over the completed load but in the case of balsa wood this had a greater significance than just protection; any little gap or loosely tied fastening would allow the wind to catch under it and give the barge a momentum quite independent of where the lighterman wanted it to go. Even trying to get the wind to work with him was difficult because its effect was so great, the eight foot rise above the gunwale made a barge difficult to handle even in a light breeze and the wash of a ship when out on the river would set it swaying uncontrollably like a cork bobbing in the surf.

Within a short period of time during the 1950s London and Rochester joined up with Browns and in the process replaced their fleets of sailing barges with bigger motorised craft. These two companies had the great majority of sailing barges still operating and when they were sold off, the craft virtually disappeared overnight from the docks. Up until that time they had been common and the inherent frustrations and inconveniences associated with them were simply part of dock life. With the loss of this fleet, sailing barges became rare and peripheral to the central business of dock work. Although picturesque they had small cramped holds and their manoeuvrability, even with auxiliary motors remained extremely restricted. When two ships were lying at neighbouring berths they had a tangle of mooring ropes crossing the space between them and it was this gap which barges had to negotiate in order to get to a working position between ship and quay. These mooring ropes and anchor chains proved no problem for dumb barges which were able to slip under them but were a major obstacle to the sailing fleet whose masts would get snagged. Only if a ship were riding high in the water was there a chance of a barge's mast clearing the ropes; alternately the master might try to angle his craft's nose in close to the quay around these ropes in the hope that the quay crane might stretch out far enough to reach the tiny fore hold. Even if it were possible it was always slow, painstaking work. In the years before London and Rochester's decision to pension off its sailing barges, if a ship's clerk heard that the importers had ordered up a 'sailerman', he had to recognise the gang would have trouble working it. This slow, fiddly operation became increasingly disruptive the rarer sailing barges became; the docks wanted to move on.

A major inconvenience with them was their unpredictability. With local lighterage companies using dumb barges, time keeping was good, indeed it had to be for the docks to function at all but with a sailing craft's dependence upon the states of the wind and tide, arrival could be significantly disrupted and this had to be allowed for by the men supervising off-loading. Even with the barge in sight it could take an age for her to make her way up to the berth; tugs were never used and the entire workforce could be looking over the side at the tantalisingly sedate progress of the 'sailerman' tacking through the crowded jostle of craft.

Traditionally of course, sailing barges had fulfilled a particular role in water transport. Dumb barges operated substantially around the industrialised waterways of the Thames and the waters that fed into it while sailing barges carried goods down river to the Estuary, the Medway and the rivers of East Anglia. Dumb barges towed by a tug were permitted down to the Medway but this was rare and was the extreme limit of their range. Sailing barges on the other hand, during the summer months were able to cross the Channel and work out of Rotterdam and the Continental ports. Again such journeys were rare but in benign seas these craft were seaworthy carrying 140 tons. For the most part though sailing barges, when they were a force, were kept busy working the coastal routes up to Ipswich and Norwich. There was a vogue amongst importers to transfer deliveries over to road haulage but often it was found that off-loading onto lorries for goods bound to factories lining the canals and rivers of East Anglia had little advantage over waterborne deliveries. Perhaps the fashion for switching to road haulage spurred London and Rochester to abandon sail for motor barges.

Once this decision to convert to motor barges had been taken the advantages of the new craft were so obvious that sailing barges generally were quickly replaced. One thing that surprised me was the manner of the change for it seemed that masters who had spent their whole lives working 140 ton sailing barges were suddenly in control of 500 ton vessels, quite a quantum leap I should have thought. In any event the competence of those old sailing masters was equal to the task and I never heard of any related problems. Masters were pleased to be given one, it was seen for a while as a mark of status and of course, the increase in cargo loads meant bigger financial rewards. Like the sailing barges though these powered craft were still fitted with a tiny cabin with just enough room to sling a hammock and brew a cup of tea as a home from home on their three or four day voyages.

For ship gangs the change to motor barges was a Godsend: timings were more predictable and the capacity of their holds meant that loading was straightforward. They had another advantage which was very much appreciated for unlike the 500 ton Silvertown Services dumb barges, which we have discussed, these craft could be manoeuvred to assist loading. Whether working quayside with the crane or overside with the derricks moving a barge under the descending sets made the job of filling its length very much easier. Two ton sets could be put down with pinpoint accuracy without fine adjustments having to be continually made by barge hands heaving the swinging sets across the ceiling.

It is worth indicating perhaps, although this is outside my territory, that these coastal barges powered either by wind or diesel, were of a different tradition and nature to the up-river dumb barges. The latter were manned by lightermen who had to be Freemen of the River whereas coastal barges, whatever their means of propulsion, were under the command of a skipper. Many of these skippers or masters would also be Freemen but not necessarily so, the apprenticeships met different needs.

During the winter months sailing barges were not allowed out to coastal waters so London based operations were confined to the Thames and the Medway but in the summer they would work round to the Essex and East Anglian waterways taking, for example, mustard seed to Colman's at Ipswich or timber to Wiven Ho.

The one sailing barge which continued to work without an engine at all was Bob Robert's *'Cambria'*. This was a completely unmodified vessel used mainly as a publicity stunt so that the more sailing barges that were abandoned in favour of motor barges the more attention this one working survivor received. Cargo capacity, speed of working and convenience did not come into the owner's calculations and in a way, the more inconvenient the more it stood out. As far as the shippers were concerned it was just a hindrance while the frustrated handling gangs knew that nostalgia didn't pay their bills. This sense of the obsolete was true of all sailing barges in later years but it was particularly so with this vessel because it was completely unaltered from its original 1906 construction. All other craft, as far as I was aware, had been modified: these included being fitted with auxiliary motors, having their hatches widened and their decks tidied to some degree, but not the *'Cambria'*. The fore hold was small and an odd shape following the line of the prow while the hatchway opening was only about six or eight feet square; even loading something as basically manageable as bagged peas for Goldhanger and Tolsbury on the Blackwater may have taken a morning and half the afternoon to complete.

When he came to collect timber Bob Roberts could only take the shorter lengths. If in the shipment there was parana pine which always came in predictable 20 foot lengths then that was useful for at least you knew he could go away with something. For most soft woods though it meant that the downholders had to sort out short lengths of the right mark to be sure they would fit and this was an expensive and time consuming task. Another option, if it was available, was for the *'Cambria'* to take 'builder's parcels' of hemlock or Douglas fir which were small, neat loads used for window frames or door lintels. Picturesque it may have been and in the sixties when virtually all other sailing craft had disappeared, a reminder of a maritime tradition but in truth it was all problems. For the dockers the *'Cambria'* was less a reminder of old craft and more a reminder of old problems with the added niggle that it was, by then, an indulgence. Given the inherent difficulties of getting the masts under a ship's mooring ropes she usually had to be worked overside. As a working principal for dock work, if a crane was available, it was used because its wide sweep allowed the arm to cover the length of a standard dumb lighter. When the *'Cambria'* came up to be loaded it usually meant that quayside work had to stop, derricks had to be set up overside, the gang reorganised and the crane stood down - all for something of less than 140 tons capacity. There was an additional, problem for the barge hands; not only was the hatch and hold pokey but also the deck on this unmodified barge was littered with ropes, cleats, sheets and all the paraphernalia necessary for a traditionally maintained all-sail craft – by the sixties these were hazards that barge hands, by then, were unfamiliar with. It is sad to recall these venerable old craft as a series of complaints but their quaint features for dockers after the War had become by then just encumbrances. After London and Rochester joined up with Browns to become Crescent Shipping, with both sailing barge fleets stood down, the days of the Thames sailing barge as an integral working craft were over and the docks, it had to be admitted, breathed a corporate sigh of relief.

In the early nineteen fifties a RML ship delivered a consignment of finings. Nobody knew what they were but as they formed only a small item amongst hundreds of tons of other cargoes they were discharged without a second thought. These finings were wrapped in brown paper parcels, quite large but very light and as there were only five of them a rope was thrown around them all for the crane to take out as a single set. The problem turned out to be their lightness: heavy goods which gangs were used to moving allowed the lifting rope to bite into them and hold them securely but here the entire load was so light that the rope was given no tension and so no binding effect. As the crane was swinging them across to the quay the load shifted and spewed out onto the dock water but as 'finings' were not, apparently, for human consumption and as they were floating it seemed to be no more than an irritation to have to fish them out, perhaps washing the packages down or just letting them dry; enough, it was reasoned, to save insurance claims.

A couple of men sauntered off to find a boat hook but for those who were still watching the packages, something odd seemed to be happening - the bobbing parcels were swelling and writhing and taking on a life of their own. Very gradually the parcels were gently exploding, bursting where the paper had become water logged. The more they split, the more they rotated and the more the finings got wet, expanded and increased the set's self annihilation. Someone said that finings were fish scales, which was good enough for us and this explained why those flakes that weren't wet were being wind blow in colourful showers across the docks. Interesting but not life threatening. All the shipworker could do was refer the incident to the insurance branch of Furness, Withy with whom all their gangs had to be insured. With hindsight the gang should have sent a couple of their men the length of the dock to the equipment stores for a net but for one small load it hardly seemed worth it. It was only later that the ship's clerk received a full broadside from an irate Head Office. Apparently finings, whatever they were, were very expensive and hard to come by in those post-War years, there was no substitute and the importers had been waiting a very long time for this single delivery. Naturally they were letting Royal Mail Lines know what they thought of them and naturally Head Office was keen to pass on their disgust. It was an uncomfortable few days for the dock staff, tarred as they all were with the same brush of gross incompetence. Of course, the fouling of the water was not a consideration.

Maybe a few intrepid East End children might dabble at the side of the Thames risking the poisoning effects of its waters but in the enclosed space of the docks where, by definition, the general public were strictly excluded, dock water was simply part of the industrial fabric. It had a job to do, leisure and nature didn't come into it. It was a convenient surface for commerce to pursue its business on and it had the very great virtue of being free. The greatness of the Royal Docks, like the greatness of the Thames beyond, tended to be measured by the quantity of shipping using it; the impact on the water was not a consideration. The circulation that took place through the locks simply exchanged the pollutants of the docks with those from the Thames and the smell of both you just had to get used to. When shore gangs hosed out holds, or cabins, the contaminants whatever they were, were sluiced into the dock water; the illegal but often necessary use of a ship's toilets cast the contents into the docks while barge hands and others were required to use the water more directly as a convenience. Oil, chemicals, rotting vegetables, carcasses added to the stew and it was a moot point whether, if goods fell in, they were retrieved. Timber and non-consumables, if they floated, were easy enough to recover but food was more debatable – there were occasions when a set shed a crate or two of apples, for example and they might be retrieved, possibly hosed down and put on a lorry with no-one any the wiser in order to help insurance premiums. On the whole, though it was a dumping ground, deliberate or accidental and nothing living was ever expected to be seen in it, apart from the occasional rat. It was not a good place to drop in.

Bill Holland the big hearted Furness, Withy shipworker whom we have already encountered, tumbled in one day. He was essentially a practical man who liked to get in amongst the action and did not much care for the isolation that tended to go with top deck supervising. On this occasion he had left the holds and was down among the barges helping to shove them around to keep the work moving. Suddenly he lost his footing and the gangers had the rare sight of seeing one of their supervisors thrashing about in the drink. The proper response of course was to get him out immediately and rush him to hospital but this was a moment to savour: amongst the jeers someone had the inspiration - and I don't know where he found it - to toss him a lump of soap, not antiseptic enough though to save him from the obligatory hospital visit and stomach pump.

One of the common names for the working water was the 'suds'. This was something of a misnomer in the docks for it was only if a ship turned her screws over that the water here became agitated enough to form a froth. Outside on the Thames though, the huge paddle wheels of the old Woolwich Ferries constantly pounded the water into a brownish yellow foam; the term, if not the suds themselves naturally found its way into the docks. My view was, the less that bacteria soup was disturbed, the healthier for everyone.

In charge of the water was the Dockmaster, responsible not for its quality but its quantity. It was his primary task to ensure an adequate draught for the ships using the Royal Group which in turn meant preserving the existing stock. For perhaps an hour and a half either side of high tide shipping had sufficient draught out on the Thames to enter and leave the Royals but the further away from high water, the greater the disparity in levels and the longer it took ships to get through locking in. It was down to the dock-master's judgement whether the time taken to pass the lock would risk depleting water stocks and his decision was final. In practice this was never a problem. If Royal Mail Lines had cleared a ship for the next high tide, there was always time for it to be sent on its way whatever the press of shipping. Smaller craft such as tugs and lighters, because of their shallower draught, had a much greater timespan for using the lock – so much so that on most evenings at around six to six thirty, as we noted earlier, the accumulated barge traffic from a day's work was able to make its way out onto the Thames causing long delays for weary dockers marooned on the wrong side of the lock.

*   *   *

MR WARWICK
For the most part Furness, Withy Head Office staff across the River in the Surrey Docks left their shipworkers alone to get on with discharging in the Royal Group but occasionally they liked to pay a visit. On one surprise visit by Mr Warwick an ex-ganger himself and FW Chief Cargo Superintendent, the shipworker I was working alongside (I was ship's clerk) was smugly happy to be able to report that everything was in hand and going well and there was no need for him to concern himself. Mr Warwick watched the discharging for a while then pointed to the set boards. As the gangs were attaching the chandeliers to the set boards they were placing the hooks inwards into the eyes at the four corners of the board, this being the easiest way to join them – especially if you are trying to preserve your fingers. "Are you aware", said Warwick, "That each time they do that, the four crates at the corners of the set are being damaged by the hook points biting into them. That means that Furness, Withy is paying for four damaged crates each set, that's twenty damaged crates each delivery out of the five holds. Tell your men to put the hooks through the eyes pointing outwards or get them to protect the crates with dunnage immediately". Exit Mr Warwick leaving a somewhat deflated shipworker. When he retired George Fairfield took over. He was an ex-ganger too and had a brother who remained a gang's top hand; the docks at that time were a close community.

*   *   *

MEASUREMENTS
For general cargoes the rule of thumb was forty cubic feet to the ton – used in assessing hold capacity and weight distribution.
Exports were measured according to volume.
Imports were discharged according to weight.

87

Captain Spinks was the Marine Superintendent for RML during the period when I was just beginning my association with the Company. Later Marine Supers could be unpleasant individuals but their power to intimidate lessened as the world changed. To conscientious men who had grown up in the early decades of the century and who had experienced hard times his viciousness invariably struck home. He would threaten the sack to anyone who, in his eyes let RML down and to employees for whom dismissal carried all the Victorian connotations of disgrace, destitution and family degradation his power was absolute. To my great good fortune I was ever only casually employed as a Company clerk during his tenure and so was able to maintain a modest level of detachment. His actual duties were the maintenance of the fleet out of London and Southampton but such was his wide ranging authority that he was able to impose his Draconian standards far beyond the levels of paintwork and cleanliness. His responsibility was considerable: he decided, for example, when a ship needed to go into dry dock for an overhaul, a major Company expenditure, but it was his irascible character that imposed itself so traumatically on the workforce. I have seen Dockmasters, men of some authority in their own right, quite literally with tears in their eyes anguished by his ferocity, usually over something like letting another company's ship through the lock before his. At the time I believe, RML controlled something like a third of Britain's mercantile shipping and to threaten the withdrawal of the entire fleet because of one individual's less than full blooded commitment to his cause literally had men quaking in their boots. If it came to his attention that equipment had been faulty or unavailable, PLA officers would be castigated mercilessly. So great was RML's economic leverage at the time that the threat of transferring business to another port, usually Rotterdam, all because of the inadequacies of one particular individual, as he angled it, devastated decent, hard working officers. For conscientious family men for whom the Depression of the inter-war years was not such a distant memory any humiliation was preferable to the spectre of unemployment. But Captain Spinks went back further than that; he had sailed on RML ships since Edwardian times and had gained a firm, Admiralty-based understanding of how to keep the lower orders in their place. When he retired from the sea to become RML's marine superintendent, the financial insecurities of middle aged clerks played right into his hands.

The main dock office of RML had been deliberately positioned so that it was immediately visible when entering Gate No.6, Royal Victoria Dock. This prominent position had been chosen, of course, to impress and assist visitors but conversely, from the offices, the gate could be clearly seen. The only respite Captain Spinks' permanent staff had from his despotism was when he visited Head Office or Southampton. If he were away for a few days, the relief was palpable but as everyone knew, it wouldn't last. The imposing placement of the dock office meant that Gate No.6 suddenly became the focus of attention of every clerk rooted behind his desk. With his return imminent, one of the clerks would ask a friendly policeman on the Gate to signal when he saw Spinks' chauffeur driven car gliding majestically into view. Someone would have been elected lookout and at the wave of the constable's arm the whole office knew that now was not the time for correcting reports, balancing books or generally sorting out paperwork. Everyone who could suddenly discovered an urgent need to be deep in a hold somewhere, preferably at the far end of the docks. And this was not Victorian deprivation this was the nineteen fifties.

His chief clerk had no such bolt hole and was left to face whatever short-comings Captain Spinks could accuse him of: the invective and humiliation were taken for granted. When the Marine Superintendent was established in his office and his 'phone rang this clerk used to leave his desk, tip-toe quickly across to the door and crouch down hoping to hear something of the conversation through the keyhole. With luck he would be able to learn enough to locate the necessary documents or familiarise himself with the situation before Spinks began his castigation; such was the atmosphere that those few seconds seemed, deep in his psyche, the difference between employment and destitution. This degradation went on for years. Spinks thought nothing of ordering him to be at his house sharp at nine o'clock on a Sunday morning to collect a message, refusal was inconceivable.

When RML took over the administration of Nelson Line they discovered that the company had only one set of ships' manuals so Spinks gave them to his chief clerk on Friday afternoon and demanded a second set by Monday morning. The poor man spent the entire weekend working all hours copying them out.

Whether Captain Spinks was merely acting as all previous Superintendents had acted, I do not know – perhaps, perish the thought, he was a more benign incarnation – but in many respects he was fortunate to have held his position when he did: carrying his despotic, Victorian regime into the nineteen sixties would have proved unworkable, the climate had changed. Until his retirement though, around nineteen fifty, RML and its standing in the Royal Docks were dominated by his presence. Masters of vessels would salute him and be on their best behaviour when he was around. Marine Supers particularly through the nineteen fifties continued the well established tradition of treating their staff with contempt but the world was changing, female temps when they arrived, would just walk out. Once it became clear that Royal Mail Lines itself was no longer the force it had been, the position of later Marine Superintendents naturally weakened both within RML and the Royal Docks but for long serving clerks this autocratic world was hard to shake off. It continued with his replacement, Capt. Connell, who happened to be Spink's son-in-law, then Capts Chamberlain and Cutler.

Captain Spinks had his own Company launch which ferried him around the docks. He would make a point of standing erect in the stern, dressed in his smartest marine superintendent's uniform, arms folded, eyes darting as it made its stately passage down the centre of each dock. There was more than a touch of the Royal Navy about this, more Pompey than Southampton, as if RML's links to the Admiralty gave him authority to inspect the entire Royal Docks. He was the only person as far as I knew to do this and somehow these tours of inspection were considered legitimate. Every transgression would be noted and a scathing report issued with no excuses accepted. A ship's clerk could only hope that from launch level his five working holds would pass muster.

The master of his launch was a man called Horace Sturgeon who took great pride in keeping his craft looking immaculate. Spinks in any case would have demanded it but Horace was an ex-guardsman so their passions for presentation were well matched. When Captain Spinks retired, the launch was sold and Horace became one of the ship's clerks but while he operated this craft he was able to earn a worthwhile second income. When he knew that Spinks was not going to be in the docks, he used the launch to ferry dockers across the water to opposite berths saving them having to walk round the quays. He charged a penny per person, that was a shilling a gang.

* * *

CAPTAIN SPINKS - GRATUITIES
Whenever he was in the docks, Captain Spinks always had his midday meal on one of RML's ships where a skeleton crew would include someone capable of serving him a substantial meal. No one else in the docks was allowed this privilege except, perhaps, the ship's master when he was preparing for his next outward voyage. As an added bonus Spinks' wife used to phone down to say what cut of meat she wanted him to bring home from the ship's store for their next meal. This didn't go down too well with the rest of us who had to make do with ration books

* * *

RODNEY BEAUMONT
Rod Beaumont reminds me however that it was through Capt Spinks' recommendation that he had a career at sea. His father worked in the RML dock office and proposed his son as a Cadet Deck Officer. Following an interview, Spinks agreed and so in large measure, Rod owed his time at sea to Capt Spinks. His first ship as a Cadet was the *Empire Chieftain* built by Furness Shipbuilding for the Ministry of War Transport in 1943 and bought by Royal Mail Lines in 1946 when she was renamed *Loch Ryan*. Although grateful of course, Rodney still refers to Capt Spinks as 'notorious'.　　MES

90

Mechanisation might have been changing the way cargoes were being worked but within the offices of Royal Mail Lines clerking and paperwork remained deeply traditional. Information technology lay decades in the future and the working environment appeared little changed from Victorian times. Mechanical typewriters were established but of no use to export ship's clerks, for them the great advance had been the advent of fountain pens – older personnel remembered the days when peripatetic clerks wore a little reservoir of ink clipped to the back of their lapels for use with their dip in pens. Women were never allowed to work in Royal Mail Lines offices not as long as Perce Arnold was in charge and it was only after he retired around 1960 that a series of temps arrived with no loyalty to RML or its traditions. The culture shock was substantial, particularly when clerks were faced with a girl who had come to work dressed in jeans.

There were office staff who never went on ships preferring to put up with Captain Spinks and the other marine superintendents because office work was what they did best: men like Charley Scannel, husband of the authoress, Dorothy Scannel, and Mick Gilmore who spent their days collating and presenting the mass of information flowing in from ships into a form acceptable to Head Office. Neat, copper plate writing together with clear and precise details of each shipment were necessary to ensure that, should a claim from an importer come through at some future time, the records would be legible and accurate. I remember once being asked by Captain Bryden, the ship's surveyor, about a cargo I had supervised as a ship's clerk eight years previously, the legal proceedings were only then taking place.

For a ship's clerk the problems associated with getting commodities out of holds and into barges were the overriding concern but the company's viability rested as much upon preventing importers' claims from wiping out profits: an accurate assessment of every bit of damage to every consignment had to be noted. It was the work of the office staff to collate all this in a manner which could be quickly retrieved if necessary and immediately understood.

My earliest contact with RML office work was through being engaged at the Call as a casual planning clerk. This work brought me into contact with the export staff there and it was only later, as an inside clerk, that I came to know the personalities involved with imports and consequently the men in the Royal Mail Lines offices with whom, ultimately, I would most consistently deal as a permanently employed import clerk. Heading the import staff was Percy Arnold a tall, gaunt, grey man who never smiled but who was bearable – until he got his hearing aid. He used this weapon with great cunning: you never knew when he had it switched on which for men who had been used to swearing at him behind his back for years produced some painfully uncomfortable moments. He was a leading light in the big

West Ham Methodist Church, a man who hated drink and was formidably straight laced. Mick Gilmore's wife was dumpy and unlovely to most eyes but to Perce's enduring admiration ran the Methodist Youth Club; she also ran her marriage. This didn't stop Mick from having an eye for the ladies to the abiding horror of Perce, meaning that poor Mick was never able to do anything right in the office as far his import superintendent was concerned; that hearing aid became a formidable weapon in the *realpolitik* of the office.

Bill Woods and George Mendham were two import ship's clerks working out of RML's offices but were interesting because they remained resolutely casual preferring the independence of the Call to the security of a permanent post with the Company. Being semi-detached from RML also allowed them a greater freedom in where they based themselves and it was less claustrophobic for them to work out of the remote 3, King George V Dock Office as the opportunity allowed. They knew as much about the ships, commodities and importers as anyone but their greatest expertise was in knowing the personalities who could provide them with a steady supply of alcohol: their loyalties were to the rum rather than Royal Mail Lines. When George retired around 1960 it was the end of an era for he had been the branch secretary of his union for over fifty years accepting the post soon after entering the docks before the First World War; his memories would have been riveting. As it happened though, it was with Bill Woods that I regularly worked in those early days as his somewhat bemused inside clerk.

Bill had been a cavalry officer in the First World War – the docks seemed to attract the type – he always maintained an air of neatness and I can only say, punctiliousness. While working as a RML representative in Vigo after the First War, he suffered a bad riding accident which resulted, by the time I knew him, in him having a severely hunched back causing him constant pain. There were extenuating circumstances for his addiction to the rum. He had had a tough Second World War, everyone acknowledged, forced as he had been to severely moderate his intake but now as I was becoming acquainted with the situation he was making up for lost time. There were occasions when Bill sat at his desk with a bottle beside him and as the afternoon wore on you could watch his normally immaculate script dissolve into an unfocused scrawl. On two consecutive days I was sitting beside him in the office as his inside clerk waiting to enter up his figures and could do nothing but watch his head sink lower and lower onto his chest, his mind far away from manifests and one hopes, pain. The best I could think to do was to surreptitiously slide the sheet he was working on out from under his hand and take the figures home to get the books in order for the following day. When I got to work on both occasions Bill was still at his desk – he had been there all night – and in front of him lay another completed set of figures beautifully entered in his precise accountant's script. The trouble was that the new figures bore no relationship to those of the day before and I had wasted another evening. From then on if I were Bill's inside clerk, Head Office could wait for the figures he ultimately passed me in his beautiful, faultless returns, their accuracy beyond my control. The sad spider's scrawl long since destroyed.

Perce Arnold, of course, loathed this dependence on drink but Bill and George both knew their jobs and presented their material with such skill that they were indispensable. One day in 1949 Perce came up to me as I was tallying a RML ship and asked me if I would consider trying my hand as a ship's clerk. Bill and George were already occupied on other vessels and someone was needed to supervise a new arrival. I was told that it would be a sugar ship and therefore a relatively straightforward job so I agreed. There were no major hitches and with the job done I went back to tallying and occasionally working as an inside clerk. Obviously my supervising had been acceptable and over the next few months Perce asked me to do more. I was getting the hang of the job and as every ship I worked seemed to be a sugar ship the pattern of work was becoming clearer; I also appreciated the kindness of Perce Arnold in keeping me on this relatively easy option. Gradually the penny dropped: his kindness had nothing to do with it. Perce knew that I ran a physical training class at the East Ham Central Hall and that although not a committed Methodist I was untroubled by the regular consignments of rum these ships carried. Bill as far as possible was being restricted to the teetotal ships of the North American fleet in the fairly futile hope of making a new man of him. In practice it had little effect; if a sugar ship was in, somehow Bill Woods got his rum.

Although that first experience as a ship's clerk had been trouble free, completing the mass of paperwork was another matter. The other clerks were, shall we say, unforthcoming, perhaps they sensed competition and it became clear that it was up to me to dig out the information; it wasn't going to be offered. Initially I tried the creative approach setting out the details in a way that made sense to me but I was told that individualism was not welcomed. There had to be one system and I had to learn it. The obvious solution eventually dawned and I spent some time examining earlier records in the office stores. Getting the information was not actually difficult, just reserved. I suppose all apprenticeships have an element of this but I suspect that it might have been more to do with not wanting unscrupulous gangers or casual clerks knowing precisely what records RML could draw upon to settle disputes. It paid not to be too free with Company information.

One winter's evening with a rum ship in Bill finished work in a terrible state: George drank a lot but somehow it didn't show; Bill however became senseless. We knew he intended going home and so some of us decided to help him on his way, much to the relief of the dock police, it was one less for them to have to deal with. We stood at his bus stop and Bill in his best cavalry officer's voice roared out that whatever bus came along wasn't his: it was the wrong number, wrong destination or wrong colour. We humoured him for a bit but it was cold and getting late so we just bundled him onto one and travelled to the Abbey Arms bus stop. We half-carried him to his next stop, told him what bus he wanted while he still ranted and raved then reckoning we had done our bit, went off to catch our own transport home. Next day the message came through to say that Bill would not be in that day.

Somewhere around midnight his wife called the police to say that he had not come home and could they go and look for him. They eventually found him in the early hours collapsed on a bomb site near the Abbey Arms. Apparently instead of getting on his bus he had decided to pop across to the pub for a few extra drinks. It had been a cold night; he had succumbed to severe pneumonia and had lost the use of both legs.

In his brighter moments Bill was keen to remind everyone that he was independent of Royal Mail Lines, Marine Superintendents and the dock office – but his commitment we all knew was actually to rum. He might protest that at the Call he could accept whatever was the most lucrative job on offer but in practice his contacts with RML and Furness, Withy staff meant that if a ship with rum on board was working in the docks he would be able to get hold of a bottle or two. That was the hold. When Perce Arnold told him what ships were berthing in a day or two's time, he would always be at the Call to be re-engaged. When he returned to work those of us who had had some survival training used to try and help him, largely of course, out of a sense of corporate guilt. During breaks we took turns vainly trying to massage life back into his legs, he appreciated the effort. It was painful just to watch him drag himself up the gang plank to supervise his next ship; once on deck he took up a position and virtually stayed there until it was time to crawl back down again. Throughout this time though, his overriding priority remained the rum and we realised we were fighting a losing battle. Within a few months he was dead.

*   *   *

HQS 'WELLINGTON'

The Honourable Company of Master Mariners has as its Livery Hall the sloop HQS 'Wellington' acquired from the Admiralty in 1947 and now moored at Temple Stairs on the Victoria Embankment. It was there on the evening of Tuesday 26th September 1989 that the Royal Mail Twentyfive Club celebrated the 150th Anniversary of the granting of the Royal Charter to the Royal Mail Steam Packet Company, precursor of Royal Mail Lines. By this time of course the Royal Docks had closed and the Royal Mail Lines, as a maritime force, was extinct and these celebrations honoured the greatness of a shipping firm which only existed in the memories of those present – members of RML who had served twenty five years or more with the Company. The memory of RML's operations in the Royal Docks was even more limited. I was the last dock representative.

Working out of the dock offices were a group of men with roles less clearly defined, but no less vital, than those of the clerks; as lads straight from school they would have been called messenger boys but as mature men they were known as 'runners'. From our technological perspective it may be difficult to appreciate the problems inherent then in providing a two way flow of information and documentation across an extended field of operations, across ships, docks and scattered offices. Runners were the channels of information carrying messages round the quays and sheds to supervisors down holds or taking bundles of papers by train up to the City. The work was menial and poorly paid, appealing to those who wanted a regular job but could not cope with office work and who didn't mind spending their days outdoors chasing between the Company's wide flung commitments. The job was a very traditional and in fact it was as a messenger boy that I began working in the City in 1929.

Dan Hughes had his own office which gave the function of runner some standing within the administration and although designated principal runner his own role was more demanding than that. He would take valuable packages, legal documents of confidential information to and from the City, he would guard gangways if valuable commodities were being moved and on occasions would watch expensive exports as they sat in a shed waiting for a ship. He was an ex-policeman and his duties spanned those of a runner and security guard, he maintained the bearing of a policeman still and carried a useful air of authority.

In the autumn of 1990, Allen Purdey who had been a cashier with Furness, Withy paid me a surprise (retirement) visit. Because our two companies had worked so closely together over a long period of time they had set down offices next to each other and when the ancient wooden offices were replaced after the War, they constructed sister buildings on the south side of Victoria Dock. Although Allen never visited ships permanent staff from both companies knew each other well and it was good to see him again.

During our get-together we naturally talked about old times and Allen raised the name of Johnny the Runner. I remembered him well as he had worked in the docks for Royal Mail Lines for many years and Allen had recently bumped into him again. Johnny had made a positive career out of being a runner. At school in the East End, he had never bothered much about education and was not naturally academic enough to become a clerk. He joined RML as a messenger boy, he was keen and conscientious enough and in those days there was plenty for him to do. Although he never set his sites above being a runner, he became in time very useful to the supervisors, not so much by deliberate application, more by good typecasting. During the time when industrial relations were poor with tempers often on a short fuse, Johnny became a very useful intermediary. For example, each RML ship had, as we have seen, a resident shore gang appointed to clean while the holds were being worked. The range of their duties could take them to all parts of the ship with the possibility of extra jobs arising at any time, especially from ship gangs working their way down through a hold. Over time, Johnny got to find his way around all the ships far better than any ship's clerks who hardly explored further than the top decks, holds and the nearest toilets, if he were lucky. Each shore gang was allocated a refreshment area, usually the crew's common room, where the men could brew up, rest and have a base for their buckets and brooms. This room was known as their 'crib' and was usually located deep in the bowels of the ship somewhere; Johnny knew them all and all the other places members of the gang might tuck themselves away in. When new work came up, the ship's clerk had no time to play hide and seek with shore gangs nor was it politic in the existing atmosphere to suddenly appear in their midst when perhaps they were brewing up something stronger than tea and enjoying a game of cards. Neither he nor the Company wanted an incident, but work needed to be done, Johnny knew how to find anyone and had the great advantage of not being a threat.

When shore gangs were paid off they sometimes took pleasure in going straight to a pub, staying there until closing time then sleep on the benches or under tables until opening time the next day. Thus their weekends might pass between drinking and sleeping without ever leaving the pub or the neighbourhood of the docks and against the advice of the office staff, Johnny would sometimes join them.

Shore gangs answered him truthfully because he was one of them and he could set extra work or find out how their jobs were going without endangering the overall politics of the ship.

He became so useful that in time he was given the honorary title of 'clerk' and that was no mean achievement for him. His job was unique, he didn't mind covering vast distances and he made industrial relations and ship layouts his speciality; he had been encouraged in that direction as he was found to be good at it and he appreciated the opportunities that had been offered to him. With the collapse of the docks and the shipping companies a host of modestly educated runners and other menial employees must have been left with precariously uncertain futures. When Allen Purdey had last seen Johnny he was selling handkerchiefs on the corner of Rathbone Market.

*   *   *

At the Main Dock Office, Royal Mail Lines at the end of each voyage paid off the lower officers – they had their own door into this office. The ship's master would go up to town to learn how much was going into his account and at the same time find out about his next ship. Crews by comparison were paid off in their ship's common room by a union representative with a RML staff member in attendance, each crewman's pay being calculated according to a list of allowances and stoppages.

For a ship's clerk working with RML, the interlocking complexity of the docks often meant that the sight of a particular lighterage company's barges immediately suggested specific destinations or cargoes. We have seen how Silvertown Services were linked to Tate and Lyle but most lighterage companies seemed to work for a specific wharfinger or to be owned by one; Union Lighterage for example, worked either side of Tower Bridge for Butler's Wharf, Humphery & Grey covered all the work for the Hayes Wharf Group while General Lighterage moved cargoes between docks for the PLA. Other companies that Royal Mail Lines worked with had long standing contracts with importers, for example Thames Steam Tug carried our copper imports to the Enfield Rolling Mills on its fleet of narrow barges designed to negotiate the Lea and local canals. The impression I got was that many of these contracts went back generations, perhaps to my grandfather's time and beyond when agreements could be made on a nod and a wink. At least this is the only explanation I can offer for a company as large as Royal Mail Lines linking itself to one of the more modest lighterage companies, Perkins and Homer.

As a feature of Empire many goods coming into the Royal Docks were not destined to stay in Britain but by passing through London could achieve the best prices. An infrastructure of importers, buyers, speculators and financiers existed in the City who traded in a wide range of commodities from furs and ivory to coffee beans. The Royal Docks had no storage facilities, only 'In, Out' sheds, so that the vast warehouses of the old London and East India Docks, were used for shipments that needed to be set out, auctioned and re-exported around the world. Because these docks were too small to take modern, ocean going vessels, the traffic in them was confined to lighters and small coastal steamers such as those of the General Steam Navigation Company where the average ship size might have been around two thousand tons. From these docks purchases could be taken directly around the coast of Britain, across to the Continent or even round to North Africa. From our viewpoint this use for the old docks seemed very comfortable with the City close by and an easy barge journey from the Royal Docks.

Royal Mail Lines contributed to this trade with a number of commodities such as coffee beans from Brazil, West Indian spices or Chilean wool and to take these items round to the London Dock they employed the services of Perkins and Homer; a neat, efficient little organisation. This company always had a general air of tidiness with clean well turned out lighters and as far as I could see they seemed to survive almost exclusively on the Royal Mail Lines contract*: when there were cargoes for trans-shipment their lighters were busy around our ships but when RML didn't need them they seemed to vanish from the Royals.

*But see 'Dumb Barges' p35. They must have had other contracts.

After the War though and through to the late nineteen fifties their presence in the docks was constant, taking goods from our ships round to the warehouses of the older docks.

They had only one runner – name of Jim – who looked after and organised their fleet of perhaps forty lighters. He acquired a number of apt nick names but was most generally known as 'Tanglefoot', a common enough term for anyone who shared his natural clumsiness. He was a very pleasant, capable chap, completely in charge of the disposition of his lighters but he was gangling and loose limbed seeming never to be in complete control of his extremities. His knack of colliding with things was unfortunate in an environment like the docks: if a piece of metal protruded from a housing he would crack a shin on it, if a piece of dunnage was left lying on a deck, he would discover it by stumbling over it. Miraculously he seemed never to be seriously injured and both he and his company flourished: they were a good organisation to work with.

Perkins and Homer only had dumb barges, they were too small to employ a motor launch but the short haul from the Royals round to the London Dock hardly needed power and as this seemed to be the entire scope of their operations, the assumption was that lightermen would scull, hitch a lift or improvise their way up river. Apart from wool all RML goods for trans-shipment came in sacks which meant that lighters could always be stowed neatly.

Trans-shipment, Perkins and Homer and well stowed barges go together in my mind as does the technique known as 'out the window'. It was a common practice with all good lightermen but because of the nature of the cargoes and their insistence on neat stowage I have come to associate it in my memory particularly with Perkins and Homer.

Briefly the technique was as follows: The first sacks into the barge were laid out round the edges of the hold under the coamings down both sides of the craft to avoid listing, starting in the prow and working along to the stern. Out the window required the barge hands to stop their loading some four to eight feet short of the rear of the hold. Sacks were next laid in rows towards the centre so as to form an even layer across the entire ceiling, allowing a second layer to be set on top, again leaving a gap at the stern. Continuing in this way, the barge hands would add layers until the lighterman decided that he had a full lighter. He would then assess the lie of his craft. If he decided that the prow was sitting too low in the water he would ask the barge hands for a few sacks 'out the window' which meant dropping them into the well space they had created with their stowing. As the sacks were added the lighterman would watch, usually from an adjacent barge, to see how his craft altered its position and when he was happy that it could make good way up the Thames he signalled to the barge hands to stop loading and he was ready to cast off. Out the window then was a way of building in a fine adjustment to the balance of each lighter by the way the main load was distributed.

The same technique could be used for all solid or packaged goods – timber and metals were regularly stowed this way – and so it was also used for wool. The big difference for the gangs handling wool compared with other trans-shipment commodities was that wool came in bales weighing 8cwt. It was hard work manoeuvring objects this size even for the downholders who had the advantage of a winchman – the winch would be used to ease the bales to the hatchway for the crane to off-load. The barge hands depended on correct placement by the crane driver to supplement their muscle power. Ideally, the men could simply release the chains leaving the bales where the crane had dropped them but it was rarely so simple in practice. Once again the cargo had to be packed tight which meant that the initial bales had to be pushed and squeezed under the coamings away from where the crane could set them down. It was gruelling work and any assistance the crane driver could give was welcomed, for example just holding the set a foot or two above the working surface for men to swing into position as the crane driver then dropped it down. Close co-ordination was essential for the gang to maintain its work rate. The lighterman could not allow loose or sloppy loading even though the work was demanding for the wool had to be kept clean and protected from the elements; rain was bad but the dock or River water was ruinous.

When the lighter was stowed high with bales the lighterman would tie a tarpaulin tightly over the load - but this was only effective if it stayed tight over the whole journey. If the bales could settle the lighterman might find himself in mid-River with a section of tarpaulin flapping free. These open lighters used for carrying wool or other easily contaminated items used the tarpaulin effectively to lock cleanliness in. Photographs of the period might suggest a general air of grime but this did not extend to the inside of ship or barge holds which were kept scrupulously clean. Serious attention was needed to keep the elements out and the starting point was tight stowage.

Sometime during the month of April, one or two PSNC ships would arrive from the Pacific Coast of Chile with a large shipment of wool. This represented the annual production from the big ranches or co-operatives running down towards the southern tip of Chile near Cape Horn and it was, according to the officers*, a long and pretty disagreeable voyage calling at ports which were little more than a hut or two on the quay in a bleak and stormy landscape.

Ships would call in at perhaps fifteen ports of Chile and Ecuador picking up wool but also copper, potash, fishmeal and aros beans all bound for Britain. As the ships travelled further south, ports became increasingly more desolate with perhaps only a nitrate store to mark their existence. Finally right down by Cape Horn, wool would be picked up from two or three ports in Chile or Argentina such as Ushuaia on the Tierra del Fuego or Punta Arenas just on the mainland, before commencing the long haul back.

The crew on these runs would be the ones no one else wanted. Respectable seamen were offered the comfortable voyages to North America with work

*My father had no direct experience of these voyages.   MES

99

on passenger liners. Trouble makers and the more dissolute merchant seamen were only offered jobs which were difficult to fill – tides could vary so much down in those regions, it was told us by the ship's officers that men would have to work the hawsers almost twenty four hours a day to keep a ship at its moorings. Cabins were always small, typically ten feet by fifteen for six crew men on the assumption that three would be on duty at any one time. With such long, tedious voyages fights were common and drinking, endemic. As the ship entered the last leg of her voyage home, drink was consumed at ever greater rates with men regularly throwing up. When they heard a wool ship was returning, the RML dock staff knew that there would be plenty of disagreeable work for the shore gang.

The wool was bound in bales some of which weighed up to half a ton and as each ranch or station took care of its own bailing, the bundles took on different appearances depending upon the type and age of each baling machine. Through experience, we knew where the wool came from by the shape of the bales: Oszy Harbour were tall and thin, tightly wrapped with nine steel bands weighing eight hundredweights, while Estantia O'Higgins were fatter and more open with fewer bands and weighing around six hundredweights. Whatever their shape, 300 tons would be worked through a day. Each bale of course bore its exporter's mark but this was largely unnecessary for sorting the wool into separate lots.

Very occasionally, wool was loaded onto the quay for delivery by train directly to a manufacturer in Britain and a steam locomotive would bring up thirty wagons to take the bales to a glove manufacturer or perhaps to a tailor for flying jackets. With these deliveries manufacturers would be buying the goods unseen, relying entirely on the name of the shipping agent. From our point of view this meant additional handling by quay gangs and an increased risk of damage but the main fear was the possible exposure to British weather. If the train were delayed, for example by a 'bridger', the bales might have to sit on the quay in the open for an uncomfortably long time.

Most wool though went out by lighter to be auctioned at the PLA wool sheds. Jacob Hoare were the agents for Chilean wool and they would pay a deposit to the exporters before selling to London buyers. The PLA issued a brochure on the strength of the ship's inventory and a date was set for when the wool could be inspected and auctioned. These arrangements were made when the ship was still at sea and any delays to the ship's progress could be agonising: a week of fog would disrupt work causing a backlog of ships queuing at Gravesend with the auction date drawing ever closer. In such a situation with so much at stake, any number of people would be demanding results but practically all the ship's clerk could do was to make and adjust contingency plans with gangs and lightermen. Depending on when the ship finally appeared quick decisions might have to be made on the size of the shipment and the time available to get at it. There were times when a frantic morning's session would be spent clearing hatchways to get to the wool then a barge perhaps half full would be sent round to the London Dock so buyers could inspect at least a sample. The precise expectations of the City, the long and unpredictable voyage home and the uniqueness of the cargo all contributed to some pretty heated exchanges between the docks and Head Office when the weather threatened schedules.

A time came when wool became scarce. Russia, it was said, was buying all the wool it could get and increasingly consignments were bought while ships were still at sea. It denoted a dramatic change in the pattern of world trade which hit the docks hard. In a seller's market it became apparent to Chile that they no longer needed Jacob Hoare or the PLA to sell their produce and instead began selling directly to foreign manufacturers; overnight the Royal Mail Lines wool trade vanished. This situation seemed to be part of a much larger global realignment as newly independent colonies and developing nations re-assessed their relationships with Old World powers. Trans-shipment was badly hit and in time the London Dock was forced to close, its warehouses empty. Less and less did RML have work for Perkins and Homer and their presence in the Royals became a rarity. What became of them I never knew but quietly and unobtrusively Tanglefoot and his pristine little fleet disappeared from the docks and our perceptions.

*   *   *

OIL CHECK

A particularly niggling little task that import ship's clerks had to undertake was that of collecting oil readings from the Chief Engineer. Royal Mail House needed to know how much oil each ship had used on her voyage and it was down to the Engineer to take the readings and us to forward the details - nothing onerous, just unfortunate timing. For the Chief Engineer it was the end of another tour of duty, shore leave beckoned and he was in party mood. This was often literally the case, the officer would have some of his friends in and the drinks would be flowing, heads none too clear. To have a ship's clerk suddenly appear in their midst in the role of party pooper for nit picking oil readings did nothing to encourage good relations between RML crew and dock staff. Trivial, of course, but as it represented the only contact Chief Engineers and ship's clerks had with each other the possibility was there, given the wrong personalities, for enduring antipathy. This ritual took place each time every ship berthed.

As well as a relieving officer on board every working ship in the docks, RML also employed a relieving engineer and among his duties were to take daily oil readings. This was to give Head Office an indication of how much oil was being used by the ship's winches during discharging. This could be 5 tons a day.

I had been ill for a couple of days which didn't happen very often and was always a bad move because of what I might find when I got back. By the time I found out what ship I was working and got myself round to it, I discovered copper ingots were being off-loaded and stored in the shed. The casual, stand-in ship's clerk had somehow overlooked advising the importer, a regular customer based over at Wapping, so transport was unavailable. Normally he would have been told precisely when to get his lorry up onto the quay for the copper to be loaded directly onto it. This time we had no option but to secure the shipment in the shed's lock-up. By the time the lines of communication had been straightened out between the importer and the ship, it was late morning and he promised to get his lorry over as soon as work began again after lunch. At twelve o'clock I saw the last of the ingots into the locker and saw it secured, at one o' clock when the lorry arrived we found the lock smashed and two stacks of ingots missing. Perhaps with a bit more time we might have arranged for Dan Hughes or a watcher to sit with the consignment over lunch but that was hindsight; it was a useful reminder that crooks could always organise themselves quicker than the authorities and that if something was worth stealing and was available, it would go. I was ready to crawl back to my sick-bed.

Metals never formed a cohesive group but whatever type or shape arrived, general cargo gangs worked them without too much trouble. The variety was considerable from ill shaped, dirty old pieces of machinery, much of it in the process of being converted from war to peace time use, to sacks of walnut sized chunks of titanium or bismuth and easy to handle. When they came in sacks they were usually in the form of metal ore for refining in Britain and were of limited interest to casual thieves. We'll narrow our focus to just three metals which arrived in various stages of refinement, zinc, lead and copper.

Unit shapes varied according to their place of production but whatever their form or pattern of stowage as long as they could be worked from a crane hook, gangs could maintain a good rate. Impure copper in need of further refining arrived as 'pie dishes' or 'plates'. Pie dishes were rectangular flattened shapes about 20 x 20 x 2 inches and weighing three or four to the ton with lugs protruding from opposite sides. These were stacked vertically and it was easy enough to wrap a chain around the lugs for the crane to remove eight at a time. The slightly smaller plates had no lugs and were stacked horizontally in tiers of five on dunnage pallets which could be used to simply crane lift out. The main problem would be if the ship had encountered heavy seas and loads had shifted during the voyage, then the neat stacks would be transformed into a confusion of copper and dunnage. This 'shot' cargo meant gangs had the back breaking task of lifting each individual plate into a new set. Gangs would have to divide up so that some restacked while others off-loaded the completed sets, alternating between the jobs. Usually one of the ship's winches would be brought into service to help manoeuvre plates and sets ready for the crane. Piece rates were low for copper and for intact loads a shipment could be quickly worked through but the slow, heavy task of re-stacking four cwt plates, was so disproportionate to standard pay rates that special deals with the unions had to be sorted. Any job working one to three hundredweight metal plates, with chains and a crane hook seriously risked the loss of fingertips but clambering amongst haphazard drifts of them imperilled ankles and toes as well as hands and back. For the ship's clerk though these plates and pie dishes of impure, blistered copper had the big advantage of having little black market value and in consequence were relatively safe. Later on, presumably as a result of upgrading their refining processes, Chile sent purer forms of copper across in the shape of long, square cross sectioned bars which tapered towards each end to make it easier to get a lifting wire under them; they were known as 'torpedoes'. Typically they would form only part of a consignment and while the plates and pie dishes were neatly stacked, torpedoes, weighing two and a half hundredweight each, were just scattered across the ceiling of a hold. Lifting them had to be a two-man job, and downholders would use 'cheese wires' – wire attached to two wooden handles - to lift them into sets of perhaps four wide by five tiers high built up on dunnage timber. With a set formed in this way and weighing in the region of two and a half tons, a wire was simply wrapped around it and attached to the crane hook. Metal against metal forms a pretty slippery bundle and gravity and friction were not always enough to hold these sets together. To avoid the load being shed, dangerous as well as distressing, pieces of wood were often tucked under the wires and against the torpedoes to give them something to bite onto – then you watched each one very carefully out of the hold.

By the time these purer forms of copper were arriving, so were the sloppier scratch gangs. If they could get away with it, they would simply wrap the wire round a bundle of torpedoes and pull it out by the crane hook, hoping that a reasonable number of bars would go with it. Plenty fell out but that was expected, downholders took evasive action, but there was no possibility of predicting how many torpedoes would be lifted or what load was being taken by the crane. Copper is a relatively soft metal and by casting them around in this way many of the smooth, well formed torpedoes ended up with dangerously awkward gouges and abrasions for the barge hands to have to negotiate.

So long as copper was built into neat sets, whatever their shape, they could be accurately placed in lighters without any manual lifting. Normally the barges were especially narrow to be able to navigate the canals up to the Enfield Rolling Mills; copper sets would be simply stacked in three rows one against each of the sides and one down the middle. Adjustments to the placement of each two to three ton load could be done once again by the men slightly swaying the load as it hung on the crane or by adjusting the barge. Placement could be accurate and the lighterman would leave with a well balanced cargo.

Once scratch gangs had dispensed with regular set construction, barge hands always had some shuffling to do and risked slicing their hands on a jagged edge, but they were not going to do their downholders' job of stacking the sets neatly. The lighterman might order a better weight distribution but by this time he was no longer able to require a well formed load; he took what he got and so long as his craft was balanced, made do. This lack of professionalism also caused problems later on for the men at the factories who were used to crane lifting well constructed sets and who now suddenly had their work increased enormously having to off-load an indiscriminate jumble. Organising the bars into sets was a time consuming task, someone had to pay and arguments between shippers, stevedores and importers grew more common. Dangerous handling was banned both by the supervising bodies and by the unions – for the unscrupulous though there was an advantage in producing a chaotic cargo in making the copper bars harder to count. So long as copper was shipped as blistered impure plates, its value on the black market was limited, but as pure copper torpedoes, the load became very desirable.

On average perhaps fourteen torpedoes out of a thousand might go missing at each delivery which represented a large proportion of shippers' profits. It shouldn't have happened; torpedoes in themselves were easy enough to count. Tally clerks, ship's supervisors, lighterman and gangs ought to have been able to agree precisely what each lighter contained particularly as on metal consignments an extra tally clerk was always employed. One tally clerk stood on the top deck counting torpedoes out of the hold and a second counted them into the barge. It ought to have been straightforward but never was in practice. Even during the days of neat, clearly visible sets, torpedoes went missing. Sets were lowered onto pieces of timber so the wire or chain could be released from around them and it was easy enough to slip a torpedo in the space between the timbers or to replace one. Well made sets laid along a ceiling had the advantage of looking innocent and it took a determined tally clerk or supervisor to make a careful on board examination. With just a jumble of copper from a scattered set, losing a couple of torpedoes would have been relatively child's play. It became a mind game amongst permanent staff during quieter moments to try to fathom how the copper could be disposed of.

If additional copper had been secreted on a barge then somewhere between the docks and the Rolling Mills along the canals and back waters the torpedoes had to be off-loaded. My preferred theory, without a shred of evidence it has to be admitted, was to assume that, although these narrow barges were securely locked, a crooked lighterman could still get at his cargo and in the middle of the night take it up to a bridge where an accomplice with a 'handy billy', a pulley block and tackle, would lift the extra torpedoes out. The barge could then return to its moorings with no one any the wiser.

Even at this distance it would be interesting to find out what actually happened to all those torpedoes and ingots, presumably as the situation never improved all our speculations were wrong. Employing an extra tally clerk was no match for whatever system they used, shippers and importers seemed prepared to write off the losses and to our discomfort, the rate of pilfering continued to tick over.

From the United States came lead and zinc, both immaculately packed probably by specialist stevedores who concentrated on just one commodity. One was easy for discharge gangs to work, the other agony. Lead was produced in flat plates known as 'pigs' and weighing one hundredweight. These plates had ledges at each end for lifting, we assumed, but were always stowed upside down preventing fingers from getting underneath, presumably in America lifting them by hand was unheard of by this time and shot loads unconsidered. Fortunately this rarely mattered, pigs made up into sets of twenty on pallets and could be lifted out easily using a chain or wire wrapped round them. Only very occasionally would a scattered load have downholders cursing the seemingly bizarre 'upside down' stowing. One advantage of working lead was that being such a soft metal, the lifting wire bit into it to help secure the load which also made placement in the barge both easy and accurate. Again, with nice neat sets it was easy for a lighterman and tally clerk to agree the quantity.

The problem was zinc or spelter as it was called. From an import clerk's point of view it was easy: beautifully laid out rectangular plates perhaps 18 x 9 x 1 inches and weighing half a hundredweight stretched out across half the ceiling of a lower or tween deck hold. Perhaps four hundred tons divided into eight or more lots with each plate correctly numbered on its edge and with the red or black paint mark requested by the shipper. As one lot ended tar paper was introduced to separate it from the next so that standing on the ceiling the strata of zinc had tar paper rippling across it confirming different consignments already well denoted by their mark. For me as a supervisor the clarity was a rare blessing.

The problem was off-loading; the edges were bevelled so that each plate was like a very truncated pyramid with a sharp acute angle precisely where they had to be gripped. As with so many uncomfortable cargoes, the real problem was the number that had to be worked; they formed a tight, compact mass making it difficult to get a dockers' hooks or fingers underneath. Presumably the plates were stowed mechanically but no equivalent means was available to FW gangs. A 'head down, arse up' job, each plate, or with the best gangs pairs of plates, had to be lifted separately and stacked onto a pallet making the same unrelenting demands on back and fingers. Once formed into a set, extraction was easy – it was getting it there that took its toll. The pallets that carried the plates were square with metal rings in each corner allowing two sets of 'brothers' to raise them. Lifting a pallet out with forty plates on it was straightforward so long as you remembered, once again, to keep your fingers out of the way of the tightening ropes.

For barge hands the work was equally tough. The first couple of sets were put down in the centre of the barge as a table for later sets to be placed on and the four barge hands then had to carry each plate, or pair of plates, and stack them four deep against the side of the hold under the coamings. The empty pallet was rested against the table to be hooked onto the next returning 'brothers'. Once the mid section was stowed, they moved up to the prow, set up a second table and repeated the exercise stowing the plates under the coamings. Finally they worked at the stern and the lighterman could say how many he wanted there to balance the craft as an 'out the window' exercise. Once the sides of the ship were fully loaded, the three tables were dismantled and the spelter plates laid out along the centre of the barge. Once again it was back breaking work; one or two half-hundredweight plates tucked under coamings was easy, four hundred tons and you knew you had done a good day's work. The process which experienced barge hands had designed for themselves, minimised lifting and carrying but it still took its toll.

Back in the ship's hold if the zinc was stowed away from the hatchway a bogie could usually be discovered by which downholders could push loaded sets to the hatchway and the crane hook. Bogies were pretty basic platforms with four small, metal wheels and if the surface of the ceiling were sufficiently uncluttered they helped but when loaded with a ton weight they were not easy things in themselves to manhandle. For ceilings with rivets and cleats, it was often easier to carry them.

Getting towards the end with the final sets far from the hatchway, the temptation was to forget the bogies and simply build sets on pallets and just drag them out using the crane - banned of course but after four hundred tons, it was a powerful temptation. Once again the main problems were damage to the crane by exceeding its limit or fraying the hawser as it scuffed the coamings. There was also the common problem that as the load swung free at the edge of the hatchway it would pendulum but in this case, being a substantial mass of solid metal, it could do serious damage to the hatches and manways. Gangs knew all this of course but with aching backs and split fingers it was, as I said, a powerful temptation.

The worst time for working any metals was in winter when torpedoes, pigs, plates and ingots were all painfully cold. Hands were cut, chafed, gouged and frozen as gangers worked through shipments which, by then, ought to have been removed mechanically. Gloves whether industrial or home knitted were unheard of at that time.

Open hatches couldn't help but be dangerous places and the danger was variable. Fall a couple of feet onto a sack of dried peas when the hatch was first opened and you just felt an idiot, fall thirty or forty feet onto a similar sack two days later and you might end up like Uncle Ned, alive but permanently disabled. But if the cargo were a jumble of angular metal you wouldn't have to fall far to terminate a promising career. Five gaping holes along the top deck were obviously hazardous with the risk increasing as the holds were worked. It was fifty feet to the ceiling of the lower hold and the danger increased, not only because men on the top deck might fall to their deaths but also because a swinging set could scuff a bar or plank on any level and send it plummeting down onto the gang below. Top hands and supervisors constantly had to look out for clutter inadvertently placed on top or tween decks that might cause accidents; equally dangerous was material lost off a set board which could prove slippery or hazardous. The area around the hatchways had to be scrupulously clear of extraneous items, coamings themselves were a risk but had the small advantage at least of predictability.

A general cargo meant a potentially wide range of specifics each of which might be worked differently and might swing and bounce in a variety of ways on the end of a crane hook – and usually weighing two tons each. Working fast with a crane meant skewing the set out of the hold and into a lighter in an arcing curve; cranes didn't lift vertically, swing horizontally then descend vertically and for this reason it was as well to be very clear on the trajectory of the crane's two ton projectile if you spent your working day around hatches: and that projectile came into its own particularly with those ships which had dispensed with a man hatch.

There was another type of danger though associated with these traditional hatches: the work of opening the hatches at the start of every day and 'hatching up' in the evening was carried out by each ship's gang working their hold. Stevedores saw the operation as confirming their competence over quay gangs but it was also important that they recognised that they worked within the conditions they themselves created; if they left the hatch boards lying around dangerously or failed to secure beams, the risk was to the gang members. All the older ships had hatch covers formed in a similar way and it was the business of dealing with these that was the first duty of a ship gang taking on a new hold.

These traditional hatch covers were substantial affairs necessary to protect the cargoes from whatever the Atlantic threw at them, yet they had to be manageable for a gang and crane to dismantle. Initially there were three layers of tarpaulins, each covering the hatch and held down at the coamings by a series of half hundredweight metal bars which in turn were secured by wooden wedges so placed that, if heavy seas were breaking across a deck, they were forced in tighter, not loosened.

With the tarpaulins removed, the main impression was of a smooth wooden surface covering the entire hatch area, perhaps fifteen feet wide and thirty feet long. This covering consisted of heavy timber planking, known as hatch boards, each about six feet long and laid in tightly fitting rows across the width of the hatch space so that usually each hold had five rows of these boards along the thirty foot length of its hatch.

Holding the boards in position were a series of metal beams stretching the width of the hatch and secured by pins at the coamings, each main beam shaped like an inverted 'T' in cross section with the boards resting on their ledges. Secondary beams, known as 'sisters' provided additional support for the boards beneath their centres, again spanning the width of the hatch. All these beams weighed a ton each and had to be removed by crane.

This system of parallel metal bars in-filled with wooden planking had to be removed and replaced each day - and each day the hole beneath the hatch covers became deeper and more treacherous. To begin, the gang started from the centre with two men, one at each end of the middle board, lifting it out and carrying it to one side. Other pairs of men followed lifting the boards to port or starboard and the hole widened across the width of the hatch. Gangs earned their livelihoods by teamwork but dismantling and replacing hatch covers was carried out with military precision, each man knowing exactly what he had to do. The boards were heavy and had recessed metal handles at each end so that gangers were frequently lifting, and manoeuvring, while standing on a beam with a vertical drop beside and before them. A slip could have been fatal. For this reason it was crucial that there were no protuberances that gangers could catch their heel against, the hatch surface had to be perfectly smooth and even. It was easy at the end of an exhausting day to be a little casual in replacing the structure; the metal beams were all numbered, so there wasn't any real excuse, but the temptation was to put the most accessible beam in the nearest slot and get off home. This had to be resisted because the wrong positioning of a beam often meant that the boards did not sit comfortably and it might be at the start of the next day with the previous day's carelessness forgotten, that men found boards they were balancing on wobbled or that half inch steps had been built in just waiting to be tripped over. Such possible discrepancies were increasingly perilous of course as each day's work took them deeper into the hold.

The top hand, the ship worker and ship's clerk all took time to see that hatch covers were replaced correctly but above them the Port of London Authority employed a safety officer with special responsibility for hatch work. He was known universally as 'Charley Hatches' and if he was spotted coming along the quay the cry spread rapidly down the length of the dock. Correct placement of the beams was his particular concern but also to make sure the securing pins were in place. One situation which he watched like a hawk was when two gangs were working the same hold. In this situation gangs maintained their integrity working at opposite ends of the hold and to keep things tidy they would often agree to keep the central row of hatch boards in place so that cranes had a clearly defined area to work out of for each gang. If, at some time in the past, beams had been badly positioned or securing pins had been left out, it would need only the merest brush by a rising two ton load to set the whole partition, beams and boards, crashing down on the gangs.

Equally, Charley Hatches was insistent that all the boards and beams were removed well away from the hatch openings when the hold was being worked. This applied on all decks for as a gang excavated through tween and lower decks each level was separated by a similar arrangement of boards and beams which, as they worked through them, had to be removed to the side walls of the hold. Once these lower hatch covers were removed the hatches could be left open but top hatches were always covered to keep out the weather which meant that towards the end of a hold's working, a gang returning for the final day ran the risk, as they took off the covers, of falling through the complete depth of the hull. Some gangs piled the hatch boards by the coamings then got the crane to lift them as a group to the ship's side or even, if there was a lot of deck cargo for example, have them put down onto the quay. So long as they were away from the action, Charley Hatches was happy.

One of the great psychological perks of finally finishing a hold was that a gang could move straight on to the next job, or go home if it was towards the end of a day. The shore gang would have to clean the hold before exports could be taken on board and they needed all the hatches open, including the top one. It was a relief for the gang to just collect their tools together, get out and forget the irksome and demanding task of hatching up. Sometimes in order to save themselves the long climb up the manway from the lower hold to top deck, the men hitched a lift on the final set board to be raised by the crane. Officially this six foot square of wood was only used for cargo and the last one lifted out the shovels, ropes and chains used by the downholders but tired men would hitch a lift if the top hand signalled that supervisors were elsewhere. But there could be a drawback: on occasions I have seen crane drivers with an evil glint in their eyes gently raise the set with the men on board and just as gently lower it over the side of the ship into the dock water. Then with the men screaming obscenities as they stood knee deep in the suds, the driver would lift them back out again and onto the quay. Just the thing to end a gruelling day before setting off on an uncomfortable cycle ride home. This of course could only happen in the old days of tightly knit gangs – try it with a scratch gang and murder or litigation would have ensued.

Soon after the War ships were being fitted with the new, all metal McGregor hatches. These were opened by simply fitting a chain to a winch which pulled the cover back in a concertina movement – much quicker and safer to open, much easier to replace any time rain threatened. For the ship gangs though, traditional hatching up was gradually lost, and with it a bit of their particular expertise. During the transitional stage they continued to work the wooden hatches whenever they appeared but the new hatches were given over to shore gangs as part of their official 'preparation of the ship'; in the past this term had meant only clearing the decks of clutter and maybe setting the derricks. These McGregor hatches were a definite improvement in all respects but the improved technology inevitably diminished the prowess of traditional ship gangs

*   *   *

SECOND BOTTOMING

When the docks were at their most busy with ships queuing down at Gravesend waiting for a berth, it was sometimes possible to increase the congestion still further by requesting the Dockmaster to permit 'second bottoming'. If a RML ship was at berth somewhere in the docks and was off-loading onto the quay, permission could be sought to bring a second ship up to the same berth, moor alongside and work overside into lighters. This could only be allowed if the arrangement didn't conflict with other traffic movements in the dock and only made sense if both vessels could work their respective cargoes in this way for a reasonable length of time. Perhaps one ship was finishing up with quay work and was due to change berths next day to receive exports from an annual rent shed. A second ship berthed alongside and working into barges would not affect the quay work and by second bottoming, the shipping company was not only getting more efficient use out of the dock facilities but also was reserving the berth for their second ship to pull into once the first had left. Even if cargoes couldn't immediately be worked, second bottoming allowed other jobs to be carried out: empty holds could be fumigated, certain cargoes might need gassing, general repair work, for example mending winches, could be undertaken. There was an element of queue-jumping in all this and Dockmasters could always refuse if they felt the operation worked against the overall effectiveness of the docks.

For the shipping line this arrangement had a second economic virtue: once berthed, the ship's crew could be paid off while the ship's clerk was expected to supervise both vessels, potentially ten working holds. The worst situation I experienced was being in charge of five discharging ships at three adjacent berths (2 ships at 1, 1at 2 and 2 at 3 RVD, South Side), with two sets of second bottoming.

In a perfect world free from bomb damage and with spare parts readily available, for every ship which berthed wherever it berthed, five cranes, one for each working hold would have been standing by. The reality of course was that after the War cranes were often in short supply and their allocation frequently required some fairly tortuous decision making at a local level, which gangs got them, which ships, which companies and this was all part of the day to day management of the docks. Decisions were rarely arbitrary and had to be made in good time. Top hands needed to know a day or two in advance if they were going to be asked to work from derricks (usually called 'the sticks') on their next engagement as it needed them to get across to the FW equipment store and arrange tackle for the range of goods they expected to be working. In addition there was a manpower complication: a crane only needed a crane driver whereas working from derricks needed two winchmen and the top hand would have to find someone competent who could earn his place working a winch. Given the choice, gangs would always choose cranes, they were more straightforward and had a greater span but derricks, in the right hands, had the advantage of being faster.

When deciding which gangs should have the cranes and which the derricks, supervisors had to consider the types of cargo, the transport items would leave on and the abilities of the gangs they had taken on at the Call. We have seen the problems that could arise if barges at Nos 2 and 4 holds became wedged between the ship and quay (see 'Loading Sugar Barges') or if they needed to be stood off. If lighters had to be manoeuvred and it interrupted work, one option for gangs equipped with cranes was for them to ask if they could 'extend the limit'. This meant seeking permission to lower the angle of the crane arm to a more horizontal position so that it could reach further and hopefully, make the hatch. This of course increased the moment on the arm and safety regulations only allowed sets of half the normal weight to be worked in this way, thereby halving the work rate but maintaining a level of throughput.

There was an upgrading scheme in operation in the Royals by which the sixty five foot cranes were replaced by eighty footers. Naturally, there were never enough to go round, all the gangs wanted them as they solved all their logistical problems but the PLA was obliged to spread the few they managed to get among the older stock so that over time most working berths had some access to them.

For a ship coming up to a berth, there were only two real alternatives: either she pulled up against the quay for quay and shed work, or she stood off against a pontoon or dummy for barge work. A top hand who had been told that his gang would have to work from the sticks would also have been told what the cargo would be and how the ship would berth. Accordingly he made his decisions on the equipment and tackle he would need and the configuration he would deploy for the derricks:

Union Purchase

For our purposes it is good enough to think of derricks as masts hinged up from the top deck and located near holds. When not in use, they were carried horizontally, about six feet off the deck beside the hatches. Each main hatch usually had four sets of derricks, one near each corner facing each other in pairs, while the smaller 1 and 5 holds in the bows and stern generally only had two, one on each side of the hatch. If the sticks were to be used, they had to be used in pairs transversally across the deck so that loads suspended between them could be moved from hatch to ship's side. All standard derricks were capable of lifting three tons maximum which practically meant that they were designed for continuous work lifting approximate two ton sets. Derricks were very quick to work and the different alignments gave them a great flexibility in use on either side of the ship.

Power to lift and move the cargo sets was produced from motorised winches, one being situated just behind each derrick. For any arrangement of the sticks, two were needed, each with its own winch and winchman.

Generally speaking, if a ship berthed directly alongside the quay, the top hand chose a union purchase rig and in fact, throughout the docks this rig was a common sight. Setting the derricks would take perhaps an hour first thing in the morning and the work could be carried out either by the shore or the ship gang. The point here was that derricks, winches and stays were part of the ship and so were Royal Mail Lines property, the pulleys, hooks and tackle blocks belonged to Furness, Withy; altogether, the gang who were going to operate them needed to satisfy themselves that the equipment was as they wanted for safe and efficient use. There was rarely any problem with these straightforward rigs but the vested interests were considerable, and all the representatives made a point of satisfying themselves with the arrangement each time derricks were used.

The simplest way to think of a union purchase rig is to imagine runners coming from two winches each over the top of its derrick and meeting in the middle with the load suspended beneath forming a 'Y' shape. In this position, the cargo set would be situated half way across the deck.

Let us suppose the right hand derrick had been secured directly over the centre of the hatchway by wires to masts or stays. If the left hand winch was played out from our 'Y', the load would gradually sink until it was hanging directly under the right hand derrick i.e. directly over the hatch. By playing out both winches the load would then descend into the hold.

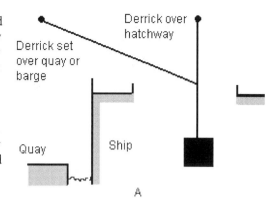

Returning to our 'Y' shape, if the right hand winch line were played out, the load would eventually hang vertically under the left hand support, which in this case would be the overside derrick fixed by stays to a position over the quay. Letting out both lines now would lower the set onto the quay.

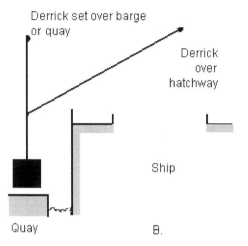

So by co-ordinated play between the two winches, winding in and letting out, a set could be moved from hatch to quay. The great feature of this rig was that both down holders and pitch hands knew exactly where the hook would descend as the two derricks were in fixed positions. At this stage, incidentally, it might become clear how important good communication was and how unhelpful it was to isolate winchmen away in cabins (see p. 72).

In fact, RML did not use the union purchase rig much, most of the general cargo ships loaded into lighters with any cargo destined for the quay taken out by crane. However, union purchase was used by Scruttons on the meat ships at 'Z' shed where carcasses were discharged. There were no cranes at this berth so derricks had to be used and the pitch hands, waiting on the quay for the nets of meat to come over, needed to know exactly where they would land in order to place their electric trolleys there. Using a union purchase rig where one derrick is fixed overside, precise placement is assured. In this situation it was no impediment not to have cranes: derricks were fast and efficient with the nets just skimming the coamings and gunwales on their course to the waiting scooter.

In practice, the union purchase rig was rather more sophisticated than this with pulley blocks helping to produce a more even distribution of weight as the set moved between the two derricks, but the distinguishing feature of the rig was that the wires from the two winches both supported the weight of the set.

Swinging Derrick

In the swinging derrick rig, one derrick did all the work mimicking the action of a crane arm while the second derrick acted only as a stop. When derricks were loading into lighters, if the gang used union purchase, either the barge would have to be constantly moved so that sets were put down in different parts of the ceiling, or the barge hands would have to do a lot of carrying. Setting the loads down in one place on a ceiling had little value in this context and the swinging derrick arrangement was designed to offer a greater coverage.

As with union purchase, one derrick was fixed firmly in position over the centre of the hatch by ropes or wires to masts and stays. The second derrick took on something of the character of a fishing rod with the winch as the reel, the derrick as the rod and the lower pivot like a fisherman's wrist. This second derrick was arranged so as to come to rest against the first in a fixed position over the hold. As the winch played out, the hook would descend to receive the cargo set. The set was raised and as it did so, the derrick would begin to move towards the side of the ship. This was achieved by using the winch of the fixed derrick, through a system of pulleys, guided the swinging derrick out over the side of the ship. How far it swung depended upon how much the winch was worked so that the top hand could see each set out of the hold then run across deck to look down into the working barge and see where the barge hands wanted it positioned. By hand signals the top hand could direct the winchman to pull the swinging derrick out to the best position for the men, saving them much manhandling, and the gang a deal of time. It was a very flexible system.

The problem was that once the set was released in the barge, there was no automatic system by which the derrick could be returned to the hatchway; winches could only pull, not push. With union purchase, the weight of the hook and block was sufficient in itself to descend into the hold while the winches, working in opposition, could provide the outward and inward motion. For the swinging derrick, the mass of the derrick itself had to be overcome in order to return it back over the hatch and this was done using a 'lazy guy'. Two forty gallon oil drums, part of the equipment picked up by the top hand when he collected the rest of his tackle, were filled with water and suspended by pulleys to the fixed derrick arm in such a way that, as the second derrick swung over the lighter, the drums rose up the first.

Effectively, the winch swinging the derrick out to the barge, transporting the set raised the lazy guys in the same operation. Immediately the set was released in the barge, the drums started descending pulling the derrick back to its rest position over the hatch. It was a good system, quick and flexible enough to minimise the repositioning of the barge, if in practice rather more complicated to set up.

You won't lose points if you don't follow all this but it might help viewing old photographs with a more informed eye.

'Frisco Rig

There was a third method of using derricks which was interesting in the way it was allowed to be used. Officially it was banned in the docks being considered too dangerous – but this ban only applied to Britain. This translated in the docks to 'British ships'. In Britain, Royal Mail Lines were the agents for the Holland American Line and the ban did not cover foreign ships so, if necessary, gangs could use this rig on HAL vessels. Essentially it was a way of lifting large weights on standard derricks allowing loads of around ten tons to be raised with all four, three ton derricks working together around one of the bigger holds. The problem and the reason for its prohibition in Britain, was that it needed very accurate balancing work between the four winchmen. A slight miscalculation or moment's inattention could cause the entire weight to be thrown onto insufficient purchasing power, sending the whole mass crashing back down into the hold. In practice, the men were always equal to the task but everyone was easier when an operation using the 'Frisco rig was completed. For RML, if a large piece of machinery had to be carried, it was usually taken on the 'Loch Ryan' which was specifically designed with a 'jumbo derrick' for bearing large loads.

As a coda perhaps the technique known as 'whip end' ought to be included. If the situation arose that two gangs were working from a restricted hatchway, almost always No.3 hold in practice, it was difficult to find space for both gangs to work separately. Winches had a sort of boss or barrel on the end of their drums and if one gang were using a winch it was possible for a winchman from the second gang to stand ready with his set's rope and slip it round the boss so that as the first gang's empty hook was returning the second gang's set could be raised. The rope had to be slipped on at the right moment and in such a way that it bit onto itself to hold fast as the rope was being wound on the drum in the opposite sense to the main runner. To do this with precision for each set off-loaded was extremely risky, the forces too great, the technique too uncontrollable and fingers too vulnerable; all the unions were against the practice but if men were prepared to endanger life and limb to maintain their gang's work rate, there was little anyone could do about it. Securing that rope and the timing of it had to be done by a cool and experienced head, there could be no room for error.

Although ocean going ships and lighters formed the great preponderance of craft in the docks, there were occasionally others. The General Steam Navigation Company was one of the largest operators of small coastal steamers of around two thousand tons, concerned in great part with the trans-shipment of cargoes from the London Docks to other ports around Britain, to the Channel Isles and across to the Continent. They formed an important link re-distributing goods from around the world to more local destinations. Direct contact between Royal Mail Lines and these steamers was rare, there was too much investment involved for them to be dependant upon each other's schedules.

If a steamer entered the Royal Docks to receive a cargo directly from a ship, it was an important operation; off-loading into a coaster meant a dramatic increase in overheads and it did not take many delays to make the whole process uneconomic.

There was one such memorable occasion which involved 'Big Fred'. He was a six foot three, seventeen stone Norwegian whose only intelligible English was "Hello, mate", spoken with a thick accent. He had been a Bo'sun during his time at sea, mostly in sailing ships, had the respect of all the men and was employed by Furness, Withey as a gearer. Most of his time was spent in the gearing shed, a building alongside RML's main dock office, where he repaired tackle, checked chains and life belts and serviced blocks to make sure they would pass safety standards. He was famous for being able to splice wires with his bare fingers, "fingers like marline spikes", was the general consensus.

While most rigging jobs for derricks could be sorted out by the gangs using them, when situations got more problematic they always called in Big Fred. On this occasion one of the Dutch boats, the 'Dongedyke' or 'Duredyke' berthed at one of the annual rent sheds on the south side of Victoria Dock, was working outside the ship into a steamer. The derricks were being used and so as not to delay the steamer which was scheduled immediately to take a cargo up the Rhein to Switzerland, the work was being carried out on a Sunday. However, one of the ship's derricks had been damaged and although it was due to be repaired in Holland on the ship's return to her home port, it was needed now. The rig was for a swinging derrick over No.4 hold but because of the damage, the second derrick down which the lazy guy should run, could not be operated. Various pieces of tackle suspended from stays and masts, had been introduced to overcome this deficiency, a winch at No.5 hold supplied the power to swing the active derrick but the net result was that the lazy guy was descending from the mast's yard, down onto the second winchman. He was not very happy about forty gallon drums swaying over his head and his refusal to work could have proved very costly: Fred was called in. He arranged for the pulleys to be realigned to an apparently more precarious position running the drums down a stay instead of the mast.

The problem was to appreciate the forces involved. Derricks and masts were designed for specific loadings like the weight on a crane arm. Rigging up innovative structures to bear the forces set in motion by a moving two ton load was a risky business and the choice of tackle and its deployment required a gut understanding of the stresses involved. It was the practical experience of Fred's years at sea that were needed here. His solution frightened everybody else but he believed in it, the winchman was happy to escape his Sword of Damocles and the steamer got on with receiving its cargo. As always, when he had completed something special Fred sat his massive frame down beside the rig, folded his arms across his chest nodded slowly as he watched his handiwork in operation repeating to himself "Jaaa…jaaa…….."

If the safety officer had been around, he probably would have banned the whole operation but Charley Hatches didn't work on Sundays. The important point for RML was that their cargo superintendent, who had ultimate responsibility for the loading, had complete confidence in Fred's judgements. Big Fred was over seventy when he finally retired – his experience and talents were irreplaceable.

In fact, such was the standing of gearers and riggers in the docks that they formed an elite having a separate branch and offices within the White Union.

Across the Victoria Dock on the north side by FW's gearing shed, RML employed its own ex-Bo'sun to look after their 'Loft' – more correctly a ships chandlers, though no one ever called it that. Bob Boyd looked after all the general maintenance equipment, paint, grease, tar, tools and tackle, for the use of shore gangs and also replacement items such as linen, table ware and cutlery, but the long, deep shape of the loft was dictated by the age old need to lay out ropes, hawsers and chains for checking and splicing. In time a new 'Factory' was built just outside the Victoria Dock to replace the Loft but for a while after the War, Big Fred and Bob could drop in on each other to discuss mutual problems and exchange yarns, Bob seemed to be one of the few men able to understand Fred's dialect.

Bob had four sons, one was chauffeur to the Marine Superintendent, a second was a tally clerk, while the eldest, Dougie Boyd, was the charge hand or leader of the permanent RML shore gang. The fourth son was the only one to escape the dock environment, playing football for Birmingham City. Bob hoped that when he retired Dougie would take over the Loft but in fact it went to Bob's assistant, Frank Young, another ex-Bo'sun*. It was Doug Boyd, incidentally, who introduced Johnny the Runner to serious drinking: his shore gang would drop into the Tidal Basin Tavern on Friday evenings, straight from work, and not emerge till Monday morning sleeping on, or under, the benches.

* *Frank, knowing my interest in these maritime traditions, passed on to me Lord Kylsant's silver plated inkwell that sat on his desk when chairman of the Royal Mail Steam Packet Company. RML had been taken over by then and the Loft's contents dispersed.* ME

Within the Royal Group there were three scruffy tugs belonging to the PLA to take care of ship movements within the docks. The *Plagil, Plagent* and *Platina* were small tugs well suited to the still waters of the Royals but not powerful enough to take on estuary work. As they were permanently confined to the docks they were a common sight towing ships up from the locks around high tide while away from high tide they were kept busy taking ships from one berth to another, taking them to a dry dock or hauling the floating cranes up to working ships. If PLA equipment had to be moved on the water – and this included the floating cranes and grain machines – then their own tugs always did the work but for moving ships, when the docks were at their busiest, this was not always possible. Lighters had no need of these tugs; lightermen moved their craft individually by whatever means they chose, collecting them together around ships or up to the locks for locking out towards high tide. Lighterage companies large enough to own their own tugs - often not much more than motor launches - as a rule kept them on the river towing large flotillas of barges in re-distribution exercises, there was rarely any need for them to enter the docks.

When the docks were at their most hectic with many ships leaving and entering, it was often the case that the powerful river tugs which had brought a ship up from the estuary would be further engaged to complete the journey up to her berth. If the logistics permitted, traffic officers would try to ensure that their own PLA tugs towed each ship through the docks with the estuary tug controlling the stern but with large numbers of ship movements even this was not always possible. Naturally tugging companies whose tugs had brought a ship up from Gravesend and seen it into the Royal Docks would try to arrange for their craft to pick up another making its way seawards on the same tide. When the docks were choked solid with every berth taken this circumstance would be likely and these large estuary tugs would be a regular feature of the Royals around high tide. Contact between tug masters and us involved in cargo handling was non-existent: they dealt with ships as transport, as moving craft; we were concerned with ships as vessels, static containers. Indeed it was a tug master's primary duty to get his tug out of the docks while the water levels permitted; to miss the tide would be to condemn the craft to twelve hours unprofitable inactivity and this never happened.

Royal Mail Lines kept the two functions, those of bringing a ship up river and of 'turning her round' in the docks, separate within its own organisation; dock staff usually heard from Head Office whether a ship would be up on the next tide. At the same time Head Office was in touch with Lofts, its agents at Gravesend, to monitor each ship's progress. Lofts provided a staging service for both incoming and outgoing vessels and would be in contact with each ship as it made its approaches to the Thames Estuary. They would already be working out what tide it might make, notifying Customs of the ship's arrival and arranging moorings at Gravesend if there were delays in getting up to London. Whatever the circumstances, they were well placed to advise RML on the likelihood of each ship's progress. Lofts would also sort out the paperwork to smooth her entry to Britain, engage a pilot to take her up river and sort out any special problems like making quarantine arrangements or notifying the Port Health Authority if the master suspected difficulties. Quarantine was one of the rare times that Lofts would be in direct contact with the dock office, another would be if the ship were carrying explosives - which sometimes happened - and was having to delay her arrival to off-load them at Hole Haven. Routinely, all dock staff needed to know was if an incoming ship would make the tide – from their copy of the manifest they already knew what the ship was carrying – and that information would be passed to them from Royal Mail House.

Head Office needed to know when the ship was likely to berth so that it could let importers know when they should prepare transport, either lorries or lighters; dock office needed to know what tide it could come up on to help in the scramble for berths. During the forties and fifties, everyone wanted their ships to berth in the Royals and energetic discussions with traffic officers and dock masters would plead the case for each company. With three annual rent berths and Captain Spinks, RML was in a strong position but then it also had a substantial fleet to organise. The actual import berth for each ship was not important, barges and lorries could reach almost everywhere (as could ship's clerks – their amount of leg work was not a consideration), the main job was to get her in somewhere. There might be a vacant berth for a couple of days at which a Company ship could off-load its shipment before a rival company's vessel came to claim back its own annual rent berth. For those two days, while the rental company filled its shed with future exports, RML would have to be off-loading into barges to keep the sheds and quays clear, but that would have been part of the deal with traffic officers. The ship's clerk would have known what goods were accessible, once the hatches were removed from his copy of the ship's plan. As the rival ship came through the lock, towed by her tug, another RML ship would be leaving her berth outward bound allowing the 'squatter' to be taken by a third tug across to complete its off-loading at a more legitimate berth. The pressures to get ships turned round and to maintain estimated schedules were immense.

Once ships at Gravesend had been given the signal to go up to the docks, they had to leave immediately so estuary tugs had to be available and standing by. RML always used the tugging services of Alexander Vessels and left it with Lofts to arrange towing for each new ship. Alexander called their vessels 'Sun' and numbered their twenty four tugs one to twenty five – 'Sun 13' was never allowed – and these powerful craft were used specifically for the movement of ocean going steamers between Gravesend and the London berths. Ships could not be brought up river and left waiting for high tide because of the congestion they would cause on the already busy waterway. At peak times six or seven ships might leave the Royals and the same number enter, usually through King George V lock, so the organisation of tugs could be quite a complicated operation in its own right. Most of the time taken to get a ship through into the dock system was due to the adjustment of water levels and as 'locking in' took place further and further away from high tide so the greater the inequalities in water levels and the longer the time it took to get a ship through. It was the dock master's responsibility to judge the tides and water levels, setting that against the two hour journey it took ships to come up from the estuary, and he made his decision on the assumption that the ship was ready. This was a routine operation requiring regular contacts between docks, Lofts and Alexander Vessels. The signal to come up meant, as I say, immediate response, delays would cause a depletion of the water stock out of the docks or even the ship running aground at the dock entrance which a dock master could not risk – the alterative for a shipping company would be a costly twelve hour wait. Ships had to be ready to move.

For a ship coming up to the Royals, the tugs would take her into the King George V Lock which was big enough to take both the vessel and two tugs. Here the water levels were adjusted to those of the dock system. Meanwhile RML would arrange a shore gang and their first task was to guide the ship safely into the lock by lowering fenders to prevent her scraping her sides against the quay then by using restraining ropes looped round the 'dollies' on both sides of the lock, hold her central. These ropes would need constant readjustment as the boat rode on the changing water levels but once safely locked in the shore gang was then able to go on board to begin preparing her decks for work as the tug towed her to her berth.

Ships passed from the lock into King George V Dock and if she were to berth in there, she would simply be taken up to her moorings and the general principal of 'bows to the west' was easily established. For ships berthing in the Royal Albert or Royal Victoria, progress was not quite so straight-forward; a ship could not come out of King George V lock and turn into the Royal Albert – there simply was not enough room so the tugs took the vessel into King George V, 'spun' her in the wide breadth of that dock then towed her past the swing bridge into the rest of the system. RML ships which used the Royal Albert and Royal Victoria a lot, frequently had to use this manoeuvre but other companies, like Port Line, were based in King George V and so only exceptionally needed to spin their ships round.

Following these procedures, all the ships in all the Royals could, as a rule, be neatly arranged facing the same way and a sideways photograph of a dock reveals whether the camera was pointing north or south from the direction the ships were facing. There were occasional exceptions to this rule however and these would have been worked out by superintendents and traffic officers long before the ship arrived. For example, if a ship carried a large piece of machinery which was too heavy for the quay cranes to move out and

120

if, in the 'bows to the west' alignment, the cargo was in a hold space closest to the quay, then the ship would be turned and berthed bows east. In this way the large floating crane the 'London Titan' could be brought up by PLA tug to the outside of the ship and work the cargo from the hold space close to it. This was rare, certainly on Royal Mail Lines ships, as heavy machinery was usually exported not imported. With the Titan predominately used for exports, the ship would be berthed 'bows west' as a matter of course and it was then a case of organising a suitable space for whatever large scale items were to be loaded.

Ships left the Royals by the reverse process: tugs would take the vessel, stern first down the narrow Royal Albert Dock, give a toot on the tug's whistle to warn the swing bridge operator to open his bridge between the Royal Albert and King George V, tow the ship round into King George V so that the tug at the bows was then able to take the ship into the lock and out onto the Thames.

This manoeuvring work performed by the tugs could be made more difficult by strong cross winds, by a congested dock limiting the turning space or, in later years, by the less satisfactory newer PLA tugs which lacked the power of the *'Plagil'* and sister craft but the work was routine and accidents unknown.

In theory, I believe, no ship needed tugs to get her up the river, a ship could travel under its own steam but the power and mass of an ocean steamer in the confines of a busy river made tugging standard. RML always did things properly and used a minimum of two tugs while some companies in order to cut costs would get by with one. Sometimes, especially if a ship were riding high in the water and there was a strong cross wind, RML would employ a third tug positioned amid ships to gently nudge the vessel back on course should she begin to drift. This decision would be left to Lofts who were on site to assess the conditions and needs of each ship.

Once the river pilot was on board, he was in charge of the ship's movements. How the ship reached the docks was not his concern but the course it steered was; he did not mind if the ship used her own power, tugs or galley slaves, he told the master where he wanted the ship to go and it was the master's responsibility to follow that course. In normal circumstances it was slightly different, the tugs would usually be placed one fore and one aft for maximum control and two ship's officers, one at the bows the other at the stern, would pass instructions from the Bridge to the tug masters. On the whole manoeuvres were routine and it was more straightforward for the pilot to signal to the tugs through a series of whistles sounded on the ship's siren and these muffled wails and pips were part of the background environment for those of us who worked or lived near the lower Thames.

Although one tug fore and one aft was the usual deployment, it was up to the tug masters to decide what the conditions demanded and it was not uncommon to see two tugs together towing a ship behind them. There were times in the docks when a lot of nail biting went on wondering if a ship would make the tide. Usually this would be because a vessel had been cleared ready to sail but it had had to wait for tugs to collect her and they might be suffering difficulties with the ship they were bringing up. In the event, the fears were always groundless; the work was standard, dock masters, pilots and tug masters were all experts at their jobs and I never knew of a ship missing its tide once clearance had been given.

As an incoming ship was making her way up Channel, other people would be preparing for it: the ship's clerk and shipworker would be meeting to discuss the order of working at each of the five holds, top hands would be assessing what tackle they needed and organising their gangs, Charlie Hanley would be deploying his barges and Mrs Brown would be shuffling her two. And somewhere round the Essex coast on the 'Cambria', Bob Roberts perhaps might be tacking at a stately pace for a more leisurely encounter with the incoming vessel.

*   *   *

CONTAINERS

As the merchant fleets of the world switched over to containers, there was a transition period when Tilbury was coming into operation to work containers but occasionally they would appear in the Royal Docks on traditional general cargo vessels. In these cases neither dock cranes nor ships' derricks were capable of lifting them; specialist gangs had to empty these containers where they sat, down a hold or on deck, for them to be lifted out empty onto a waiting lorry and repacked again once the contents had been set down on the quay. A very expensive and time consuming operation – precisely the obstacles that containers were designed to overcome. It was a clear demonstration though that traditional ships and docks could not handle the changing order.

*   *   *

LOST SHIPS

As Royal Mail Lines declined, it became a common and depressing sight to see familiar vessels which, when they flew the RML flag were proudly maintained to Admiralty standards, return later in their lives as little more than rusting hulks, the property then of some eastern freighter company.

There came a time when the 'Potaro', discharged and being loaded, was sold to the Greeks. They changed the name while she was berthed in the Royals and put in their own crew - but the cargoes remained RML commitment. The solution was for RML to put one of their own Cargo Superintendents on board to sort out the paperwork and regulations so that the voyage to America became a one way charter. According to the Super he also taught the crew to sail the ship and to navigate her across the Atlantic. Once the shipments had been off loaded in the US the Superintendent left to make his own way back and the Greeks took over.

Joining the Royal Docks and more particularly joining Royal Mail Lines within the Royal Docks meant becoming part of a well established order. How contracts were formed, how long ago, why particular companies were chosen were factors lost in the mists of time. Our commitment was to specifics, not overviews: we dealt with each particular tree as we came to it and move on, the wood could take care of itself. Here we briefly consider RML's cargo handling arrangements.

Royal Mail Lines had three mainstay commodities filling holds year round and providing the Company with substantial trade but each commodity in itself belonged to a separate aspect of consumerism with different importers, processors and distribution networks. RML was simply one link in each much larger business and had to respond to the demands and pressures of each market; I have already commented that for a ship's clerk moving from sugar to meat was like changing jobs so different were the problems and priorities.

It is fortunate from our present perspective that each of these three major commodities were worked by a different stevedoring organisation as it emphasises the mix of firms and spread of contracts forged some time in the past. Contracts between the big companies were important to men working the cargoes because they created patterns of work the gangs could link into. We have already looked at Furness, Withy's general cargo gangs, and we will soon come to consider both Scruttons, who handled RML's meat imports and the Port of London Authority's gangs working grain. Although we are looking at the relationship between RML and each of the stevedoring companies it is worth mentioning that each was a large organisation in its own right, Royal Mail Lines' contract was important to each but it was only one of many.

By the time I was working for Royal Mail Lines, most of the docks of London were worked by PLA gangs. Whether this had been a wartime rationalisation, which continued into the fifties, I don't know but if, for example, the Royal Docks were completely full and the Authority ordered a sugar ship up to the West India Docks, it was no longer Furness, Withy who handled the cargo but PLA employees. In the Royal Group though, the older tradition of independent stevedoring organisations continued alongside PLA gangs, maintaining their own contracts with the different shipping companies.

The single cargo which brought PLA gangs onto RML ships in the Royal Docks was grain. The Port of London Authority owned the machines that extracted grain from ships' holds and to ensure they were used correctly they employed their own specialist gangs; 'cornporters' only worked grain and as the process was simple there was little need for the ship's clerk to be involved in the mechanics of discharging . In addition, as the PLA allocated work in strict rotation from a broad base there was no close association between particular gangs and RML staff. Because of the uniformity of the cargo, a gang emptying a hold knew precisely what pay they should be entitled to for a trouble free shipment but if there were problems a system of 'allowances' could be employed to enhance their income. It was in each gang's interest therefore to discover problems and it was here that a ship's clerk discovered his new role. Allowances and enhanced income could only happen at the expense of the shipping company whose representative the clerk was so that working grain tended to be a constant battle of wits.

All South American meat imports were handled for us by Scruttons which seems to have had a more ancient lineage in the docks than Royal Mail Lines, stretching back, I believe, to the very early nineteenth century. The understanding was that the company had initiated many of the innovations and specialist equipment which had gradually improved cargo handling over the years. They were experts in their field and ship's clerks could not offer any useful advice, we just let them get on with it – in fact Scruttons insisted upon it.

Scruttons ran the meat berth at 'Z' shed, Victoria Dock deep in RML territory and on a RML ship yet a clerk felt almost an interloper in a Scruttons' enterprise. Personally this situation wasn't helped by the memory that a number of the personalities had been the ones who regularly tried to cripple me when as a tally clerk I refused to help them with their black market operations: unsurprisingly this memory diminished camaraderie, it wasn't wanted and it wasn't needed. Scruttons were routinely efficient at their work and the ship's clerk could concern himself with other matters. Relationships between ship's clerks and meat gangs tended to stay uninvolved which allowed a clerk to focus his attention on the conflicting demands of meat importers. .

One oddity in the stevedoring contracts should be mentioned: although PLA gangs only handled RML's grain imports and Scruttons only their meat shipments, Scruttons for some reason, also had the contract for re-loading her meat ships. To facilitate this Royal Mail Lines maintained an annual rent shed at 3 King George V Dock, well away from its main centre of activities, to collect exports bound for the River Plate and the Atlantic Coast of South America. For a peripatetic import ship's clerk, whose working ship could be berthed anywhere within the Royal Group, it was a useful contact point.

Wherever grain or general cargo ships were discharged within the Royals, they were taken to the Royal Mail Lines sheds on the south side of Victoria Dock for loading by Furness Withy gangs while meat ships discharged at 'Z' shed were towed to 3 King George V for Scruttons' general cargo gangs to load. Meat ships were odd in the sense that they had compartments capable of refrigeration, rather than holds, making access restricted and awkward but it was nothing that Furness, Withy gangs couldn't have coped with. As I said at the beginning the contracts were givens, we just prepared for the next ship making its way up from Gravesend.

GRAIN

Grain was a major import for the Royal Docks as well as for Royal Mail Lines and much of the south side of Victoria Dock was occupied with flour mills belonging to Spillers, Ranks, CWS and the PLA. The grain RML carried came from the Pacific Ports of North America and long before the Second World War the industry had become highly mechanised there. The stories we heard were of combine harvesters roaming across the wide open plains following the ripening corn through the Mid-West States and up into Canada – a mental image in stark contrast with our bombed out world. Much of this grain was exported and RML ships were able to collect wheat from Seattle and Vancouver year round, thanks to the huge storage capacity at these ports. As the British Government had determined not to ration cereal products post-War, whatever quantities shipping companies could import were welcomed, the pace in consequence was frantic. The quicker ships could be turned round, the sooner they could be steaming towards their next profitable shipment which in turn, within the docks, meant plenty of work for the cornporters.

Maybe older ships in the RML fleet had carried grain in sacks, I don't know, but from the Thirties certainly, America was only interested in exporting bulk grain. Loading facilities had become highly specialised with gangs of men erecting substantial sub-structures in holds to secure the thousands of tons that were delivered. Grain was cheap and to keep it cheap meant providing the industry with a fast, efficient system of considerable sophistication, or so it seemed to us looking down from the top deck on the feeders, separators and grain stowage.

The most effective RML ships transporting grain were post-War vessels like the *'Loch Garth'*, launched in 1947, whose capacious main lower holds were capable of carrying one and a half to two thousand tons of grain in each. Getting the grain out was, in principal, straightforward, for the PLA had purchased specialist grain machines from the United States, so making the entire process of both getting grain in and out of our holds a largely American installation. The trouble was that there were never enough of theses machines (or 'floaters' as they were universally known) and ships would be queuing up to use them.

These grain machines required their own way of working and the PLA organised gangs of its own employees to operate them. As these cornporters were permanently employed, there was no need for them to attend the Call and as they only worked one commodity, any general cargoes in the upper holds of grain ships – a usual practice – were worked by Furness, Withy gangs. Through the circumstances of their engagement, for us at least, cornporters were rather separated from the rest of the work force forming their own tightly knit groups like the Corbetts gang or the family gangs such as Bentham, Clark and Reid where group loyalties were reinforced by family ties. Incidentally, cornporters were generally known as 'toe rags' from their custom of tying pieces of sacking round their shoes and lower trousers to keep the grain out of their boots.

From a shipping company's point of view, because the Call did not operate, there was no choice in the selection of gangs to work their grain so ship's clerks contacted the PLA Grain Superintendent based in Victoria Dock, told him when the general cargo gangs would be finished then waited for the floater and toe rags to arrive. In practice, this lack of selection did not affect the speed at which holds were emptied as gangs fed the machine as fast as it could suck. Gangs were paid at piece rates which kept them working hard but in addition the PLA engaged its gangs in strict rotation which, if another grain ship was waiting to be discharged, introduced an element of intense competition.

For the ship's clerk though other factors had to be considered and the gangs the PLA sent materially affected stress levels. Gang leaders had a whole raft of dodges for increasing their pay through a system of 'allowances'. If grain were contaminated or difficult to work for some reason, toe rags would demand extra incentives from the shipping company to complete the work, and some gang leaders had got the bargaining down to a very fine art. The ship's clerk had the prime responsibility to keep costs down for his company and to distinguish genuine problems from invented ones; if grain had been contaminated for example, who had done the contaminating? Rows were constant.

As the general cargo gangs finished their off-loading and the ship was preparing to turn over to working grain, there were some gangs he just didn't want to see. Once the general cargo gangs had finished work in the upper holds, ship's clerks prepared for the removal of the wheat. Grain machines were capable of self propulsion but were usually towed up by a PLA tug and with their arrival cornporter gangs would be making their way up the gang plank. Floaters were fairly ungainly pieces of equipment whose operators were employed essentially to keep them working, movement of the suction pipe was a simple vertical operation - there was none of the finesse that crane drivers or even winchmen using derricks could achieve. To begin work the pipe was dropped into the grain and began sucking. As a well was created the pipe was further lowered and at this early stage the free flowing grain naturally rolled down the slopes towards the pipe mouth. For a short time there was little for the downholders to do but watch gravity and suction do their work for them. This didn't last for long and as the sides of the well broadened, men jumped down into it and began shovelling the grain fast towards the pipe mouth. Cornporters could work safely around the suction pipe with none of the inherent risks associated with, for example, swinging sets and the pipes themselves remained static except for occasional signals to lower them further into the grain.

Clearing the hatch was easy enough but for the rest of the hold space toe rags had to shovel fast and furiously to keep up with the capabilities of the floater. The work was not particularly inspiring – general cargo gangs said that all toe rags knew about were shovels – but it was relentless and the glistening surface of their shovels where the abrasiveness of the corn grains kept them polished, bore testament to their efforts. As bigger and more powerful machines were introduced so was the effort needed to feed them but this was recompensed by a substantially enhanced take-home pay.

Grain was usually stored in the large No 2 and No 4 holds but not infrequently in No 3 hold also, although the configuration of the hold space there, especially on ships like the 'Loch Garth', made working it more difficult.

The next ship in might have thousands of tons of grain but it might be unevenly distributed between the grain holds. Gangs would be well aware of this and as they were re-employed in strict rotation, competition to finish first and select the best hold was acute, partly of course for the money but also for gang pride. Gang leaders would be keeping an eye on other gangs' progress and would be urging their men on: holds had to be completely cleaned and sweat would be pouring off rival gangs as they shovelled and swept the final remnants towards their suction pipe. Once the hold was entirely clear the gang leader would signal to his machine operator to 'sound off' on the floater's siren to indicate that his men were available for re-employment and I have known gangs after moving a thousand tons of grain to finish within seconds of each other: as one siren fell silent, the next would sound off.

Problems could arise in discharging even the most apparently straightforward shipments and these would usually be caused by contamination. Cases could leak from general cargo in the upper holds, oil or grease could enter the consignment but most commonly damage was caused by water. In most cases pollution was slight – typically 1 to 2 tons per hold - but if a ship's water pipe burst, fifty tons of wheat or more could be soured. All damaged grain had to be scrupulously removed from the human food chain and was given over to RM shore gangs to deal with. This could seriously interrupt the work rate of the cornporters. In some holds, notably No 3, extensions had to be fitted to the suction pipe to get to the further recesses and fitting them took time – typically ten minutes but gangs might claim an hour's lost work. Whatever the problem, unions and employers had worked out a system of allowances to compensate for interruptions and as far as possible a well structured pay scale was in place. Unfortunately, human nature being what it was, life was usually more complicated: gangs knew their pay rate, everyone knew the tonnages in each hold and therefore what each gang member would get for completing the job – and as a working principle, it was never enough. A culture had grown up where gang leaders strove to discover problems which might offer their men allowances. Standard dodges included leaving a little grain at the end of the day in a near empty hold. If overtime were allowed, and it usually was, it would be worth paying the gang an hour's overtime rate to clear the hold for

15 minutes work. This then freed the grain machine for the PLA engineers to relocate to another vessel saving the shippers hiring charges. Again, if overtime was to be allowed, gangs would make sure their grain hopper was absolutely full at 5 o'clock and this grain would be included in the enhanced pay rate (1 hour trimming rate –standard – plus one hour 'meal rate', effectively doubling their pay). It was amazing how much grain was shifted during that hour.

Gangs worked in isolation, each determining their own rate of working but the personality of each gang leader seriously affected the stress levels for clerks as some turned a fundamentally straightforward operation into a creative exercise for supplementing incomes. All gangs naturally sought to maximise their earnings but the predictability of working grain, particularly in a time of industrial unrest, lead to a good deal of acrimony as reasons for allowances were newly invented – and contested. Another source of friction was over soured grain. RM wanted it declared 'lost' for their shore gangs to discharge into old refuse barges for dumping, but if no other work was in prospect, gangs would want the importer's agents to save it for animal feed. The cost to RM was huge. The gang would have to shovel the grain into sacks and a crane driver hired to off-load them onto the quay. For the shippers this added up to around £5 per ton.

For one gang leader in particular this determination to pursue creative opportunities for financial rewards became obsessive. For him it was the cutting edge of the class war with every ship's clerk marked down as a capitalist lackey, running dog. He was very intelligent, very political and as devious as a ship's clerk allowed him to be. As a consequence he had to be watched like a hawk. It was his mission in life to exact revenge on the whole capitalist system by demonstrating to his gang how much smarter he was than every clerk he encountered, his ability for creative argument was formidable. He was known throughout the length and breadth of the docks as the 'Wicked Uncle' and when a supervisor saw this cocky little individual striding up the gang plank, he knew that the Fates had dealt him a bad one. There were situations where polluted grain interfered with the gang's rate of work, or a hold's clutter of ledges had to be worked round or extension pipes took time to fix but his endless capacity to invent new problems then argue their seriousness from every angle was, for the ship's clerk, exhausting – and he had four other holds to supervise. One option the Wicked Uncle employed was for his men to pee on the grain, or worse, then claim contamination allowance while Head Office would want to know why grain was suddenly so expensive to work out of this particular hold. The merest indication that grain might cling to a slightly damp stringer meant the patch was carefully worked round so that when the hold was empty his gang could claim 'overhead work'. This meant in practice climbing a ladder and sweeping it off but he could make a major issue out of it. If a lower hold was full of grain he would claim 'lack of head room', if the grain started some way down in the hold he would claim 'raised separation' indicating that the surface was uneven. Sometimes the ten by ten foot metal plates dividing the lower hold from the ballast tank were lifted and set against the side of the hold so that the tanks too could take grain as a sort of lower, lower hold. A series of service pipes were built into these tanks which the Wicked Uncle would use to claim 'awkward working' which in practice meant changing the angle of the broom. Astonishing, looking back that a less confrontational system couldn't have been introduced as a matter of organisational urgency, but it never was: and all over the modest task of sucking grain up a pipe.

*　　　　　*　　　　　*

PAPER ROLLS

Paper rolls of stiff, brown paper weighing 3 tons, and standing 6 or 8 feet high were very vulnerable and unstable items needing to be worked by good gangs. Brought in from Canada on the 'Loch' boats, densely rolled with a wooden central core, these rolls were stowed mechanically by equipment unavailable to us in the docks and would be either 'on their head' (horizontal) or 'on the roll' (vertical) according to how best they fitted into the hold space. If they were stowed horizontally, they were stacked on top of each other and very great care was necessary to get them out to the hatchway. A bat, a long wooden handled instrument with a wide metal blade, was inserted between the top and second roll and levered gently to force a crack into which a 'shoe' could be slipped. Shoes were 'L' shaped pieces of metal, one side with a hole for attaching to a crane, the other side serrated for gripping onto the paper. Very carefully the crane and brute force had to guide the roll off the stack and onto the ceiling so that it ended up 'on the roll'. Pads of hessian sacking were used to buffer contact with the ceiling and the paper rolled out to the hatchway where, again carefully, it was lowered horizontally in a net for the crane to lift out. The crane and shoe helped but it was hard physical work. George Fairfield who was the stevedores' Chief Superintendent, introduced – maybe invented – a double shoe device which, attached to the crane hook, acted as a grab and was sufficiently secure to be able to lift the roll out directly. This single innovation considerably reduced the amount of physical effort the gangs needed to expend manoeuvring each roll. Once in the barge they was assessed for damage, the size and depth of each cut or scuff recorded and agreed between the supervisors and lighterman.

There was an incident during the period when only one shoe was used when late one afternoon in failing light a father in the gang saw his son crushed beneath one of these rolls; as the downholders were manoeuvring one towards the hatchway the one behind became unstable and toppled over on top of the lad.

129

There were two ways to discharge grain in the Royal Docks: either directly to the Victoria Dock mills or indirectly using grain machines. Most of the grain RML carried was destined ultimately for these local mills but to arrange for a shipment to be actually discharged there, meant that if there were delays, the entire ship would be tied up until the grain was removed. Delays were a major feature of grain shipments and the most flexible and economic way to circumvent this was to order up a machine and get the grain out into barges so that the ship was then free for receiving exports. In practice, there were delays both at the mills and in queuing for the floaters but the latter was a quicker and more adaptable option. Newer and faster machines were regularly introduced but were always inadequate for the quantity of grain imported and each new introduction was no more than a stop gap. It is worth mentioning here that the PLA sold grain in its own right sharing part of a grain shed with CWS and Spillers so an efficient throughput of grain was also in its best interest. The lasting solution was to build a Grain Terminal at Tilbury and so bypass the Royal Docks altogether. Our story though is with the floaters.

To sustain Britain's policy of not rationing grain after the War, the PLA had two machines, 'Turbo I' and 'Turbo II' both of ancient construction and the newer 'Phalanx' and 'New Yorker' capable of moving six hundred tons a day each. The New Yorker soon broke down irretrievably and was replaced by the 'Thomas Wiles' which in its turn was capable of processing a thousand tons a day. In spite of this improvement, congestion grew as the increasing capacity of the mercantile fleet outpaced dock facilities at every stage. The Ministry of Transport sent two machines from somewhere, 'MOT 7' and 'MOT 8' which could achieve one thousand five hundred tons daily until the PLA introduced their own similar machines, the 'Sir John Anderson' and the 'Douglas Ritchie'. This was the best grain moving facility that the Royal Docks ever achieved and historically that whole twenty year post-War period can be seen as one long series of bottlenecks until Tilbury finally came on stream. At the time though, it seemed to us who had to make the system work that the frustrations would never end.

One minor point was that in spite of all the pressures to feed the Nation, grain still had to be tallied. As it was sucked out by each machine the grain fell into a hopper which, when it collected two tons, then spewed it out into the waiting lighter. This intermittent action was the only effective way that could be found to maintain records so this vast international bulk trade had to be filtered through a stop/start hopper. Once, during one of the strikes the Army was sent in to move essential cargoes which included grain. The officer in charge was astonished to discover his men intermittently tipping grain from the machines into the barges. It was not good enough, wasting time when the Nation needed feeding, and so on. He issued instructions that in future the off-loading was to be continuous, recording quantities didn't matter and to get on with it double quick. Admirable of course, but in spite of the best efforts of his engineers it seemed that that was how the machines were designed to work; adaptation was beyond them and they were wasting more time trying to unravel the Americans' ingenuity than using the machine in the way it was designed. The officer and the Country would just have to resign themselves to stop-start deliveries of their grain. We found the incident strangely comforting.

For the six downholders though, in normal circumstances, working to get through six hundred tons, then a thousand or one thousand five hundred was hard, physical work. The improving earnings with the introduction of each new class of machine made sure that this greater throughput was preferred by the gangs, but they had to work for it.

There was a circumstance which should be mentioned that was increasingly hated by cornporters through the 1950's and that was bagged grain. Most of the grain that came into the docks after the War went to the big millers with a nationwide network but there still existed small local mills working with individual bakeries and food producers. Many of these mills did not have the capacity to cope with a barge full of grain and in any case, many were not sited on a convenient river or canal. What they wanted was regular supplies of small quantities and most needed them delivered by road in manageable bags. The American ports had not been interested in supplying grain in bags for decades, so to maintain the broad base of flour production these mills were supplied with grain bagged up for them in the docks, from a bulk shipment.

Before grain machines were invented to cope with bulk imports, the traditional way of transporting grain had been in sacks so, although America had long since moved away from this option, it was not considered an unreasonable request by importers. As bigger, faster machines were introduced, bulk deliveries increasingly began to dominate but during the transition period the older grain machines which alone had been designed to deliver corn from the hopper either in bulk or for bagging could not be completely discarded. Importers were felt to have the right still to order a consignment of bagged grain and to oblige them it was these old, slow but more flexible Turbos I and II that had to be resurrected. Cornporters and supervisors increasingly assumed faster levels of throughput while the ship's itinerary had begun to assume it, so that returning to the Turbos meant all round frustration. Turbo I and II could work bulk grain slowly or bagged grain very slowly and all sorts of deadlines had to be abandoned.

For the barge hands particularly, it was a tough option. For bulk grain, two barge hands only were necessary, one to direct the flow from the machine across the ceiling while the other stood on the grain mounds and spread them evenly across the hold. Bagged grain needed eight men, four standing on the platform of the floater by a delivery pipe, four on the gunwales of the barge in front of and slightly below them. Each man on the machine had a pile of sacks by him and he took one, shook it out and held it open with his fore arms round an outlet pipe. When they were all ready, the gang leader tapped on his pipe to signal to the machine operator to release the grain. Something like two hundred pounds – though the actual measure was in bushels - was shot into each sack then the men shook the grain down, folded and concertinaed the neck and tied it round with a length of string taken from a supply tucked into his belt. When the bag was secure, he tapped the shoulder of his partner standing on the gunwale to let him know the load was coming then he tilted the bag forward onto his waiting back. As far as possible the receiver just lowered his shoulder to allow the bag to roll off him into position in the hold. There was a limit to this of course and the actual amount of humping required of both men in the team was considerable. This aspect of cornportering was totally exhausting. As a comparison, in a day perhaps at best 200 tons of bagged grain could be worked compared to 600tons of shoot loose. If they knew they were going to have to work bagged grain, the gang would always start the day with bagging while they were fresh, then work the 'shoot loose', as bulk grain was called, into the barges for the rest of the day. If more than an hour's work at bagging was necessary, the gang usually decided to start the day filling sacks then return for half an hour at the end in the optimistic hope that their stamina would be restored. Two hundred tons a day represented a good work rate and an exhausting physical effort but as the barge hands sweated and toiled, the downholders, machine operators and supervisors could do little more than curse with frustration. By the end of the fifties bagged grain was already history.

*   *   *

SHORT NIGHT

If valuable and vulnerable items were being exported (for RML this usually meant whisky), Customs needed plenty of time to check the paperwork and inspect the shipments. The situation could arise that a ship otherwise fully laden and hoping to catch the next tide, would find it necessary to offer Customs 'short night' overtime for them to complete their examination. This meant offering the Custom's men overtime up to midnight. Incidentally this also meant RML had to pay overtime to the ship gangs, quay gangs, the shed foreman and the PLA to facilitate this. It was an expensive decision but getting the vessel away on an earlier tide made overall financial sense. Customs, the PLA and the gangs involved had to be notified by 4pm (later brought forward to noon) needing some careful judgements through the working day. A 'long night' was overtime paid until 7am.

A surprising aspect perhaps of grain shipments was the amount of timber work frequently needed to contain the grain, for unlike bulk sugar cereals remained free flowing with a potentially dangerous tendency to shift position during a voyage. To have a ship pitching in heavy seas with thousands of tons of grain rolling loose would have been to court disaster, so safety measures had to be taken: if the quantity of grain was small, perhaps a few hundred tons in one or two holds, then the solution was one of stowage. Small quantities could be levelled and covered with hessian to allow a heavy cargo to be laid on top; a consignment of zinc or lead plates could usually be found - sometimes North American timber - and onto this, typically, would be set large quantities of bagged goods such as dried peas or fruit. A well planned loading sequence and attention to tight stowing were precautions enough to ensure stability for smaller grain shipments.

For larger loads of half or more of each of the two major lower holds, good stowage in itself was not enough. In the cargo ships of this period, most of the older ones had rows of stanchions running through the holds as structural supports to the main body of the vessel. To the handling gangs these were inconveniences which had to be worked round but they were a normal feature of hold design and so were expected. For grain shipments though, these posts could be used to construct internal sub-dividing walls. This had to be done before any grain was loaded so for economic reasons the final quantities would have to be known in advance. From experience it had been found that it was only necessary to create one sub-division of each hold allowing the central row of stanchions to be utilised; first, each one was encased by four substantial wooden beams bolted in place then, using them like fence posts, wooden planks, known as parting boards were nailed to bridge the gaps. This planking ran down the complete length of each grain hold providing an effective barrier between port and starboard. It also cut across the hatchway to allow grain to be loaded on both sides and maintain overall balance. There was a considerable amount of work and organisation associated with these preparations; US and Canadian gangs were specialists who concentrated solely on fitting out holds as a support to the grain export industry. The net result subsequently was that however much the ship rolled in heavy weather, each great mass of grain could flow only as far as the parting boards and overall stability was maintained.

Sometimes even parting boards were not enough. With very large shipments of around one thousand five hundred to two thousand tons in each of the main holds, the lower holds would be filled completely with, on occasions, further grain overlaying them in the tween deck. The problem here was that the space occupied by the grain did not necessarily stay constant. There could be air pockets produced as grain filled the lower hold and in any case, it was probable that grain would settle during the voyage like the contents of a cornflakes packet. So there was the possibility that, in rough seas, grain could destabilise the balance of a ship by flowing into spaces unplanned. There was no way of telling.

To get round this difficulty, feeders were built into the hatchway. Occupying half or a third of the hatchway space, feeders would stretch up out of the grain to the height, maybe, of the top deck. In effect they formed a vertical hopper above the mass of the shipment which when filled with grain acted as a reservoir to fill any developing spaces. As the motion of the ship caused the grain to settle, the surplus in the feeder dropped down to plug the gaps and keep the cargo tight. The size of the feeder needed for each hold and for each shipment was naturally a matter of some prudent judgement by the exporters.

Once again the feeder, like the parting boards, was a substantial affair; it had to be. Four six by six inch timbers formed the corners of the construction with two of them built into the corners of the hatchway; between them were secondary bracing beams and the entire scaffolding wrapped around with layers of thick craft paper, to keep the grain in, and bitumen to keep any water in neighbouring cargoes out. For No. 2 and 4 holds this was an impressive structure but if a feeder was necessary for grain stowed in No.3 hold then, passing as it had to through the height of the cabin areas, the arrangement was formidable with the feeder itself containing a significant fraction of the hold's grain.

The amount of work necessary then to prepare a general cargo ship to receive grain could be considerable and this work had to be repeated for each voyage. Incidentally, building timber supports, barriers and cages was a regular aspect of loading for many other cargoes and when this work was carried out in the Royal Docks for encasing exports it was known as 'Tomming off'. For example, export cars would need to be protected from general cargoes where perhaps hundreds of tons of goods could envelop the vehicle. In this situation complete cages would have to be built round the cars and stevedoring companies employed full time carpenters to do this work.

Returning to grain, what could not be predicted was the level to which grain sank in the feeder during each voyage and this in turn affected the work of the general cargo gangs. Sometimes the feeder was empty and could be immediately removed by the ship's shore gang but frequently, particularly in No.3 hold, it could still contain substantial amounts. Ship's clerks and shipworkers would have to inspect the levels and decide if the general gangs engaged to clear the upper holds would have to work round the feeder. In itself, this was not a major problem; half the hatchway would be available for off-loading and that was usually plenty. General gangs could not touch the grain itself - that was strictly the province of the toe rags - so if the feeder did make life awkward, it was just too bad. Normally though, even in the restricted vertical space of No.3 hold, the job could be done.

Of much greater significance during this work were the hatch boards. With the feeder still in place, the hatch boards and beams covering it too had to be left to protect the grain. As half the hatch was still covered, the danger lay in the constant rise and descent of the crane tackle and the possibility of it brushing against the boards and dislodging some. They were, as we've mentioned, large heavy pieces of timber and metal, the prospect of having them crashing down particularly in this restricted space had to be avoided. Certainly Charley Hatches would want to be involved and this was exactly the sort of situation that needed his attention. Hatches were always dangerous but this extra level of risk meant the inspector would need to be reassured that the various securing bolts were firmly in place.

At some stage the feeder would have to be taken out, ideally before the general gangs arrived but often only after they had completed their restricted off-loading and had departed. The grain machines and cornporters then took over and might have to spend half an hour clearing the feeder as their first task. It was convenient, though not always possible for this to happen just before lunch so that the shore gang could be left to remove the construction in time for the afternoon session. A major disadvantage of this otherwise eminently sensible arrangement was that shore gangs, when unattended, were not noted for their methodical approach to a task. When supervised they would reduce the woodwork one beam at a time until the main corner posts could be independently raised out. This took time and effort and shore gangs tended to be short of both. Over a lunch break, with no one watching, they would knock out a few planks then fasten a chain round strategic lengths and haul it out using the crane. Sometimes they got away with it, sometimes not. The first danger was to the men themselves, as pieces broke free under the pull of the crane, jagged timber stumps, crane hook and half ton ball could all suddenly catapult in a totally unpredictable way. A second danger was the crane itself for the three ton maximum loading could easily be exceeded; there was no way of calculating the tensions being imposed by the men fixing the chain. They chose a chunk of woodwork and signalled to the driver to pull. The crane could be seriously overloaded with costly damages resulting but it was a far more common occurrence for a sudden collapse in the timber structure to cause the ball to fly upwards and jerk the wire off its pulley wheel at the top of the crane arm. It was an awkward and time consuming problem to put right especially at a time when there were never enough operational cranes – and someone had to pay. The PLA owned the crane and hired it out to FW, Royal Mail Lines employed the shore gang who had strict instructions not to use it. This situation was bad enough in itself but so long as it was the cornporters who were returning to the hold after lunch, they at least could return to a functioning grain machine. If on the other hand a general cargo gang still had work to do the loss of their crane hugely increased the scope for recrimination and demands for compensation.

Because of the way ships had to import the commodity, bulk grain was capable of yet one more level of conflict. There was a subspecies of clerking in the docks known as cargo superintendents whose job it was to act as agents for the many importers who were not personally interested in visiting the docks to inspect the condition of their cargoes. These agents were mostly ex-tally clerks who now worked independently on behalf of outside clients – in a similar role to ship surveyors but without their professional standing. Cargo superintendents looked for trouble to furnish evidence in future claims against shipping or stevedoring companies and had two main duties: to look for cargo damage and to note shortfalls in their clients' allocations. Unfortunately, grain was an ideal commodity in which to discover discrepancies of both kinds.

Although grain was shipped in bulk, it was not a uniform commodity. As harvesting proceeded across the United States and Canada, different wheat types were gathered according to the seed which best suited each region. Thus, at various times through the summer and autumn, and for the rest of the year from silos, different wheat types were available: Hardwinter, Alberta 1 and 2, Manitoba 1, 2 and 3 and so on. These grains would be offered at the West Coast ports to RML and other shipping companies with a range of types usually for sale. Each type was also offered at a different quality indicated by the numbering system, three was poorer and cheaper, one first class, and a ship taking on grain would usually carry a range of different types and grades. The separation could not be done by holds for a ship taking one full consignment in one hold would become unbalanced. Each grain consignment had to be distributed throughout the holds with, perhaps, each hold a quarter full. Before the next consignment could be loaded, hessian sacks had to be laid across the levelled surface (though never level enough for the Wicked Uncle) and wooden dunnage placed on top to keep it secure. A different type or quality could then be poured on top and the process repeated until the holds were full, or the top of the parting boards was reached.

For PLA cornporters in London this meant working carefully each time they came to a separation. The same grain type might exist either side of the parting boards but at different levels or perhaps different types might sit next to each other across the divide. If a ship had encountered heavy weather the top layers in each hold might have become mixed or removing the parting boards as the gang worked could cause different grain types to become confused. The ability of grain to flow was a constant problem. The grain machine's suction pipe had a grid fixed over it called a camel, to prevent pieces of wood disappearing with the wheat but this would not prevent it sucking at the hessian and confusing – the cargo superintendents would say 'contaminating' – the different layers. Each layer had to be thoroughly cleared, no grain could be left on the hessian from a top layer – you couldn't have picked up a handful of grain - before the next layer was started or the agent would claim a shortfall. Damaged grain in one layer had to be carefully removed so as not to contaminate the next and all the while, of course, all the gangs wanted to do was to get on and make their money. Quantity was their overriding priority.

With the cornporters' minds set on speed and profit, tearing or scrunching pieces of hessian was not a high priority so the likelihood of 'contamination' was ever present; just tripping over or removing a piece of dunnage could confuse types. Even the way men worked could increase the risks; if extension pipes had been fitted, different operations might be underway at each outlet – for example, while some downholders might be finishing a top layer, getting into the corners with their extensions, others would be pulling back the hessian and throwing aside the dunnage to expose the next. Men would put their shovels over the ends of unused extension pipes to increase the suction in those still clearing and also to prevent newly exposed layers, cleared and ready for working, from accidentally being drawn up. It was not a foolproof procedure. And all the while the agents would be watching like hawks and the ship's clerk would be watching the agents.

The chemistry between ship's clerks and these agents could be complex. The agents in the docks were representatives of cargo superintendent companies and they took work from importers inspecting a miscellany of cargoes but particularly bulk foodstuffs like grain, coffee beans, animal feeds and fertilizers. While larger companies tended to be well manned and in control of their commitments, smaller ones were often overstretched needing to resort to more creative stratagems. One agent might find that, as ships were worked, he was supervising the discharge of one cargo at Tilbury and at the same time officially watching a second client's goods in the Royals. In this situation the superintendent needed the help of the shipping company for if he was on good terms with the ship's clerk he might, at a later time, be allowed to go to the shipping office, see the inside clerk and get a copy of the lighterman's receipt. From this he would know the quantity and condition of the goods as accepted by the lightermen so allowing him to make out his report. With such an understanding his flexibility increased considerably, as did the amount of work he could take on but if some damage had been noted on the receipt, it was in the interest of the agent to exaggerate it, first to meet the costs of his services showing his effectiveness to the importer and secondly, of course, to give the impression that he had been there when the goods were unloaded. Ultimately though, his intention had to be to help the importer claim damages against the shipping company who had just helped him.

Worse situations were known: if a cargo superintendent was on hand, particularly with a commodity like grain, the ship's clerk had to make sure that 'accidents' did not happen in his vicinity. Sometimes, if he thought he was not being watched, an agent might inadvertently scuff back some of the hessian separation sheets as he was carrying out an inspection and then claim contamination – or he might find a way of introducing some liquid contamination of his very own. Given that a ship's clerk was supervising five holds with perhaps half a dozen or more agents milling around, it is not difficult to imagine that strict scrutiny was not always possible. There might well have been honourable and right living cargo superintendents amongst their fraternity but to the stevedore and shipping companies they were universally known as 'The Forty Thieves'.

When there was spoilt grain left over after a hold had been worked, the cornporters were keen to finish tidying the good stock and get onto the next ship, leaving the refuse for the shore gang to dump into a rubbish barge. Some cargo superintendents would not allow this, they would insist that the damaged grain be put into sacks and placed on the quay for later collection. This meant that the grain was not rubbish and so could not be handled by the shore gang, the bagging up had to be done by the toe rags. Presumably these bags were sold off cheaply as animal feed and although small in quantity, would be pure profit for the importers. For the shippers though, the cost was enormous. The time taken to bag up grain at cornporter rates meant that those sacks of animal feed were vastly more expensive than the good grain removed by machine for human consumption, with the cost having to be met by the shippers not the importers. Cargo superintendents taking this line would have been well advised not to ask for favours from the shipping company for a good long while.

*   *   *

Allowances to cornporters - see 'Grain' and Illustrations at the back of book.

```
                           COPY

R. 4008.                                407  13  472  1586.
                                            1618.
              "LOCH AVON"

              TRIMMING ACCOUNT.

T.  1984.12.2.6.             @ 1/4d per ton          132 - 6 - 2
                             increase 10%             13 - 4 - 7

              OVERTIME TRIMMING

22.8.55.   Hold. 1.  1 min meal hour @ 153/6d per min    7 - 13 - 6
    "        "   4.  387 meal qrs @ 64/6d per 100 qrs    12 -  9 - 7
    "        "   "   1 min O/T hrs @ 76/9d per min        3 - 16 - 9
                     increase 10%                         2 -  8 - 0

              ALLOWANCES TO CORNPORTERS

20.8.55.   Hold. 1.  Caked grain on boards (8 men each 1hr)  1 - 11 - 1
22.8.55.    "    "     "    "    "    "    (                  1 - 11 - 1
    "        "   4   Dunnage on seperation cloth.
                     (8 men each 1 hr)                       1 - 11 - 1
    "        "   "   Brackets on bottom (8 men each 1 hr)    1 - 11 - 1
    "        "  4.4. 2 tanks no grids( 8 men each 1 hr)      3 -  2 - 2
23.8.55.    "    "    "    "    "     "    "                  3 -  2 - 2
    "        "   4.  Brackets on bottom of tanks
                     (8 men each 1 hr)                       1 - 11 - 1
    "        "   4.  Bagging & Lnading damaged grain
                     (8 men each 15/-)                      11 - 17 - 4
22.8.55.    " 1 & 4.Shifting pipes tp facilitate dis-
                     charge.                                 1 - 12 - 7
                     Lighterage Gratuituies                      8 - 0

                                                      £199 - 16 - 3
```

Of the three major commodities we are looking at the greatest status was given to meat. A plentiful supply of beef and lamb was seen by the government to be the most effective way to convince the country that it did, in fact, win the War. The trouble was that if the British mercantile fleet was short of ships generally, it was desperately short of the refrigerated hold space needed to import South American supplies. The meat trade had not been nationalised and with each shipment importers were anxious to get their hands on as much meat as they could to re-establish, or better, their market position. Inside the docks, men were very keen to join meat gangs for the regular and well paid overtime that government backing encouraged. In the early post-War years when meat was still rationed there was also the opportunity for the less virtuous, a not inconsiderable number, to claim their share in the black market trade.

Meat changed as a commodity over the period we are considering from precious luxury item to dietary staple. Priorities for the supervisors changed in parallel from minimising theft in the early years to placating importers later on who, with supplies regularised, wanted their shipments available to meet the country's renewed purchasing pattern. As rationing ended, with increasing meat supplies in the shops customers returned to basing their purchases around the Sunday roast. Importers needed their consignments so that they would be in the shops for Friday or Saturday; refrigeration was only just becoming an option at home and for a while was still severely limited within the trade. These changes in availability were brought about in large measure by improving numbers of meat ships and also by improving refrigeration technology which allowed importers the opportunity to trade in premium chilled South American meat. Shipping companies wanted to exploit this demand but the technology was not always secure allowing considerable scope for debate down in the cold meat lockers as to whether a shipment was chilled, frozen or refuse.

'Z' Shed was deep in RML territory with an annual rent berth alongside and main Dock Office close by but it was Scruttons which worked the meat with specialist gangs. Occasionally, if RML didn't have a meat ship on its way, Holder, Donaldson Line or Blue Star might hire the facilities.

For Scruttons' meat gangs the pressure was relentless over the first two decades after the War. As meat ships arrived gangs worked non-stop to get shipments out to importers to such effect that rival ports assumed that there was some operational sophistication that they were missing. In fact it was no more subtle than hard physical labour. Of course the gangs were working piece rates and of course they were being paid double on Sundays but there was no disguising the fact that the daily number of carcasses they moved was unmatched anywhere in the world. And still the importers were not satisfied.

Ship and Quay Gangs

When meat was plentiful it was considered a low prestige item in the docks with correspondingly poor pay rates but in the post-War climate with men able to work all the overtime they wanted – and especially with double time allowances for Sunday work – everyone wanted to join a meat gang. With good pay for long hours, Scruttons' gangs were tough, stable and hard working and although the company was constantly experimenting to advance productivity it was the quality of the gangs themselves which ultimately determined the throughput.

The gangs on the quays achieved their impressive results using a technique known as 'backing'. When each metal net containing frozen carcasses came over the side it was lowered onto a hand pushed or electric scooter which, as the crane hook was released, was run across to where two teams of men were waiting. A short distance away lorries reversed and waited to collect their consignment. Each team organised themselves so that a tall and short man each lifted a carcass from the trolley. Because of their discrepancy in heights they naturally held the meat at an angle under which slipped the back of a ganger whose job it was to stagger, bent backed, across to the tailgate of the lorry. For every two 'lifters' there would be six or seven 'runners' so that two teams would constitute a gang of sixteen men –larger than the twelve gang uniformity that tidy minded organisers tried to impose but essential if the gang was to keep working. Actually this increased gang size had to be kept unofficial by a conspiracy of silence; Head Office would not have paid Scruttons for extra men, their additional pay was always put down as 'expenses' or 'maintenance to scooters'.

Such was the success of these gangs' efforts that sometime in the early fifties representatives came across from Rotterdam, then being held up as a model port for managers to aspire to. They needed to know how these levels of performance were being achieved; they assumed they were missing a trick. What they saw were men carrying quarters of beef weighing between 120-180lbs and gangs regularly moving between 3,600 and 4,600 quarters a day. On the Continent, and for much of the world, union agreements insisted that such weights be carried by four men; 'Backing' had been prohibited, so for as long as London meat handlers were prepared to operate the technique they would continue to outstrip the world. The Rotterdam representatives retired defeated.

When meat rationing ended supplies were still inadequate but improving. For the meat importers there was still much to be done in order for them to be able to offer the levels of customer choice they wanted and into the sixties men were still being asked to work at rates more associated with the forties. As an indication I remember sometime around nineteen sixty when I supervised meat ships continuously from before Christmas to Easter without a single day off.

Meat Importers

After the War the Government thought it more prudent to work through the existing commercial infrastructure rather than nationalising the industry but maintain a regulatory role. An organisation known as MINDEL was set up and an ex-Armours man, Mr. Harris, was given the unenviable task of apportioning supplies to wholesalers based on their pre-War market share. Naturally the wholesalers' representatives were skilled negotiators each seeking to increase their company's share of the market and to be the first with each new shipment to get it to Smithfield. The implication for the docks was considerable as rivalries at these meetings tried to impose work rates and procedures on a workforce already out-performing other docks.

Royal Mail Lines

Royal Mail Lines had a representative at these meetings, as did Scruttons, and to help give him a bit more authority Percy Arnold was elevated from ship's clerk to 'Meat Superintendent', joined at busy periods by Eric Swinburne but, as I heard it, their negotiating skills were not in the same league as the professionals. In order to introduce a note of reality into the proceedings it was immensely useful to have both PLA and safety officers reinforcing what was practically possible in the holds and on the quays. Back down in the Docks our meat supers had to negotiate with Scruttons' staff, specifically, Charlie Leavis their shipworker and Percy Beckman their quay foreman. This continuity between staff was established in the hope that relations remained at least civil, and even, on occasions, good.

With the end of hostilities in 1945, RML began a period of rapid rebuilding but immediately after the War, I believe I am right in saying the only meat carrying capacity available to it were the two SAM boats, the *Tweed* and the *Teviot* sold by the US to Britain and passed on to RML to rebuild the trade. (Eventually RML had eight meat ships, the four 'Highland' vessels and their commissioned 'D' boats: the 'Drina', 'Deseado', 'Darro' and 'Durango'). Unfortunately it was only the low ceiling upper holds of No2 and No4 hold that could be refrigerated on the SAM boats which meant that both ships had to tour ports looking for less perishable commodities to fill their large lower holds before they could take on a meat shipment. The refrigerated holds themselves measured perhaps, 40ft x 60ft x 10ft high and were subdivided into a series of lockers, of very unequal size, which added to the squabbles amongst the importers and dock staff.

It was also the case that during the War the government sold off RML considerable financial assets in South America as part of the War effort so when Argentina made less meat available as the country rebuilt its stocks, RML had little leverage to influence decision making. The first priority was to improve the fleet and by the time rationing came to an end in 1954 RML had eight new meat carriers: the *Tweed* and *Teviot* were retired from the meat run becoming general cargo vessels taking on fruit, powdered eggs or dried milk, anything in fact which came in small enough units to fit their restricted meat lockers.

There were other factors affecting the docks: traditionally the RML meat trade was closely linked to its passenger service. Passenger aircraft at the time were unable to fly directly to South America and it was assumed for a while that this would always be the case. Ships as transport need to keep much tighter schedules than freighters so timetables needed to be established well in advance of sailing and they needed to be adhered to. As a consequence, the new ships designed for the River Plate run were also built to take passengers and as the competition with airlines became increasingly serious the requirement to keep to published timetables became more essential. Delays caused by fogs of rough seas for example had to be made up for by dock staff turning the ship round more efficiently – which broadly meant headaches for the supervisors and double time for the gangs.

Shore Gangs

If a ship had failed to make its expected tide the dock staff were expected to cut corners to redress the balance. Options were limited but one possibility was for a shore gang to meet the ship at locking in and not only see her through the lock but also clear the decks and set the derricks during the hour it took to tow her up to her berth so that ship gangs could start work immediately. The support of the water guard was useful here. Often in this situation a shore gang was needed at short notice and RML relied on a chap called Ralph who could always get a gang together, day or night. He was permanently drunk and would cycle – he was regularly banned from using his scooter – round the local pubs picking up men. The work was not for the most part exacting so sobriety was not important; as long as men could push a broom and were in need of beer money they were hired. In any case most were regulars, the same faces turned up time after time, they knew what needed to be done and each could find their way around a top deck.

Ships engaged on the meat run varied enormously from the new purpose built vessels launched after the War to the old general cargo vessels with severely limited refrigeration capacity. In these older ships hatchways could not be frozen so before meat gangs could start work, Furness,Withy general cargo gangs had first to clear whatever had been stowed there, often something deliberately straightforward like a tractor or car. Thus the shore gangs had to work to different ends: if a ship had first to be worked by general cargo gangs the ship would berth anywhere available and use cranes or derricks according to what was on offer. The shore gang then prepared the ship for general cargo discharging. On the other hand if the ship was new, she would only be carrying meat and would go directly to 'Z' shed. These ships had frozen hatchways with solid 'plug' hatch covers which shore gangs could remove using derricks. Either way, as the vessel berthed, the shore gang would have prepared the ship so that the relevant ship gangs could begin work immediately.

Black Market

Before the War with no restrictions on trade, importers would hang their consignments in the storage facilities at 'Z' shed for buyers to inspect before purchase but after the War the market took whatever it was offered; meat was bought unseen and rushed to Smithfield, dockside trading disappeared and refrigerated sheds remained unused. In these new circumstances Head Office had to interpret information both coming out of the MINDEL meetings and out of the docks to advise hauliers when to send their transport. This had to be a precisely coordinated operation for if meat were allowed to sit somewhere, in a shed or on the quay waiting for transport, then it would disappear, lorries had to be waiting ready as the nets came over the side.

During this time I was a tally clerk and such was the value of meat on the black market that being honest became a very uncomfortable experience. Any quarters that could be spirited away meant good bonuses for gangs working them and if only one tally clerk stood in their way he had better watch his back – assiduously. If possible the number of tally clerks at every station was doubled, one working for RML the other for Scruttons, but with so many men still in the Forces, labour shortages often prevented this. For tally clerks the going rate was five shillings for each quarter they let through so that even if there were the full quota of clerks, with these sorts of unofficial bonuses on offer, accurate tallying was not in the best interests of the community at large. In these circumstances an honest tally clerk had to stand, quite literally, with his back to the wall.

The most direct way of discouraging honesty was to maim: a scooter or trolley might run into the back of a clerk's legs or a frozen quarter might drop on his toes or collide with his back. Remember that there were six or seven runners and they all needed watching – all day long. If a clerk was the equal of these stratagems the gang would engage in endless distractions, drivers would suddenly have a problem and need advice, porters would get in his way or bump him while others called out "How many's that Bert? Eighteen isn't it?" "No nineteen" someone else would say, "I thought it was only seventeen", and so on. For someone who wanted to stay honest – and healthy - there were easier jobs in the docks and for a while I refused to work meat, settling instead for general cargoes or exports.

To give some figures: the best Scruttons meat gangs, sixteen men strong working in 2hour shifts could move 4,300 quarters of beef per gang working 8am to7pm. This was recognised as too hard and by the early 1960s gangs were contracted to off load 325 quarters per hour which was still around 2,400 for a standard 8-5 day. A fore or hind quarter of beef weighed 120-180lbs so even in the '60s gangs were still moving 160 tons a day. Incidentally, the best gangs would also discharge 15,000 carcasses of lamb – 14,600 tallied, 400 to the Black Market. Typically though 8-12,000 carcasses would be worked daily, vans had to be ready and waiting of course.

The new specialist meat ships which were introduced to supersede the *Tweed* and the *Teviot* as capacity improved had the facility to be able to transport meat 'chilled'. Even with improving technology transporting chilled meat was never easy and had to be confined to small upper holds where the temperature might be held at thirty one degrees Fahrenheit, with very little margin for error. If the shipment could be kept within these limits, it could be sold in the shops as 'fresh' and although the problems were considerable, with the public demand for quality meat increasing, it was important to be part of the trade. Only the best meat was chilled with poorer grades confined to the frozen lower holds where refrigeration subtleties were not required, the temperature was sent plummeting and held low. Thus a two tier technology produced two broad grades of meat offering new levels of discord among the importers. One obvious line of attack was for them to try and find fault with the chilling process: if the temperature dropped too low the consignment could be classed as 'frozen' and lower fees paid, if too high then the meat would be declared unfit for human consumption. All incoming meat shipments had to be inspected by a health and safety officer and genuinely bad meat, perhaps where refrigeration had failed completely, was properly condemned but the possibility of getting good quality meat cheaply was obviously something not to be overlooked. The report of the ship surveyor, armed with his spear thermometer for plunging into carcasses was crucial in deciding disputes which took place long after the meat itself had been sold and consumed.

In the lower holds of these newer meat ships, beef quarters and lamb carcasses could be simply heaped on top of each other to fill the available space but in chilled upper holds - and this was a measure of how far meat availability had improved since 1947 - in order to achieve 'fresh' status, each piece of meat had to hang from a rail in such a way that cool air could continuously circulate around it. In terms of cargo space this was particularly wasteful but the public's increasing discernment - and hence the higher prices that could be asked - made these shipments viable. Even the floor spaces beneath the carcasses could not be used as storage for once the ship had berthed and each locker door opened, surveyors and safety officers needed the space to inspect each cargo and once passed, gangs set to work off-loading; general cargo stored under the meat would just have got in the way. One factor which limited the amount of chilled meat which could be carried, one which had nothing to do with refrigeration, was the instability that thousands of carcasses swaying from their hooks could impart to a ship rolling in heavy seas. Every chilled upper hold had to have sufficient frozen meat stored beneath it in the lower hold to provide ballast.

The fundamental problem as we saw it was the technological for lockers. Maintaining a 'chilled meat' temperature was difficult, even on the newer ships, and sub-dividing the upper holds into, typically, six smaller compartments each with its restricted door to the hatchway meant that meat could only be off-loaded at a trickle. Holds were full of meat, importers and the market were desperate to get their hands on it yet men had to carry individual quarters weighing around one hundred and forty pounds out through this confined doorway and into a net. It was awkward and exhausting work made more uncomfortable by the cold gnawing at muscles and back. Compounding the problem for importers was the fact that each company would have their shipment confined to a separate locker: with a ship delivering consignments to half a dozen importers one locker only would be opened and cleared leaving five customers waiting. Chilled meat received absolute priority and the conditions which ensured it maintained its 'fresh' status were demanding, so it was impossible to work more than one locker at a time; once opened it had to be cleared, much to the frustration of those in the queue behind. Gangs worked their full quota of overtime but the meat still left the ships in a trickle. Until containers transformed cargo handling the bottleneck was unavoidable in spite of the threats from importers and the best efforts of the dockers.

The situation was made worse by the decisions to improve the working conditions of the men who were still being asked to work as if the War had only just finished. Eventually an agreement between shippers, stevedores, importers and the unions established that gangs would guarantee to move eight hundred quarters each session which for a three session day meant the men were still backing two thousand four hundred quarters daily. Even more awkward for the importers was the decision that handlers had to have more leisure time by limiting Sunday work to a one o' clock finish. This was particularly irksome for by this time the traditional meat purchasing pattern had become re-established: the Sunday roast would extend to Monday but by Tuesday or Wednesday housewives would be looking to make further purchases. For the meat trade, restricting work to Sunday mornings meant that Smithfield only had half a day's output to sell, allowing those importers who had collected their quotas to effectively corner the market. Those allocation meetings stayed acrimonious with Perce Arnold and his successors trying to maintain a sense of realism; we clerks just worked all the hours God gave us and tried to construct a sequence around importers demands, Head Office preferences and transport waiting on the quay.

In spite of the fact that everyone knew that there had to be some sort of sequencing each shipment meant a new battle with the big three importers aiming as a minimum to make sure that they held the first three places. Weddles, for example, owned the Blue Star Shipping Line and had its own berth, 'A' shed, just along the Victoria Dock from Scruttons' operations at 'Z' shed. RML shipments were adjuncts to their operations and their independence gave them extra leverage while smaller companies, we were told, committed to RML would go out of business if they didn't get a good deal. Importers would tell dock staff how many lockers they could clear in the time available and the Scruttons' representative would usually have to spell out why, with the best will in the world, their calculations were over optimistic. Of course once an agreement had been reached on whose compartment would be opened first that importer demanded a second as he did not want to send a lorry to Smithfield half full. More than any other commodity, what went on behind the scenes affected our working atmosphere. As things stood, discharging meat had to be unsatisfactory.

The ship's clerk could not be detached from these discussions for the very practical reason that they might be unworkable: some ships, as we have mentioned, were 'tender'. This was particularly true of RML's 'D' boats which were built specifically for the meat trade. Emptying lockers according to the committee's schedule might cause the ship to list, allowance had to be given to where in the hold each compartment lay: too many lockers cleared on one side could mean the derricks were scraping sets against the hull instead of reaching the quay scooters. Usually these fears were genuine but sometimes they were introduced somewhere in the negotiations to give smaller firms a more balanced position in the pecking order.

Once chilled meat had become the priority, clearing the lower frozen holds became less frenetic, especially if as sometimes happened less urgent items had been included. Blocks of corned beef were common, or horse meat destined for pet food and identified with an indelible green stain, in case anyone might be tempted to introduce it into the human food chain. Incidentally if meat for human and non-human consumption both arrived in the same hold they would be separated by barriers such as a shipment of butter making the distinctions very obvious. As gangs worked through the frozen meat it allowed supervisors to concentrate on the next ship due in and to anticipate the likely gambits of importers given the disposition of their consignments. Within a decade, say by 1970, with quality meat now commonplace, importers frequently reversed this established practice of demanding their meat immediately; instead they delayed collecting their quotas. If there was a short term glut in the market for example, it was more convenient for them to leave their meat in the ship's lockers rather than transferring it to the PLA refrigerated stores at No6 Shed (behind No29 Shed RAD) which were very expensive to hire. The shipping company of course needed their ship emptied, re-stowed and back at sea; importers gave their assurances to send a lorry but somehow this regularly failed to arrive.

Down in the holds men continued their work regime oblivious to the intrigues of various importers. In the confines of the chilled meat lockers men worked in two man teams: one stood behind each hanging quarter and as his partner ran up and turned his back, he gave a small jerk to the hundred and fifty pound load lifting it off its hook and down on to the shoulders of his team mate who ran, or rather staggered, it out into the hatchway and the waiting net. With sixteen quarters comprising a set, the meat was lifted by derricks to the quay. In the lower holds meat lay as a single frozen mass; frozen meat was always sent 'with its shirt on', each quarter sheathed in muslin and before they could be run to the hatchway, each had to be prized from the solid mass with crow bars. So long as this was the way meat had to be imported, so long would the bottlenecks, the complaints and the rows continue.

For a while there was considerable discussion amongst managerial groups about the number of men that ought to constitute a gang and some traditional formations like the sugar eaters, as we have seen, were swept away as the National Dock Labour Scheme tried to impose uniformity. For meat handlers though, there was a definite problem: if meat was waiting in the holds and the country was desperate to buy it, meat ought to be worked continuously to minimise the constrictions of off-loading. For a twelve man gang this would require men to work constantly in sub-zero temperatures over three shifts each day. There was never any thought given to providing protective or insulated clothing; men laboured in the clothes they came to work in. Even to the most ardent rationalisers this was clearly unacceptable, for there had to be scope for men to thaw out periodically and if clearing the holds was to be continuous some sort of rotation was needed. As with the quay gangs the solution was to accept the need for sixteen man gangs and engineer some way of being able to pay them. By rotating every two hours, the gang was able to keep up its work rate through the full three shifts, the only circumstance that might interrupt their flow being that, if it were raining hard and their sodden jackets began to freeze on their backs, they might just stand under for a while.

(I have a separate note where my father writes that meat gangs wore coats and gloves and tied sacking round their feet and ankles to keep out the cold. This apparent contradiction may refer to the difference between handling frozen meat and chilled meat or perhaps it may refer to conditions straight after the War and later, more controlled decades. Others may be able to clarify. MES).

*   *   *

JACK JONES

There was a needleman we used to employ from time to time called Jack Jones who enjoyed being part of the action. He had been a well-respected ganger in his time but now at nearly eighty his strength had long since turned to fat. He was big and squarely built, capable still of clearing up with a gang in a lower hold and with the aid of gravity, capable of getting down there. The problem came at the end of the day when tired, he had to make his way back up the manway – he could slowly get up the ladders but found it impossible to squeeze his frame through the man hatch. Downholders, supervisors and clerks had to help push and pull this Victorian docker back onto the top deck at the end of their own exhausting day's work.

It always saddened me that men would fight tenaciously for extra pay but hardly ever for an improvement in their working conditions. For the casual gangs who worked in the open all day at hard physical labour, often in filthy conditions the three basic requirements of access to good, solid food and somewhere comfortable to eat it, shower or wash room facilities and decent toilets were all denied them. There were many organisations with bases in the Royal Docks and perhaps some of them looked after their employees benevolently but from my experience the general level of provision even for permanent staff was always inadequate. This wasn't a result of war damage but presumably an extension from Victorian times of management's general disregard for its work force, workers had no right to expect decent facilities; it was only with Government intervention that RML, for example, gave up its wooden sheds to provide their staff with a brick office fitted out with toilets and the luxury of electricity points to brew a cup of tea. On the whole as a tally clerk and even as an import supervisor, you found toilets where you could, always as a concession, always a favour. Casual ship gangs had even less scope for a decent existence.

A constant complaint, though not one that I can remember collective action being taken over, was the absence of reasonable meal facilities. For those who came to work down the 101 bus route, 'Dicky' Bird's was the place to buy food if you didn't bring a sandwich from home. Each morning early whatever the weather, lines of dockers would queue patiently to get their provisions there. The shop was actually a grocer's with no licence to sell take away food so Dicky had to sell his items separately, a couple of slices of bread and a weighed quantity of cheese, breakfast sausage or corned beef. It was sustenance of sorts and men could at least see what they were paying for. If Dicky Bird's wasn't an option the official alternative was the PLA van which toured the docks dispensing tea, coffee and sandwiches but this was always something of a last resort: the drinks were generally reckoned to be indistinguishable while the sandwiches consisted of dainty slithers of bread with a near transparent slice of cheese or ham between them, hardly a mouthful for a hungry docker. Most regulars who patronised these vans recommended the bread and dripping – "at least you could see the dripping". The van came round at 10am and 2.15pm stopping between berths, in theory for greater accessibility but for downholders having to clamber out of their holds or men scrambling across the barges, they frequently found the allocation of food gone, snapped up by the quay gangs.

Alternatives were few. British Railways had a restaurant on the Manor Way inherited from the Great Eastern but this soon closed after the War; there were the pubs and cafés, just outside the docks but a tidy distance to have to walk from many of the berths, especially for men who more than anything, needed a sit down. In a gesture of philanthropy the PLA tried converting their mortuary in the Victoria Dock into a café, once ambulances had been introduced to render its former function redundant but somehow it was never popular. The food was of the same quality as that offered by the PLA vans and the atmosphere remained uncomfortable, most patrons having known someone who had been laid out there.

Most RML ships that were being worked had among their skeleton crew a resident cook and if good will were flowing it was sometimes possible for a top hand to collect a canteen of boiling water for a gang to brew up in their hold amongst the cargoes. Not luxurious and not guaranteed but if offered it might save them the scramble for the van or trek to a pub. It may be as well to remember that these gangs were employees of stevedoring companies, here Furness, Withy and were as far as possible, banned from the rest of the ship; they were employed to empty holds and were expected to stay within them. Very occasionally benign relieving officers, if they recognised a gang and knew their worth, might allow them access to one of the crews' cabins, but it was always made clear that this and the availability of hot water were strictly concessions. RML had no obligations to the gangs off-loading their ships, nor, apparently, to their own employees supervising them.

As a casual tally clerk you were a bit out on a limb when it came to lunch breaks. Harland and Woolf on the south side of King George V Dock had a canteen and if you were working in the area it might be worth seeing if you could slip in there, but you had no right to be there and could be turned away. The alternative, as I found, was to tally the ships of one company as much as possible, make friends with the permanent staff and hope they invited you to their company's office to escape the elements for half an hour.

Toilet facilities were grim. Those in the Victoria Dock were rudimentary and were so old they ought to have been Grade II listed. Of ancient brick construction, measuring perhaps six feet by eight feet, and set just behind the sheds they might well have been as old as the dock itself. The feeling was that they were close to the place of work not so much for the comfort of the dockers as to enable management to keep an eye on their workforce. In practice, however desperate the circumstance, they were never used. Men who were used to being held in low esteem baulked at accepting this facility, the general condition was too disgusting; the vomit and excrement might have been as Victorian as the buildings because I never knew them to be cleaned. Architecturally, they consisted of brown salt glazed urinals along one side and at the far end three locked closets for the use of officers. A key to these cubicles was always given to the relieving officer (no pun intended) of each working ship both for his use and at his discretion, for company staff of adequate standing. They offered a level of exclusivity and privacy but in fact the state of these cubicles was as abysmal as the other facilities and any officer would have had to have had a death wish - your whole life passed before you - to contemplate using them. Completing the facilities for non-officers at these 'conveniences' were the sit down loos located opposite their urinals. These consisted of a large metal tank with a wooden plank stretched along it for sitting on, with low partition boards marking out the three places but offering no privacy. Completing the degradation, there were no outside doors to these toilets allowing supervisors – and anyone else who happened to be passing – the chance to observe men perhaps wilfully delaying their return to work, as if time spent there was in some way cheering. The wind cut through carrying away some of the stench for a moment but these toilets symbolised the docks at their worst: they were designed to intimidate and they succeeded. Women, of course, had no place in the docks.

A ship's relieving officer held the key to these quay toilets as the official alternative to the ship's wc's. These were banned from use because they emptied directly into the dock from above the waterline and any lighter with its cargo unfortunate enough to be under it would suffer the disagreeable consequences. Relieving officers worked permanently in the docks and knew all the RML staff well, they also knew the condition of the quay toilets, so a request to borrow the ship's key surreptitiously was not always easy to refuse. Personalities featured large. Furness, Withy gangers on the other hand, however regularly they worked the RML ships, were strictly prohibited - their only recourse, not unknown, was to discover an out of the way ship convenience and kick the door in.

Inevitably lighters sometimes gained unexpected additions to their cargoes and more unfortunately, lightermen were occasionally drenched by something unpleasant in the congested space round a working ship. In this situation the reliving officer was in serious trouble, the lighterman could take his barge away from the ship and refuse to let work continue. The first duty of everyone was to placate him, the shore gang removing the soiled cargo and cleaning the barge, while the lighterman was given a donation from the petty cash or offered a drink or two from the ship's stores. Using the ship's toilet was always a risky operation but with those Victorian toilets as the only immediate alternative, cultivating good relations with relieving officers was essential – but they could still refuse. To those of us staff employees honoured with the privilege of gaining a key, it was always worth a quick glance over the side, judge where the outflow was and where the nearest lighter, before availing oneself of the onboard facilities.

This was the situation for import clerks but for export clerks, this was one of the few situations when their predicament could be even worse than ours. Because they were responsible for the ship on its next voyage, the master, first and second officers had to be on board to supervise loading. They were not part of the docks, usually saw themselves as superior to their surroundings and had no need to offer favours to anyone. Toilet keys were never lent. Most export ships berthed at one of the annual rent sheds where Royal Mail Lines had an office and a toilet, but exceptionally, if the loading was from a remoter shed, the clerk, and any visiting staff had a problem: locked toilets stayed locked and unavailable. A supervisor would have to run down the quay, or even catch a bus, to where he knew a Company ship was discharging and make friends right speedily with her relieving officer.

This pretty ignominious state of affairs could also extend to import clerks whenever their particular relieving officer was uncooperative.

Because I had to travel all over the docks, both as a tally clerk and an import clerk, I adopted the policy of making friends with shed foremen and their writers as their own offices situated on the top floor of each shed were equipped with reasonable facilities - foremen were more permanent than relieving officers, and their toilets didn't change berths. Another line worth pursuing was to build up links with other tally clerks at the morning Call to see who had access to whose toilets and gauging whether they would be acceptable to the ones open to you. In this by no means cast iron process, a network of strategically placed toilets had to be gradually built up to over come the gross deficiencies of the docks themselves. It was a pretty grubby affair.

The general level of facilities seemed to me to be a reasonable cause for men to threaten industrial action but they never did. With four of five pints inside them from lunch in a pub, barge hands just had to pee against the side of a ship and down holders find a quiet corner for the shore gangs to clear up later. Cornporters could avail themselves of perhaps the best retaliation by urinating on grain against the side of the hold then claim an allowance for contamination later on. It was rough justice at the expense of the shippers rather than the dock authorities but it wasn't a situation for niceties.

After the War, under normal circumstances, passengers were kept away from the unpleasantness of the docks by boarding their ship at Tilbury but when a vessel was behind schedule, it was sometimes necessary to transport them up river to the Royal Docks so that the ship could make her way directly out to sea once she had caught her tide. This naturally caused consternation amongst the dock authorities – ship toilets were banned even to boarding passengers - and to meet dock regulations 'Portaloos' had to be quickly set up somewhere strategic, strictly for the use of the passengers, and removed again as soon as the ship had sailed.

Completing the range of facilities offered to the work force, on the wall outside the Victorian toilets there stood a cold water tap at which men could wash. Usually frozen in winter, these taps at best could only be used by men to dip their faces under in the hope that at the end of the day, this gesture of civility would be enough to get them onto a bus home. Remember that many homes were still without a bathroom so hygiene was a serious issue. There was a shower room, for anyone wanting to make the trek after a full day's work, down to Victoria Dock but for most men working in the Royal Albert or King George V it meant a walk of a mile or two away from where they hoped to catch a bus. It was also necessary to do the same walk first thing in the morning before work started to notify those responsible that hot water would be needed later in the day giving them time to light the boilers. The situation was absurdly impracticable. It was more straightforward to try for a bus and if banned, put up with walking the couple of miles home. Better still, if men knew in advance the nastiness of the day's cargo and suspected a miss-match with their probable conductor, it was easier to come to work by bike.

Although gangers knew that their condition was frequently too unsociable to admit them onto public transport, they did expect some understanding from the conductors. There was one conductress who was notoriously unreasonable and officious; she wasn't going to have filthy dockers defiling her bus, in spite of the fact that the route existed for them. Men didn't need her fastidiousness at the end of the day, if there had been a more refined way of working fishmeal they would have gladly taken it. They knew perfectly well their own objectionable condition and didn't need her highlighting it - it was easier to wait the extra fifteen minutes for the next bus. She gained a considerable reputation over the time she was on the route and was universally loathed. When she finally got her comeuppance however, it was over quite a different matter:

There was a day, not long after females had begun to appear in the docks, when a girl who worked in one of the offices was told that she didn't have enough money for the fare. She thought she did, she used the bus daily but this woman insisted that she would have to get off a few stops early. To cover the girl's embarrassment a docker chipped in "Here y'are love, here's the extra", it was only a couple of coppers after all. "I'm not taking money from you, it's her fare, she pays or she gets off'. Other men joined in offering the cash but she refused them all, the girl would have to get off early. The row ended and an uneasy calm settled over the bus as it made its way along the route, everyone expecting a final showdown. It didn't happen though: a few stops short of the girl's destination a couple of dockers who were getting off, passed each side of the conductress as she stood in righteous indignation on her platform. Each man grabbed her by an arm and bodily lifted her off the bus as another docker rang the bell. A triumphant calm descended over the rest of the journey; the girl got off when she wanted to, men rung the bell for the driver who remained oblivious to the little drama that had unfolded. All in all, there was a general air of quiet satisfaction. Whether she ever caught up with her bus no one ever knew - perhaps she is still running - but she was never seen on that route again.

(In the early years after the War there was an alternative service, of course – trams ran as far as the 'Ferndale'.)

Presumably when the Royal Victoria Dock opened in the middle of the nineteenth century, railways were the future given that the alternatives were waterways or horse and cart. By the time I joined the Royal Group of Docks rails stretched everywhere giving access to quays and sheds, suggesting that trains had been planned as a major contributor to the movement of goods up to and away from ships. In this expanded system the PLA maintained its own engines which took over the delivery of wagons from the Great Eastern or British Railways as trains came into the docks thus maintaining the Authority's control over the entire infrastructure. This integrated system, I assume, was put in place before the advent of the internal combustion engine but by the nineteen fifties the whole network was in serious decline, the flexibility of lorries over rail proving decisive. For us casual clerks though, squatting in dilapidated wooden sheds the great advantage in the continuance of the railways, particularly the steam engines, lay in our easy access to fuel from the PLA coal dumps – more later.

In theory there were still in the post-War period, occasions when using rail seemed eminently sensible: for example, Fords could deliver a whole train load of cars from their Dagenham works right onto the quay, beside the ship and each wagon could be moved to where the cranes needed them for setting in the holds. The problem was that the rails ran the complete length of the dock, they didn't serve just one berth so in order to bring up a train of wagons to any particular ship, all the quay gangs working along the route of the train would have to know it was coming and modify their work to allow its passage. This of course was extremely disruptive and time consuming and a ruling came into force from the PLA insisting that they had forty eight hours notice if a train was being brought onto the quay. During these two days other berths would be warned for them to make alternative arrangements; cargoes might have to be loaded in a different sequence, perhaps taking deliveries from lighters, while gangs might have to adapt how they set consignments out on the quay, with lorry drivers and scooter operators needing to know how much of a dislocation to their routine was involved. Overall it was a ponderous and disruptive operation. An alternative was for trains to deliver their exports to the back of transit sheds where parallel sets of rails lay to save the quayside disruption but in this case special PLA 'bridges' had to be brought up to span the gap between the wagons and the loading bay, with every item having to go through the shed and out onto the quay. It was less intrusive for work directly on the quays but a long train at the back of the sheds limited access there for lorries. Once again work at other unrelated berths was affected, there was no easy solution.

There was a time when one of Royal Mail Lines' regular importers suddenly decided to have his consignment sent by rail at a time when everyone else was abandoning the system. The cargo was a large quantity of rum which usually went out by lighter but the idea here was that if the barrels went directly from the hold to waiting wagons under Custom's supervision, less of it would 'evaporate' en route to the warehouse. The train had to be put together in marshalling yards on the north side of Victoria Dock behind the tobacco sheds, then taken down across the Connaught Road towards Silvertown Station, back round the Pontoon dock, behind the mills, up to the lock then out along the quay to the ship. A 1955 plan of the docks from about the time gives a pretty good idea of the convoluted journey it had to make - most of the dock was involved. Maybe in times gone by this procedure was common but by the mid fifties, it was seen as an eccentric decision; the costs to the importer were considerable and it was rumoured, on the two day journey up to Leith, 'evaporation' was much the same as for the more established waterborne route.

Behind RML's main dock office on the north side of Victoria Dock were a great mass of railway tracks which were the dock group's primary marshalling yards. Men worked here coupling wagons as they were shunted together to form trains, one being one of the first West Indians to enter the Royal Docks. Men worked using a long pole to link or unlink wagons and to save them leg work it was possible on a rolling wagon for them to slip the end of their pole under the furthest buffer, then on top of the closest and spring onto it and so hitch themselves a lift down the track as the wagon was shunted into position - strictly illegal of course but commonly done. Unfortunately for this poor man his pole slipped or broke and he fell under the rolling wagon losing both his legs. I used to see him later in life around Wanstead in his wheel chair, he'd put on a lot of weight but seemed to remain remarkably cheerful. The incident took place on the lines just outside our main office.

*   *   *

SUGAR ACCIDENT

The basic rhythm that all discharge work assumed was that once a crane hook had been released from a set in a lighter, the time it took to rise up over the deck, descend to collect its next load and return with it to the barge, was the period needed for the barge hands to 'throw away'- that is, clear - the set just delivered. Thus the work was continuous, we might say unrelenting. Occasionally things got out of sync and very occasionally accidents resulted. Once when working bagged sugar the barge hands had not quite finished throwing away the last set as the next came over, the top hand shouted to the crane driver and he applied the crane's brakes but unfortunately the line 'ran out', meaning in effect that the breaks had failed to work. One of the barge hands was struck on the head and seriously injured. In fact he was paralysed and was away for months. He returned to the docks in his wheel chair a few times hoping that there might be some work he could do but with the best will in the world, it was just too dangerous. The docks as an environment were not geared for wheel chairs; there were just too many potential hazards.

154

Tally clerks of course spent their days in the same main areas as the handling gangs, on ships and quays and in sheds, for it was their job to monitor precisely what goods were being worked but there were other casually employed clerks, taken on at the tally clerks' Call, who worked in more remote areas sometimes with no direct contact with cargo. All came under the broad heading of 'tally clerks' but if they weren't afraid of paperwork they might prefer working as inside clerks or planning clerks, it very much depended on temperament and talents. Both roles, inside and planning clerks, were to support a ship's clerk; in broad terms while the ship's clerk supervised off-loading or loading of cargoes, support clerks maintained records. Tallying required little more than standing in one place, in all weathers, noting marks and recording quantities. It could be a cold, numbing existence but the paperwork consisted of little more than putting marks on a small card docket.

Now these dockets were issued by an inside clerk who was working to a ship's manifest. He would have been engaged at the Call a couple of days before the ship started working in order to prepare the paperwork. Once the ship had berthed, the hatches removed and the cargoes were being discharged the inside clerk, as well as distributing and collecting tally clerks' dockets also dealt with documentation from hauliers, lightermen and lorry drivers. This paperwork was demanding because it had to be accurate in case of future claims from importers and where possible it was done from an office. For a ship off-loading imports though, much of this work had to be carried out on the ship's top deck or across at the transit shed and there needed to be a clerk assigned to maintaining this paperwork as each consignment was sent on its way. Under these circumstances keeping things orderly was not easy and an office to retreat to occasionally would have been nice.

For a planning clerk, filling in or studying little boxes on a ship's plan, the work needed a large, clean desk – and this could be a problem. Import planning clerks dealt with the future: they received the plans as completed across the Atlantic setting out where different cargoes were stowed as they had come on board. Here a RML planning clerk used these plans to predict how the cargoes would be worked out of the holds and so advise importers when to prepare transport. Export planning clerks, on the other hand, dealt with history: it was their job to start with a blank ship's plan and gradually build up, in box notation where different exports were being stowed in each hold. They needed an office space but they also needed to be able to visit the ship to see precisely where each consignment had been stowed, and they had to copy out the final loading in triplicate. Planning clerks, import or export, definitely needed an office.

Now a casual clerk might be employed by Royal Mail Lines to draw up plans for one of their ships but it didn't mean necessarily that he had access to a RML office, partly because office space was limited but also because they may not have been working in a part of the dock where Royal Mail Lines had an office. Consequently there were at any one time a collection of casually employed clerks in various capacities and working for different companies armed with ship's plans, bills of lading, manifests, delivery notes or tally clerk dockets with nowhere officially to work from.

Away from the quays and the main flow of goods, various companies had erected 'offices'. These were often simply wooden huts without heating, water, plug sockets or toilets; sheds simply dropped down in a convenient spot, easy to erect, easy to abandon as fortunes changed and in themselves, incidentally, would form a fascinating sub-history of dock evolution.

Behind No 14 Shed, Royal Albert Dock, Ellerman Bucknel had a wooden office but it was in such wretched condition that it had been abandoned years before. For souls with serious paperwork to contend with and who were working in the Royal Albert or King George V, this was a useful if precarious base which I used frequently as a casual clerk. There was a single light, no heating or water and few of the windows had glass. Soot from the steam engines which clattered past outside was everywhere. There was one long, solid sloping desk and a couple of collapsing stick chairs – it was safer to stand and work – and in winter it was bitterly cold. Eventually, acting on their own initiative some of the clerks finally decided to install their own heating system. They set a big old, oil drum up on bricks, smashed a few holes in it and turned it into a brazier, taking turns to 'borrow' coal from the steam engine depot. For a short while this might have been the warmest place in the working docks and it proved a popular if smoke filled base for stray clerks. Unfortunately this innovation proved rather too effective and a group of nicely warmed clerks had the unsettling experience of watching the brazier collapse through the charred hole it burnt for itself in the floorboards. The office was in a bad way when we moved in but as we were only there under sufferance we did feel more than a little guilty every time we stepped over that hole. The brazier was dug out and the hole patched up with dunnage but from then on we just put up with the cold. Whenever I was taken on as an export planning clerk I found it easier, on the whole, to cycle the couple of miles home and work on the kitchen table but it did mean returning usually three times a day to see how the cargoes were being loaded; at least the plans stayed clean. If any of those tidy plans still exist, don't underestimate the effort it took to keep them that way.

As I increased my links with RML and my face became a bit more familiar, access to Company offices became more generally available, the working conditions didn't get any easier but they saved the cycle rides home. The best of Royal Mail Lines' wooden sheds was the one on the south side of Victoria Dock near the annual rent sheds. Facilities were familiarly basic; bad lighting, no heating, toilets or running water but it had survived the Blitz with glass in the windows. The furniture was dominated by a large, solid wooden desk running down the centre of the shed, sloping on both sides so that clerks could work facing each other down its length. Between them above the 'ridge' of the slope ran a brass rail on brass supports for clerks to hang their sheets and charts on. That was pretty much it: it was a place of work not relaxation and it was nobody's job to supply home comforts. I believe these RML sheds were set up when the jetties were removed during the re-organisation of the Dock before the War but that central clerks' desk and its dominance of the office seemed more properly Dickensian. Until about eight years after the War this shed was the best facility the Company provided its dock staff to re-establish its authority in the docks.

Across the dock on the north side, RML had a clutch of wooden sheds which functioned as their main dock office - I have already referred to these (see 'Captain Spinks'). These offices were also useful for export staff in that they were an easy delivery point for lorry drivers to drop off delivery notes but they were, as working offices, a bit remote from the main action on board ships and were little used by casual or import staff. Further, they had been seriously damaged by bombs and in spite of various patching jobs offered little in the way of basic office comforts.

Incidentally, the collection of buildings, strung out in this area between the back of the transit sheds and the mass of the railway tracks, in themselves formed an illuminating side light on the work in the docks. Swifts had its cold store next to the Royal Mail Lines' buildings – including their 'loft'- Furness, Withy had its gearing shed where Big Fred the Norwegian worked. Next to this were the PLA Tobacco Sheds, warehouses really, where leaves were left to mature, again bomb damaged but secure as far as I could make out due to the presence of strategically placed Customs posts nearby. Along from these were administrative buildings then the mortuary which nobody liked to dwell on too much and finally came the storage warehouses for lost property, impounded cargoes and non-permissible items where goods went after oversights or skirmishes with Customs Officers. One of my last jobs before retirement was trying to unite importers with long forgotten cargoes left in corners of remote sheds – a fairly depressing, end-of-an-era task.

There came a time in the early-fifties when RML discovered bricks and mortar – or more probably it was due to government legislation – and the era of the sheds ended. Suddenly there was adequate lighting, plug sockets for cups of tea, heating and even toilets: for staff who worked permanently in these offices this was a real advance but for import clerks working from wherever their ship had berthed the improvement was less useful. To show their commitment to the docks, it was here, just outside No 6 Gate that Royal Mail Lines also built its 'Factory' where everything was stored from crockery and linen for the liners to the records' store. Within another ten years that too was to pass into history.

Before this flurry of building activity, RML had a third wooden office behind their annual rent shed at No 3 King George V and this was used regularly by Company import clerks working ships in this general area. The office lacked the usual basic facilities but had the additional inconvenience of lacking much of its roof; half hearted attempts were made to weather proof it but it was clearly not a RML priority. It was just better than nothing and once I had become a permanent staff member, I used it frequently to sort out my paperwork. RML had the good grace to employ an ancient needleman to tidy up but with the general state of decay, soot, pigeons, rats and rain, his impact was marginal. He would clean a space to allow plans and documents to be set out but anything more substantial was beyond him.

Apart from acting as a base, there were advantages to this shed: being remote from RML's main presence, it was infrequently visited by the Marine Superintendent – dirty and uncomfortable it may have been but without the anxiety. A second advantage, much appreciated by certain members of staff, was that it had been constructed of four by two inch timbers with cladding on the inside and out. Because sections of the timber were rotting, it was easy to smash discrete holes in the panelling to hide emergency rum rations from the sugar ships. For men who had grown used to a steady supply of drink during the thirties, the deprivations of War had proved a struggle. With the stuttering re-introduction of the rum trade the old tendency to stockpile took on a new urgency and being able to utilise these hidden panels was, to old hands, both nostalgic and reassuring. Bottles could be amassed, cherished and enjoyed at a moment's notice. The trouble was that for serious drinkers like Bill Woods and George Mendham, their collections were not Fort Knox secure and for a while paranoia got the better of them; they got it into their heads that the needleman knew where they were concealing their hoard. They assumed that he was as desperate for rum as they were and their only option was to drink as much as they could before he came in at the end of the day. A sound enough policy in itself but it did nothing to help build up reserves. Worse still, in these early days after the War, rum shipments were by no means regular and there were times still when the two of them had to go without. During one such fairly desperate period they convinced themselves that they remembered a cache of rum being tucked away in the loft of that very shed just before War began. They both decided to take a break from ships' plans and have a reconnoitre. Even with his deformed back, Bill managed to join George in the loft – but neither was there for long: the ceiling joists were as rotten as the rest of the building and they both swiftly re-joined their colleagues along with half of what had been left of the ceiling, records, timber, pigeon droppings, dust etc. Neither was seriously hurt fortunately but they had done nothing to improve the general working conditions in the office - and they hadn't found any rum. The accident had to be reported and the Marine Superintendent learnt that they had fallen through the ceiling while looking for old records.

There came a time when we were still working out of these wooden sheds when someone listened to our complaints. The main dock office was being re-built about this time and had the luxury of electric fires and power points, so it was decided that, as a stop-gap measure, something had to be done to warm up the two sub offices. From somewhere the Company got hold of two Canadian stoves, four feet high, one for each office. It seems that they were built, for a climate substantially colder than ours - they just ate coal: a hundredweight was lost in one of them. It took the office regulars the best part of a morning collecting dunnage and raiding coal dumps just to get the things going, then they spent the afternoons suffocating. Even with open doors, broken windows and makeshift roof, clerks were still passing out from the heat, there was no happy medium. And painstaking accurate work still had to be done. In reality looking back, the working environment in those offices was awful.

*   *   *

One curious PLA building that we shouldn't overlook was No 7 Shed on the south side of Victoria Dock and near RML's annual rent sheds, for it had a model of the Thames laid out along its full length of perhaps three hundred feet. It featured the PLA controlled section of the Thames from Teddington to the river-mouth showing not only man made objects like wharves and jetties but also tributaries, mud-banks and shallows. It had a PR value and was always shown to visiting VIPs but its primary purpose, we were told, was to try to work out how to prevent silting, especially at the Tidal Basin Lock.* I suppose this would all be replaced by a computer programme now, and to greater effect but it was a nice model for anyone able to study it.

In fact studying it might have been its greatest value, for apprentice lightermen used to scrutinize it to help them understand the Thames and its tributaries towards gaining their Freemen of the River qualification.

It seemed something of an oddity but for those with time on there hands No 7 Shed, RVD was a pleasant distraction from the rigours of dock life.

*   *   *

'TWEEN DECK HATCHES

If a lighter failed to turn up, meaning that some upper cargo could not be off-loaded, the stevedore company – Furness, Withy for us – had to pay for opening the between deck hatches so the gang could keep working in a lower hold. When the barge finally appeared, it was the ship owners who had to pay for the re-covering of the hatch: work could not be restarted in an upper hold with the hatch left open. This was safety precaution and Charley Hatches would make a point of checking that pins and hatch boards were both sound and in place.

159

General transit sheds were exactly what their title said they were: storage units for general cargoes passing through the docks by road. They were large, undistinguished buildings of brick or 'tin' (corrugated metal) of between one and three stories high, some joined in pairs at first floor level, where their shed foremen had their offices. Large doors onto the quay allowed trolleys or, later, scooters to deliver goods too and from a ship, while those at the back gave access to a standard loading bay for lorries to drop their tail gates onto and hence be easily loaded. At the side of each shed was a ramp allowing lorries in specific circumstances to drive up onto the quay. These were the sheds which some companies hired from the PLA as annual rent sheds for permanent use and into which exports could be gradually amassed to fill the holds of their outward bound vessels. These functional sheds stretched along each dock down both sides and might only be distinguished by what goods passed through them: shippers worked particular trade routes and exporters would regularly use one company, so that looking around a range of exports and seeing their destinations, an employee could recognise his company's presence. On the whole, whether annual rent sheds or not, these buildings in themselves were functional rather than distinctive, their size being their purpose.

General transit sheds extended approximately the length of a ship's berth and were capable of holding, on their ground floor, the entire contents of a ship's five holds. They had been designed as an integral part of the economy of the docks for it was assumed that much of their revenue would come from rents charged on every item stored in them. In practice this policy was destroyed by a Government decision to allow lighters free access into the docks and importers quickly learnt that it was more economic to have their cargoes loaded directly into barges rather than pay rent for storage in sheds. Even less economic for the PLA was the storage space on the first floor, intended for long stay commodities or more valuable items making them less easy to steal but in practice this vast space was rarely used.

Sheds and berths went together, the name of a shed logically being the same as a ship's berth. Through the large expanse of each ground floor, a series of stanchions held up the roof above and these were used to improvise bays for arranging commodities. For imports using the sheds, items came off the ship and were set out according to each importer across the floor space so that in an ideal world, lorries could back up close to where their importer's goods were stored. For exports, the separation was by port: as a general rule Britain imported produce and exported products and these latter were accumulated by a chalked name on a stanchion indicating their delivery port thus non-perishable items gradually came together under a range of destinations – typically seven - defining the ship's next itinerary.

Occasionally exports arrived by train in which case large quantities of goods quickly filled the bays but these deliveries diminished rapidly through the fifties; more commonly, road haulage delivered relatively small quantities over an extended time frame.

Because barges had free access to the docks, imports which used the transit sheds were quite specific, certainly for Royal Mail Lines, so although general cargo ships carried general cargoes, general transit sheds only received a filtered out, specific range of goods. We have seen that sugar and grain, major commodities, always left by lighter while timber and metals, fish meal, pollards and a whole mass of goods usually went out of the docks by water. Only meat, as a major import, left by road haulage but because it needed particular conditions it could not pass through these general transit sheds. Rum barrels, came onto the quay according to the importer's mark, for the Customs Officer to inspect, but then very quickly were loaded into lock-up lighters. If something valuable had to go through the transit sheds, copper bars or bottles of rum for example, the shippers would move heaven and earth to get the traffic officer to give them a berth which had a brick shed - on the north side of King George V for example – capable of withstanding the special attentions of less scrupulous dockers. Tin sheds were just an open invitation to them.

For RML imports, the main commodities to pass through these general transit sheds were those bound for Covent Garden and local markets. In those post-War years any fruit was a luxury and importers needed their cargoes off the ships, through the sheds and onto lorries as quickly as possible – partly because the produce was perishable, partly to be ahead of the competition. So in my mind, it was fruit and vegetables that were the commodities most closely associated with the transit sheds and here problems were less to do with the sheds themselves than access to them.

If there was a choice, you requested a berth on the north side of the newer King George V where a large concrete area stretched behind all the brick sheds, allowing free access for lorries. Remember that behind all the sheds ran railway tracks but at the rear of these the concrete formed what was in effect a continuous 'level crossing', equally suitable for road and rail transport. If you knew the next ship in had a large quantity of goods destined to leave by lorry then this is where you wanted the ship to berth.

Identical sheds on the north side of the Royal Albert were less well provided: behind these, the tracks ran proud, with only a few raised concrete areas, known as 'pads', allowing lorries access to the loading bays. For each shed, perhaps a hundred feet long, there might be half a dozen pads. As a result, lorries were forced to queue with loaders waiting impotently as men attempted to direct those at the head of the queue to the closest pad to where their goods had been set out in the shed. And this frustration was for every ship which berthed at these sheds – presumably, cement was at a premium after the War.

But things could be worse: there were sheds up in the Basin at the far east end of Albert Dock. Maybe it had been assumed that all goods off-loading

161

onto the quays here would leave on railway wagons for no pads had ever been laid across the tracks so, given this impediment, as far as possible ships which berthed in the Basin worked directly into lighters. To facilitate this the cargoes of incoming ships were studied by supervisors and traffic officers in an attempt to keep lorries out of the Basin but such was the pressure for space after the War that not infrequently lorries would have to bounce their way across the tracks, testing their rudimentary suspension. Men tried to help by throwing down odd pieces of dunnage more as a goodwill gesture than as an effective solution; it was bad enough watching transport jolt there way across empty but to see them leaving fully laden, brought tears to the eyes.

The worst situation though was on the south side of King George V where space was severely limited. There was simply no room for lorries to back up to the loading bays, particularly as lorries themselves were getting bigger; shippers would do anything, even accept a berth in the Basin, not to have to off-load fruit and vegetables there. Sometimes a smaller lorry could just wriggle its way somewhere close to the bay but it was always awkward and involved a lot of carrying.

Normally what had to be done was this: fruit was landed on the quay, sorted and arranged according to its mark, then stored in the shed to clear the approach. When the entire shipment of fruit and vegetables had been sorted, lorries, one at a time, had to reverse up the ramps at the side of the shed and onto the quay itself. The delivery gangs, who had just stored the goods in the shed, then had to use their trolleys to bring them back out again and lift them onto the back of each lorry – a procedure that the loading bay at the back, was designed to overcome.

These bottlenecks caused untold arguments and frustrations day after day, as lorries queued idly evaporating profits for the hauliers, with wholesalers having a ready market for fruit and vegetables which were sitting, inaccessibly in a shed. Compounding the frustrations, shipping companies were unable to clear their holds until the perishable backlog had been sent on its way. That decision back at the turn of the century to squeeze the new King George V Dock into too small a space was a curse that dockers daily had to work round - and it was the docks, not the designers who got the blame for inefficiency.

There were two systems by which a shipping company could use the shed facilities of the PLA: Quay and Shed Agreement or the London Clause. Royal Mail Lines always worked to the former contract where shippers and their stevedoring company were responsible for all the labour, into and through the shed. By extension, this also meant that RML was responsible for getting importers' transport up at the correct time as well as loading it. In this way the entire operation, getting the goods onto the quay, sorting and storing them in the shed then loading them onto the correct lorries, was under the authority of RML and FW. Importers liked the movement of their goods being under one control, while Head Office knew that responsibility for a safe delivery was in the hands of their own staff. For a ship's clerk though, the London Clause option of just off-loading goods onto the quay and leaving them for the PLA to manipulate through the sheds sounded like something of a rest cure.

Each shed had its own shed foreman who was the executive head and under him were a writer, the head of administration, assistant writers and clearing clerks who seemed to be the main liaison between the goods they were handling and Customs Officers. Above each shed foreman was a traffic officer responsible for groups of sheds in ascending levels of responsibility so that, for example, a Traffic Officer 1 might be responsible for all the sheds on the north side of Royal Albert Dock.

The foreman of each shed was of course a PLA employee who had no need to grant favours to anyone, but for a peripatetic import clerk, building up some sort of rapport was important – crucially, in the hope that he would let you use his toilet. When a ship had a large quantity of goods passing through his shed though, with the work lasting perhaps a week or more, his assistance could make a big difference to the well being of shipping clerks.

Wally Clatworthy was the shed foreman at No 29 Royal Albert Dock. I knew him well as his two daughters were members of my gymnastics class at East Ham's Central Hall. Wally was a staunch, dour Methodist, a lay preacher and sidesman. One particularly bleak winter, around Christmas soon after the War, when there wasn't much comfort to be had anywhere, we had a 'Loch' boat discharging a large shipment of North Pacific fruit at this shed. Normally my assistant would work on the top deck of a ship collecting paperwork from lightermen but when fruit was passing out of a shed onto lorries, he needed to transfer his point of operations to the shed itself, to take receipts and issue passes to the drivers.

I worked between ship and shed up and down the gangway to monitor how the fruit was being discharged and this activity had the incidental advantage of keeping my blood flowing in that bitter December. For my clerk though, the job was entirely static and I had asked Wally, as a very great favour, if he would let us use his office. It meant him having an endless flow of lorry drivers and tally clerks passing through, disrupting his office regime and he wasn't too enthusiastic but for us a bit of warmth and a clean surface to work off would be a Godsend. After some deliberation and with it clearly understood that it was no small kindness, he finally agreed.

Unfortunately my clerk on that job was Les Bradshaw, a highly intelligent, capable but restless soul who also happened to be a straight-talking, exuberant cockney. Within a day or two, cooped up in a corner of this office with an endless stream of drivers and clerks vying for his attention, it all began to get a bit too much and in exasperation, he let out a stream of fairly choice expletives - just as Wally was returning to his office. Within about ten seconds Les, his pass books and receipts were out of the office and back among the fruit. "No one uses language like that in my office". Eventually it was decided that I could stay but it was a close thing; I had vouched for my inside clerk in the first place and I was guilty by association. Poor Les had to construct a cubby hole and desk for himself, made out of uncollected apple crates, stamping his feet and hardly able to hold a pen. There was no protection from that biting winter wind, it just howled through the open shed doors carrying off any paper dockets not weighted down. I pleaded his cause but it was about a week before Wally would relent and by that time the work was nearly complete. I have to say that this was not a particularly unusual situation except that it was heightened more starkly in my memory by the personalities involved and by the size and season of that shipment. Wally needn't have offered his office at all, it was a major concession, clerks were expected to put up with their inconveniences whether on ships, on quays or in sheds. No one was required to offer them succour.

Not all transit sheds were general: we have already mentioned Scruttons' meat shed – Z Shed – and there was another specialist structure at No 35 Royal Albert Dock near where the tally clerks had their Call. This shed had no storage facilities as it was dedicated to bananas where the emphasis was on speed of throughput. Stems of bananas were loaded on wooden boards with a curtain round to contain them and lowered onto the quay. The stems were put on conveyer belts and delivered to raised loading bays, like railway platforms, either side of the vehicular access. The belief was that these bays had been built during the days of horse and cart deliveries and while the space might have been ideal for horse drawn wagons, as lorries got bigger the squeeze just kept getting tighter. Bananas were not marked, a lorry simply crossed a weigh bridge twice, once empty, once full to determine the load, while tallying was by counting the stems. Ripe bananas were dumped, importers only wanted green ones to ripen in their own warehouses. There were frequently good intentions for delivering ripe bananas to local hospitals but the cost difference between this and tossing them into a refuse barge for dumping down river was substantial and sadly, no one wanted to foot the bill.

Royal Mail Lines had few banana imports and consignments were small. Usually these were off-loaded at Z Shed as, like meat of course, they needed a level of refrigeration: both sheds were also conveniently close to a dock gate to allow their perishable goods a speedy exit. With small shipments, ripe bananas were also few in number and could be delivered to a dump by lorry, but they had to be accompanied by a Customs 'watcher' to make sure that as condemned items they didn't get deflected onto a market barrow. For the most part, bananas were problem free except that occasionally as they warmed up from their refrigerated holds, hairy tropical spiders would scuttle out to unnerve even the beefiest docker.

*　　　*　　　*

On the whole the architecture of the docks was unimpressive but America Lines suddenly appeared on the scene with a very large shiny metal shed on the south side of Victoria Dock, on the other side of the Pontoon Dock from

RML. This impressively large shed became an instant landmark shimmering in the (occasional) sun. Instantly all other dock structures looked old and tawdry. America Lines equipped the shed – it became No 4 Shed – with ninety foot cranes and became a triumph for publicity officers concerned with projecting the modernity of the Royal Docks. Probably because of industrial disputes, in no time at all the company moved out - we were unused to such quixotic behaviour - to Felixstowe I believe and it was then used as a general utility shed by other lines. This bit of American opulence was known throughout the Docks as 'Silver City' – one step up I assume from Silvertown.

Photographs reveal little of the experience of working in the docks and it is odd how particular incidents and sheds stay linked in the memory:

There was a day in the early fifties when I was working at 12 General Transit Shed, south side of the Royal Albert, sorting out paperwork in the PLA office – another concession. When I came out at around 3 o' clock I realised at once that something was odd but couldn't immediately see what it was. Suddenly it dawned on me that all the ships were looming up above the quay. The people working in the area had not noticed, so gradual had been the change but coming out of the shed onto the dockside, it was obvious. I ran on board the Royal Mail Lines ship working at that berth to warn the relieving officer, then went to tell the lightermen to get their barges out from the quay side of the ship. The mooring ropes were bar tight, straining at the bollards and pulling at the ship. The quay gang had to be quickly organised to ease the ropes as the message spread down the docks that they had a serious flooding problem. The dock quays were built higher than the surrounding land but even so water was pouring over the lock gates and through the Basin.

Normally the water level lay several feet below the quay but as we watched, it lapped over the embankment towards the sheds. All work was halted although once safety measures had been taken there was no immediate danger. Nevertheless people still had to get home and with high tide at 7 o'clock the flooding was only going to get worse. I worked till five and joined the long slow procession of men, trousers rolled up above the knees, shoes and socks in our hands; the entire population of the docks was wading its way to where we could pick up a bus or ride bikes. The low lying Kier Hardy Estate had three or four feet of heavily polluted water swamp its living rooms, while further to the west in Silvertown, the flood waters rose eight to ten feet behind the south side of Victoria dock.

This was where RML had just built its new factory, it was only about a year since its completion, and the gatekeeper* trapped in his cabin, nearly drowned. Fortunately the waters just failed to rise as high as the ceiling, giving him a pocket of air to breath until he was rescued – but it was touch and go. 12 Shed Royal Albert Dock is always indelibly linked in my mind with that flood.

When I joined the Royal Docks, ship gangs formed an elite group. Quay gang rates of pay, crucially, were four fifths those of the stevedores and it might be of value just to emphasise the distinctions between the two during the period when these divisions were clear cut. I had better make it clear that I am only considering the general cargo gangs of FW as being representative of the traditional roles between ship and quay gangs – cornporters and the meat gangs as employees of the PLA and Scruttons were in a different situation. Although ship work was no longer the preserve of the 'Blues', those White gangs which had built up sufficient experience during the War to continue working holds in peace time, were just as keen to maintain their exclusivity. When I began supervising imports it was as likely that White gangs as Blues would be off-loading goods onto the quays for other White gangs to take to the sheds but it did not lessen the divide in pay or ethos.

Furness, Withy had the responsibility for not only discharging goods out of holds but also for seeing them into sheds or onto lorries as part of their contract with RML. To fulfil this commitment they permanently employed quay foremen – additional casual foremen would be taken on if work demanded – whose job it was to engage and supervise quay gangs at the White's Call. In this they paralleled the duties of a shipworker but, I believe, their work was made more difficult by the lower status of quay gangs: it was harder and became increasingly harder over time, to hold onto good men and to form cohesive gangs. Nevertheless, quay foremen sought to build up a consistency amongst their gangs, and ensure their sphere of operations proceeded smoothly. It was significant though that however competent or experienced a quay foreman was he would never take over the work of a shipworker who was absent perhaps through illness. Until his return his place would always be taken by one of the ship's top hands.

Although a much smaller work force, the ship gangs had the edge in many respects: they passed through the areas where quay gangs worked, knew the nature of the work and knew that they could take it on if required. Quay gangs saw ship gangs go up the gangway and disappear; for years they could have spent their working lives alongside ships without ever having seen into a hold. Quay gangs worked in the open in view of shed gangs and all other gangs stretched along the quays. They knew each other's work, knew that they were interchangeable and that they were essentially porters who could be equally well employed at any of the great London wholesale markets. They were always part of a wider community on view to visitors, inspectors – and top hands.

Ship gangs worked in isolation, even the gangs themselves were split up between downholders and barge hands, they were never happy when a second gang was introduced into their hold, preferring to maintain their exclusivity even to the holds they worked. Ship work was specific: general cargo gangs in fact worked a range of very specific cargoes, needed specific ways of working, using particular types of equipment to move them involving their own particular dangers. Many cargoes always left the docks by water on lighters and never came into contact with quay gangs. Commodities which did leave by road necessarily came in, in manageable units such as crates or boxes. There were specific dangers or considerations in a hold environment: removing hatch covers, swinging crane hooks in a confined space and methods of working that were outside the experience of quay gangs. None of these problems were beyond the wit of quay gangs, as the introduction of Whites during and after the War had proved, but simply that the work was beyond their normal experience – and ship gangs were keen to keep it that way.

When the two forms of labour came together, when cargoes were off-loaded onto the quay instead of into lighters in other words, it was always the ship gang that had the controlling influence. In place of the four barge hands, when working onto the quay, a ship gang deployed just two pitch hands whose function it was to release the sets as they came over and to replace whatever tackle was involved back on the crane hook. In this way goods were delivered on to the quay at the rate that the ship gang worked; how fast the quay gang removed the items was up to them, the ship gang's pay rates were unaffected. Pitch hands effectively established a part of the ship work on the quay – quay gangs never imposed onto the ship.

This was particularly the case when gangs were loading exports and where safety was an important factor. Quay gangs delivered goods to the side of the ship for pitch hands to build up into sets for the crane to deliver to their downholders. When gangs were loading goods of a fixed unit size the men in the hold had confidence that each set was well constructed, was of a consistent size and was unlikely to cascade on top of them because it had been constructed by the mates they drank with. Fundamental to all this of course was the fact that the crane driver belonged to the ship gang and it was his rate of working that ultimately established the rhythm of the men – both ship gang and by extension, the quay gang.

This segregation of work was continually being eroded under the influence of the National Dock Labour Scheme and later decasualisation but for a while RML and FW maintained into the 1950s a distinction which was probably older than the docks themselves.

*   *   *

PLIMSOLL LINES

Ships were always trimmed of course so that they were weighted towards the stern to keep their propeller in the water but Head Office in the City liked to know this detail was being maintained. Plimsoll readings had to be taken F(forward), A(aft) and M(Mean) by the ship's clerk each morning for the 'Morning Report' for a runner to take to the Dock Office to be 'phoned up to the City. Essentially, it gave a broad indication of how much had been discharged the previous day.

My memory of general transit sheds is inextricably linked with apples; they were our largest regular commodity to leave by road. Plenty of other items passed through the sheds but mostly in small, easy to handle shipments leaving no lasting impression.

Apples, amongst these bagged and boxed quay cargoes stood out partly because of their importance after the War and partly because they could arrive in such vast quantities. Some RML fresh fruit and vegetables were bound for Covent Garden but a lot went to Spitalfields or Fulham markets and either went there directly or after storing for a few days in a shed. In general, it was worth an importer getting his consignment out within three days - storage rates were cheaper over this period - but if the tradesman was gambling on an upturn in the market, perhaps a holiday was in sight, it might be worth delaying its collection. The freshness of most fresh fruit was a lesser consideration. Traders were able to work the system much more deliberately than was possible with goods leaving by barge. Sometimes in later years, markets were so flat that it was easier to ignore the fruit, let the shed foreman have it condemned by the Port Health Authorities and just pay the bills for disposal. The sheds had become by this time a more considered part of wholesale warehousing.

Immediately after the War though, crates of apples hardly touched the quay so great was the Nation's desire for fresh fruit. Importers could sell all they could get and lorries would be queuing to rush their load across to a market. Tens of thousands of apples arrived from North America: Winesaps from New Westminster, Rowland Beauties from Vancouver and the United States, Newtons from Portland. (Winesaps, we were told, being a particularly soft fruit were sent up North where they were appreciated by people who drank soft water and had rotten teeth).The original containers for apple shipments were barrels and so they were sold by volume not weight or number.

After the War apples were sent over in slatted wooden crates weighing around 40-42lbs but the real measurement was still by capacity, namely one bushel. A great deal of standardisation had been going on amongst the American fruit industry and by this time all United States crates were of uniform shape as well as capacity. Under the same rationalising influence, Canada had also standardised its crates, but to a different set of dimensions, they were just as easy to handle but coopers engaged upon replacing damaged slats, had to check where a shipment came from and prepare their timber accordingly – there was no time to modify slats once the fruit started coming through the sheds.

Because of these handy bushel sized units, fruit could be stored in some of the more awkward corners of a ship's hold space, typically down the long narrow passages that ran alongside the accommodation blocks on ships designed with a shelter deck, uncomfortable work, running each individual box a third the length of the ship in order to gain the hatchway. Alternatively meat ships sometimes were ordered to pick up fruit as the Government sought to balance the Nation's diet; crates could easily be stored and removed from lockers using gravity rollers to send consignments out through the narrow locker doors. Eighty, one bushel crates were taken out at a time on large square boards using a 'chandelier' with four hooks each of which was linked into eyes at the corner of the board. Off-loading was straightforward.

Once on the quay, gangs using porter's trolleys ran them fourteen or sixteen at a time to their mark. Within a decade the boards were lowered directly onto electric scooters and the whole set driven to its mark or straight into the shed.

Importing thousands of seemingly identical boxes of any commodity was always susceptible to confusion but the stevedoring gangs in America who loaded apples came up with an ingenious arrangement for distinguishing different consignments. Each box had on one side or one end a bright cheerful advertising label for the farm or co-operative of origin but as two or more importers might be taking goods from the same source, the labels could not be used directly to differentiate them. Instead the labels were used as a simple binary code, the first consignment all had their labels showing 'label out', the next all turned to the wall 'label in' so that, standing in the hold with a copy of the ship's manifest, gangs and supervisors could easily see the extent of each consignment. However awkwardly consignments were fitted into ships' lockers or even passages, quay gangs and clerks were presented with complete consignments which could be systematically off-loaded and stored in a shed bay or taken to the importer's waiting lorries. You had to hand it to those American export gangs.

There was another useful concept, now probably long forgotten, which related to the size of consignments and that was the evolution of the 'carload' as a measure of capacity. Looking back, it was as if American fruit exporters were using the capacity of a container before containers existed, perhaps they were defining it. One carload became standardised as meaning eight hundred crates – US or Canadian - that is eight hundred bushels, presumably a normal load for American trucks (British lorries collecting apples from the docks more typically carried 640 crates). For a couple of decades around the time of the Second World War, orchards, exporters, shippers and the London wholesale trade all used the carload as a standard unit, which helped not only the gangs in the docks sort out consignments but also helped ships' masters to allocate hold space.

The employment of the carload was a mark of increasing maturity in the North American fruit trade. In the past, farms had sent what they picked with only a rough form of grading and London importers and traders, sometimes bartering on the quayside, would employ a 'tapstick' to give impartial assessment of each parcel of crates. With small, local deals, variations in quality within a shipment were not important, they could be assessed and traded over directly but as selling became centred on Covent Garden, the paperwork involved for the shipping companies, distinguishing between half a dozen crates at one grade then twenty at another, became impracticable. RML had insisted, by the time I joined them that only consignments of a minimum of one carload would be accepted and that each must be of the same type and quality apple. This was in any case in accordance with trends; crops were becoming predictable, the quality was rising as better trees were planted and the new chain stores and supermarkets wanted larger, more uniform fruit.

By the late fifties, gluts were occurring in the markets and shore gangs were regularly seen clearing decaying and abandoned consignments from the sheds. Shipping companies tried to stabilise the trade by keeping in touch with each other about their shipments and advised their clients accordingly. This rapid change in status for the humble apple, from a highly desirable black market commodity to an every day item, was accompanied by another trend: apples began to be packed in cardboard cartons and the sight of coopers sweating at the back of sheds to keep up with the stream of damaged crates soon became a thing of the past; a whole aspect of the coopers' craft disappeared from the docks as crates became less common, and they had seemed at one time indispensable to apple shipments.

Back in the forties, demand for apples was insatiable and the quay gangs responded with sustained physical effort, matching that of the ship gangs. Equipment was basic yet the gangs removed crates as fast as cranes discharged them onto the quay, though lorries could never be loaded fast enough. Lorry drivers were on bonuses and the race was on each time a fruit ship berthed, to be the first to get to their parcel to market. The quay gangs with FW all had to use porter's trolleys for although electric scooters were in use with some companies, notably Scruttons, their availability was erratic and FW gave the impression that they were rather a luxury, they seemed in no hurry to acquire their own. The trolleys the gangs used were 'improved' by having two sticks of wood wedged between the metal bars of the foot plate to extend the carrying area – sometimes properly constructed toe boards were available but these were like gold dust – and this modification allowed larger boxes or cartons to be held securely.

With sixteen crates piled up, it was no mean feat just to get the trolleys moving but in fact they were always pushed at the half trot so as to get over the tracks and ruts on the quays. If the boxes were for immediate delivery, once they had been tallied at their mark on the quay and ascribed to an importer, a delivery gang would take over and run them into the shed along to where the lorry was waiting at the back bay. The man running the trolley was called a 'trucker' and when he reached the bay another member of the gang known as a 'pusher' would be waiting to help get the trolley up onto the gang plank and into the lorry. It is worth pausing here just to emphasise this detail of constant aggravation. The heights of the bays may have been the same as when most goods left the sheds on the back of a cart or maybe lorries had got taller but whatever the reason men were always faced with an uphill shove at the end of their run. It seems never to have occurred to management to do something about this, perhaps it was considered too trivial but for the truckers and pushers it was an unavoidable irritation with every delivery run they made.

As the trucker returned to the quay the pusher helped the driver sort and arrange the boxes. This was all done at a lively pace and if importers were getting their lorries up in time, up to thirteen thousand crates a day could be sorted and dispatched. Once there were surpluses in the market though, importers were less enthusiastic about collecting and delivery gangs would find themselves kicking their heals waiting for promised lorries to appear.

There were times when lorry drivers themselves were keen to get fruit onto their vehicles and out of the docks, and not just for bonuses. In the early years after the War, especially before Christmas, the black market in apples was thriving and every visit to the Royals gave less scrupulous drivers the possibility of a few extra boxes. The usual technique, at least the one that was known and looked out for, was this: a driver would say how many crates he was taking from his boss's consignment and the dock pass would be made out for this number, typically six hundred and forty arranged eight wide, eight high by ten long. With the help of the pusher, the first couple of tiers were set out correctly, but in a special way. These first few rows were the time when the tally clerk supervising the loading was most likely to be watching. Once he had seen the way the crates were being set out, he might have to check another lorry, or might deliberately be distracted by gang members – or might simply lose interest. Now, although these crates were approximately square in plan, they were not precisely so and the slats of wood that made up the sides bowed slightly outwards, which meant that by laying the first rows loosely bulge to bulge, there was space enough to fit in an extra row when placed flat to flat, making sure of course that the last exposed rows seen from the back followed the original pattern. If the clerk was not watching absolutely every lorry loaded, or if he just accepted the total the driver told him, the dodge was easy enough. With the extra rows in place and a tarpaulin hastily thrown over to disguise any inconsistencies it was difficult to see what was going on; a conscientious clerk could order a lorry to be unloaded again if he was suspicious but he had to realise that smuggling was going on and be brave enough to order a recount. It may seem trivial now to be concerned about a few crates of apples but for a time it reached epidemic proportions and one Christmas around 1950, two thousand crates were 'lost' in one week from the '*Durango*'.

The problems of covering the continuous loading of lorries six or more at a time, were exacerbated by the post-War labour shortages: there were days when only two or three tally clerks turned up for their Call, with employers looking for a hundred and fifty. Apples packed in large quantities of uniform crates could lead to extremely chaotic situations, with every importer wanting his supply first, especially at a shed which was provided with a good number of pads; all day a gang might be running apples into six or more lorries for different importers once they had been organised on the quay and released. In order to keep an effective check on crates leaving five holds, something like thirty or forty tally clerks might be needed, seeing them off the ship, sent to their mark then loaded onto the lorries, some clerks working for RML others for FW. The reality might be that only six to ten men were available. It was also clear to employers that some tally clerks were negligent, others dishonest but they had no option other than to employ them. Working thousands of near identical units, it was not surprising that opportunities existed for men determined to make a bit of extra cash.

Gradually supplies increased during the fifties so that smuggling apples was no longer profitable, then an odd thing happened. RML transported fruit only from the Pacific Coast of North America, with other companies working the Eastern Seaboard. Suddenly, on the Atlantic Coast, stevedores refused to load goods bound for Britain during normal working hours; they had enough local work to keep them busy and decided that if Britain wanted their exports they could afford to pay for them at overtime rates. Farmers from East and Middle America were not happy; their produce suddenly became less competitive, so they switched their exporting to the Pacific ports. Overnight, what had been a steady, medium sized trade for RML suddenly became an inundation with ships filled to the gunwales with American apples. The market was established in Britain, so masters were happy to collect this extra trade but when the ships arrived at the docks, sheds and quays were swamped with apples; different types, different grades, different importers' marks. This situation only lasted a short time, the East Coast stevedores realised that they were doing themselves out of work but it left an indelible impression on those of us managing these freak events. Visions of sheds overflowing with apples, ship's clerks attempting to match heaps of fruit to importers' marks, while the coopers, Joe and Jack, seemed permanently submerged behind a mountain of damaged, spilling crates - and still the cranes kept them coming. The situation might only have lasted a short time but the nightmares went on for a good while longer.

*   *   *

COCHL

If I've got the derivation right, a 'cochl' literally means a 'spoonful' and it was a word much bandied around by runners and representatives of the wholesale fruit and vegetable trade, especially towards Christmas. In this context the word had come to mean a small basket of samples, a couple of apples, oranges, some vegetables and perhaps even a banana or two, offered as a sweetener to us clerks to help shipments speed their way through the docks and out onto the market stalls. With produce hard to come by after the War, a cochl could be a genuine incentive to help clerks upgrade their families' Christmas but although promises came thick and fast from the runners in the lead up to the holidays, I don't know anyone who actually received one once each consignment had been cleared.

172

Gangs hated onions: they had nothing going for them, except perhaps the shortness of the season. RML ships would typically bring three shipments from Chile in March, hoping they would beat Egyptian onions for the new season. Onions came in wooden boxes shaped like shallow trays with long slats stretching down their length and holding 70lbs. During the voyage the onions swelled slightly making the tightly packed crates 'belly'. The timber used for these crates were very brittle, thin slats and this inherent vulnerability was compounded by Chilean exporters seeming to use the smallest tacks they could find to hold the sections together. The consequence was that onion trays were always very fragile and for each shipment there might be a hundred thousand loose onions rolling around the holds, being trodden and slipped on by the gangs. In that confined space, eight brawny downholders would be working with tears permanently streaming down their faces. Needlemen did their best, gathering loose onions into sacks for the coopers to re-crate but it was impossible to keep up with the general disintegration.

Loaded in Chile, the trays would each have contained carefully graded sizes, 90's meant ninety in a crate, 180's, a hundred and eighty in a crate, and so on. These were all precisely listed on each importer's consignment but through the mayhem of discharging, the coopers repacked whatever needlemen could collect; on a good day if there was time, some sort of rudimentary classifying might be attempted but generally onions were arriving too fast and in too great numbers. The real answer was to advise the Chilean exporters that they needed to upgrade their trays to North American standards but this was never done. It was less troublesome, it seemed to apologise to importers and blame their arbitrary batches on docker clumsiness – as if gangs enjoyed days spent working in an atmosphere of onion essence.

The ultimate insult for the gangs though, was their take home pay. All boxed and crated imports were paid according to the number worked, taking no account of size or frailty of the packaging: eighty to one hundred boxes of apples could be taken out as a set whereas anything more than about thirty trays of onions risked a total collapse of the load. It may sound a trivial point when explained to someone away from the action but to a ship's clerk trying to defend a patently absurd situation, this formed a major aspect of his job. For a day's work, perhaps fifteen thousand cartons of apples might be off-loaded compared with seven thousand trays of onions, a poor reward for miserable work.

For the vast range of imported goods which were in boxes or crates, nothing was standardised except the rates of pay, so whether men were working strong bushel crates of apples, trouble free cartons of tinned goods or disintegrating onion trays, pay rates made no distinction; import gangs' financial returns were effectively determined by packaging from around the world. As an extreme example, Royal Mail Lines' ships occasionally carried consignments of citrus fruit. When they came from North America, because of their higher water content and therefore density, exporters kindly put oranges and grapefruits in slightly less than bushel size crates, to maintain the unit weight of around forty pounds. Brazil, on the other hand, from where RML also collected shipments had a different solution: they decided to double the size of the boxes to around two bushels or eighty pounds. Men quickly used up their vocabulary of expletives trying to man-handle these cumbersome crates down the narrow passages of a shelter deck or out through locker compartments. Needless to say, these Brazilian crates were made out of the same thin, brittle slats held together with tiny tacks as Chilean onions boxes and the results of working them were equally unrewarding.

I've talked about the disintegration of crates so I ought to mention the Furness, Withy coopers who had the task of reconverting sacks of fruit and shattered crates back into merchandise. The senior partner was Joe Lawless* who learnt his trade well before the War and who always assumed the highest standards right up until his retirement – by which time, with piece work just a memory, his way of working was considered eccentric. As import ships might have berthed anywhere in the docks, Joe had to maintain his own portable workshop and once he knew where the vessel was heading, he and Jack Blackman, his assistant, would set up their trestle tables at the back of a shed ready for the onslaught. They knew what cargo was coming in and from which country and by experience would know what size slats were needed to reconstruct damaged crates. These he got from Furness, Withy supplies over in the Surrey Commercial Docks, telling them quantities and dimensions and the company accepted his judgement.

Needlemen not only collected the spilt fruit but also broken fragments of crates which were passed onto the coopers, not to save timber but to try and reconstruct trays or crates back to importers' standards. Each crate bore its exporter's mark stamped on one or both ends and by getting hold of a piece of wood bearing this mark, a new crate could be built around it. They could then select from the piles of sound fruit or onions, ones which would be acceptable for the markets.

Sometimes, if marked pieces could not be found, they would knock one end out of a sound tray, if it bore a mark at both ends, put in a blank, then use the Odd marked piece on a newly constructed crate. Joe and Jack had no overseers but they knew it was their job to save the company money – and

*Joe's son, Terry, was a tally clerk in those days but neither of them liked the way things were going with Terry deciding he'd be better off as a boxing promoter. There seemed no acknowledgement from above for Joe and Jack's commitment, it was assumed that that was what coopers did. Once Devlin had been introduced and piece work disappeared, it was considered a reasonable day's work if a cooper knocked up fifty of these trays.

174

reconstructing almost entire consignments saved the company money. As sound items were collected they would be respectably crated into specific importer's lots, while those left over, of odd sizes or bruised were sorted and separately crated to be sold off as seconds. There was always a market for substandard goods in the days of austerity and they were gathered not by needlemen who aimed to gather good stock but by 'sweepers' who collected items on the borderline between merchandise and rubbish. Each of these substandard crates full or part filled would be separately marked, its contents recorded, then sold off to traders at much reduced prices. Although the whole procedure was immensely labour intensive, it was still more economic than sending the whole lot to a dump – but that was only so long as Joe and Jack were prepared to work like slaves. This they did because it was a tradition of their craft and between them they would have made or rebuilt up to a thousand trays a day.

The importation of melons was as precisely timed as that for onions but for different reasons. The Chilean melon season almost coincided with that of onions and shipments of the fruit could be expected from mid-February through to the end of March. Melon boxes were smaller, squarer and much easier to handle. The problem lay in timing; masters would be touring the ports looking for cargoes and there could be a consignment of melons looking to be exported. Everyone knew the shortness of the season and after a certain date masters would refuse to sign a guarantee that they would deliver the fruit in a safe and sound condition. Melons were no good to Chile sitting on their quays and as Britain's appetite for fresh fruit was insatiable, if there were hold space, a master might risk a shipment. This was invariably a mistake but not one that ship's officers had to deal with; nearly ripe melons in Valparaiso meant ripe fruit in transit and collapsed refuse in the docks. Melons brought in after the agreed date had to be inspected by the dock's health officer and usually the entire consignment had to be written off, leaving a shore gang the unwholesome task of getting it into a rubbish barge. Sometimes however, importers or more probably their agents, would claim that the crates could be 'garbled', in other words sorted with sound fruit re-boxed as a way of off-setting losses and then it became the responsibility of the ship gang to pick their way through the rotting load. The problem lay not primarily with the collapsed fruit, nor with fragile crates but with the flies; for some reason over ripe melons produced clouds of flies that rose in drifts and hovered in a tormenting swarm over the fruit. As the hatch covers were taken off, so the flies would swarm. If the infestation were considered too bad, the hold could be fumigated but this was expensive and time consuming, especially for men on piece work. One limitation which also had to be borne in mind was that fumigation only dealt with the top layers. As soon as they were removed the flies came out again every bit as invasive as before - with a flat cap and buttoned up shirt as the only protection. On one occasion, a Liverpool company reckoned it could salvage enough fruit to make it worth their while taking a lorry up to Liverpool instead of throwing it all into a refuse barge. The ship gang had the job of selecting the 'good' melons and off-loading them onto the quay. It was one of those ridiculous decisions that it was embarrassing to have to be involved with. I had to accompany the health inspector down into the hold sometime after the gang had been set to work and while we were all there battling, breathing, choking on the swarms of insects, trying to justify the work, one of the gangers just went for me. The flies, the collapsed fruit and the smell were just too much for the poor man; he was at his wits end and just needed to tear me limb from limb as an expression of what he thought of that managerial decision. As this gang and I were normally on good terms - I had a great respect for the way they worked and they knew how appalled I was at what they had been asked to do – it helped to see the other downholders rush to restrain him. (It also helped that the Health Officer present was a 6' 4" ex-PTI - Physical Training Instructor, RN). I had become for this ganger, the accessible manifestation of 'Authority' and he just wanted to cast his vote – the real decision makers were, of course, never to be seen.

When the carefully sorted melons eventually arrived at Liverpool, they were immediately condemned by the health officer there and RML had to bear the cost of sorting and handling.

To distant managers nice distinctions between different fruits and their containers were of no interest, their concerns were with bigger issues I suppose but it wouldn't have taken much to have eliminated large areas of discomfort for the gangs, if there had been the will.

*   *   *

FRUIT COCKTAIL

Customs Officers never went on board a ship unless something serious like drugs was suspected. For the three annual rent sheds Royal Mail Lines used on the south side of Queen Victoria Dock there were four Officers, one to each shed checking exports being stored there and imports coming into the country through the sheds. The fourth Officer 'floated' between the sheds usually concerning himself with exports or travellers' belongings.

Customs worked 8am to 5pm, ships often worked to 7pm so an Officer gained two hours overtime: so long as a ship was working an Officer had to be on hand.

All goods had to be assessed against a complicated list of dutiable goods; one particular oddity that stuck in my mind was the need for them to open sample cans of fruit cocktail to check the proportion of cherries in them – too many and the cans came under a higher level of taxation. At a time when these imports were considered real luxury items, there was not a little envy among the work force seeing the Officers opening the cans, counting the red bits then consuming the contents.

176

The only case of rum smuggling I can remember concerned Tommy Tinlegs. He was a PLA clerk who had served in the Navy during the War and when his ship was torpedoed had spent so long in the water that both his legs had had to be amputated. A crooked Customs Officer and he concocted a plan, so the gossip went, for Tommy to smuggle bottles of rum out of the docks in his artificial legs. They were caught and duly convicted. Perhaps Tommy felt the Nation owed him something and he would have settled for a few bottles of rum.

Docks were designed for the very purpose of minimising smuggling in dutiable goods and the high dock wall, Customs Officers, security guards and police as far as we clerks could see, did a pretty efficient job achieving this end. If ever we had a shipment of rum or tobacco our only concern was to get it passed over to Customs Officers, lightermen or shed foremen as quickly as possible. If smuggling took place after that, it was outside our responsibility – we were onto the next cargo. It was far easier for dockers to smuggle less valuable items like copper or quarters of meat, so the only widespread and regular smuggling of rum took place in dockers' bellies. The authorities assumed that men who handled alcohol would drink some of it: police were content so long as men could get themselves out of the docks and onto a bus.

Royal Mail Lines had the rum trade from Jamaica, someone else had Barbados, and although consignments took up modest hold space, they were valuable supplements to the main task of transporting local sugar. How long RML had had the trade I don't know but it was a very long standing contract which only ended when Tate and Lyle transferred their sugar imports to their own fleet. After that, it was uneconomic to pick up a few casks of rum from Jamaica and from then on it was carried by Geist on their banana boats.

Traditionally rum arrived in casks ranging in size from a puncheon holding 110 gallons (12 cwts or 1.8 to the ton), hogsheads 50 gallons (4 to a ton), barrels of 40 gallons (5 to a ton) and firkins capable of holding 16 gallons but which, as they simply held whatever was left over in a vat were usually only partly filled. Given their variable shape, seepage and evaporation, these measures were ever only nominal in practise.

From an early date after the War, rum was shipped in bottles as well as casks. The belief was that with the curtailing of rum shipments during the conflict, all the casks in Jamaica were used up and even after the War with hold space at a premium, shipments of empty casks back to Jamaica were halted, so exporters there turned increasingly to using bottles. Most of our shipments were a mixture of the two, with bottles in the ascendant. Like the sailing barge, barrels seemed integral to the traditional image of the docks but over a couple of decades after the War both barges and barrels were to disappear.

All casks seemed old, as if manufacture had ended years before. Some of them were alarmingly asymmetrical – perhaps the result of having been broken down for a return journey to save hold space and not having been reformed properly; no two were ever the same, which caused Customs men computational nightmares as they tried to work out exact volumes. It took about ten years, apparently, for a cask to make a round trip (at least a year in Jamaica, seven or more in the Brandy Vaults or other cellars) so that many of them may have been Victorian, all of them functioning adequately - an object lesson in recycling. Coopers believed that the timber of older barrels became brittle, but how old - fifty years or a hundred and fifty – was anybody's guess, so long as they could plug the cracks dating was academic.

Small shipments often had casks set amongst the sugar in the lower hold by the hatchway but larger consignments were stored separately usually on the Shelter (Upper Tween) deck. Most rum arrived in forty gallon barrels, stowed 'on the run', so that they could be rolled to the hatchway opening but with each delivery, there were always a few puncheons which stood on their ends in the hatchway itself, often used to help brace the barrels behind. Because they were so heavy, it made sense for a crane in Jamaica to simply drop them into position and for another to haul them out in London, so puncheons were always the last in, first out. Casks were stowed away from the hatchway, with the hatchway itself and the spaces beside the casks filled with easy cargoes such as bags of turmeric, ginger, pimentos or quasha chips (used to make insecticide before DDT). If the hatchway had been filled with scrap metal, a wooden bulkhead would have been constructed to prevent damaging the barrels during the voyage. In these upper holds, barrels normally filled the height of the hold, usually five rows on top of each other.

A considerable amount of timber work might also have been introduced to brace the barrels in position, particularly when they were stowed on the run and this would have to be dismantled by the shore gang. The slightly larger hogsheads though, were always stowed on end and for some reason always put at the furthest end of the hold. To get hogsheads to the hatchway and presumably to get them in initially, demanded a disproportionate level of manhandling; all right on smooth welded holds, not so good on the more usual riveted and braced older ceilings. Fortunately hogsheads were relatively uncommon.

To help downholders get casks to the hatchway, the men were allowed to use the ship's winches together with a set of cam hooks. Each hook was placed at opposite ends of the cask and the tension of the winch caused the hooks to bite into the wood and keep them in place. In fact each pull of the winch drew out four at a time using four sets of hooks. Traditionally this was the only way cam hooks could be used to move casks – to drag them, never to lift them – because it had always been assumed that the weight of a full barrel would be too much for the timber.

To lift the barrels and hogsheads, the technique was basically the same as that for lifting sugar bags; because of the bulge on barrels, it was easy enough to wrap a continuous loop of rope around both ends as they lay on their sides and fix it to a crane hook. The rope thus acted with the metal bands to keep the staves tightly together during the period of greatest strain as they were being raised out of the hold. Once again, casks were moved four at a time (six or eight if the casks were smaller) using the 'brothers', two large hooks each attached to a two foot length of rope in turn joined to a metal ring. This ring was placed on the crane hook and stayed there for the duration of the work, while onto each of the hooks were set two rope loops holding two casks. By using two sets of brothers, eight barrels could be lifted at a time and once more the greatest danger in this otherwise straightforward operation was the risk to fingers by the tightening rope as the crane hook changed from lowering to lifting and the eight loops rapidly fed onto the hooks. The pitch hands waiting on the quay by contrast, had only to release these ropes and slip them back onto the brothers for the downholders to re-use, a far less tricky operation.

During the War, cam hooks had been used to lift out metal barrels of oil from holds without using a rope loop and during the late forties the same method was tried on casks. It was found that one set of hooks was sufficient for barrels, two for hogsheads and puncheons and the more prudent use of ropes gradually declined. If this caused structural damage to the casks importers did not complain, perhaps they knew that casks were being phased out and a few extra gouges would give them added character set on patios as water butts in later life.

Something like a hundred barrels a day could be discharged and these would have to be set out on the quay by quay gangs. Rum was a very variable commodity and a shipment never consisted of one quality with one destination. Varieties of type (dark through to light), of maturity (shown by year markings) and all from different estates, had to be matched to importers' listings. This was a major job for the quay gangs, carried out under the gimlet eye of a Customs Officer. Initially all the barrels were set on the quay and their marks examined by everyone with an interest in the contents, from ship's clerk and Custom's Officer to thirsty gangers. The more disinterested observers tried to find some correspondence between what they observed and what the ship's manifest listed. This was never easy: no universal system of marking existed, each estate using its own key, which made sense to them and presumably, the importer but for us, faced with poorly stamped marks with worn or scuffed patches, accurate identification was almost impossible. In this confusion, the casks were vulnerable. Customs Officers would be sounding the barrels, coopers repairing them, tally clerks trying to count them while quay foremen and ship's clerks, anxious to get them beyond their company's jurisdiction, tried to decipher the symbolism. Meanwhile, the quay gangs would be shuffling the casks around according to instructions but with their main attention fixed upon gaining a few 'tasters'. Now these men were not fools, they had no intention of drinking rubbish and it was the commonly held belief that if anyone had succeeded in sorting out the marks, it was the quay gangs – after all, their vested interests were the most immediate. By making two small gimlet holes in their chosen cask, usually one of the remoter ones, air could get at the top and the ambrosia collected beneath. Someone would have remembered to bring in one or more of the old wooden meat skewers which neatly plugged the holes and rum was then available on tap. If a supervisor appeared or the barrel had to be moved, the skewers could be broken off with no one any the wiser. The entire enterprise was a constant and long running game of cat and mouse – as long, presumably, as rum had been coming into London.

Meanwhile the ship's clerk would be trying to get the casks moving onto the dozen or so barges, sometimes with a coastal steamer or two, to get the shipment beyond RML's jurisdiction; once the receipts had been signed and collected from the lighterman, everyone could breath a sigh of relief, but in order to achieve this, the marks had first to be sorted. Each craft had been hired by one importer, some would only receive three or four barrels, but each importer expected a precise consignment of type, maturity and colour. Every cask would be examined by the cooper, passed to the Customs Officer, checked by the clerk against the tally clerk's identification and then committed to a barge. Obviously the most desirable situation was to call up each barge in turn and accord to it its correct and full consignment but in practice it was more common for just a few barrels to be identified by deduction or elimination, loaded onto the barge then told to stand off until more of that mark appeared. The longer the casks sat on the quay, the greater the 'evaporation' with a corresponding increase in general lapses of concentration.

One Custom's Officer – and only one, all the others were very strict – actively encouraged consumption; perhaps he reasoned that if men were drinking from the casks he allowed, there was more supervision. I had known him though, in the Navy, which was where he got his taste for rum and I suspect that he just wanted to be in on the action.

In any case, he would set up two firkins between the men, one with 70% proof, the other 139% and call out "Men on this side, boys on the other". Through all this, fitfully the work progressed. Lock up barges would get their consignments and set off for the Brandy Vaults, the Pickford and Hayes Group Wharf or Cotton Wharf while the coasters would be loading bound for Liverpool, Leith or Glasgow.

While the supervisors worked hard to maintain order amongst the quay gangs and discover order amongst the barrel markings, the FW coopers, Joe and Jack, worked physically hard sounding and repairing the casks. A shipment of rum might consist of three thousand barrels, perhaps one thousand from each of three holds, and the first job the cooper had to do was to 'sound' each one. Inevitably during the length of time the rum had been in the cask, some would have (genuinely) evaporated, sometimes seeped out, leaving an air pocket. With the barrel on its side, the air pocket would sit just under the greatest bulge of the staves, like a huge spirit level bubble. By tapping this midriff area with a two pound hammer and listening to the sound, Joe could decide if the rum loss was unacceptably high. Clearly no-one wanted to pay the full import duty on one quarter full, or half empty barrels so hollow sounding casks were marked with a cross in chalk for more accurate assessment by the Customs Officer. Once all the casks had been off-loaded and sorted to their marks, the officer would inspect them then turn his attention to those that the cooper had ullaged. Each cask in turn would be set up on 'scotches' bung uppermost and using his 'flogger' - a narrow mallet of lignum vitae on a bamboo handle – Joe would tap each side of the bung until it popped out. The customs man then took a dip stick to measure the depth and using a set of tables, estimated the likely spirit content. This had to be approximate, even with full casks because of the variety of shapes and distortions but with partially filled barrels, short of draining the contents into a measuring tank, accurate estimates were impossible. Nevertheless, there were rules of thumb requiring measurements of girth, diameters and length to check against the set of tables and in an era before calculators, the arithmetic could be tricky and time consuming - which conveniently played into the hands of the quayside consumers. In these early days, Customs was only interested in the damaged or ullaged casks, with spot tests on the others for alcohol content. Later as casks became rarer, Officers insisted on measuring every one which again was fortunate for the local connoisseurs.

In between this assessing, coopers also, as a matter of urgency, had to repair damage as they discovered it. If one of the staves was cracked it was usual to fill the gap with spills of twisted newspaper then tack a piece of lead or 'togger' (tin covered zinc) over the crack using short tacks that would not pierce through to the rum but would help prevent further cracking. This might be a major undertaking, depending upon the state and number of damaged staves but the rum that remained had to be secured. Alternatively, the staves might be intact but rum might be seeping from the joints and it was then the cooper's job to close them: first he had to rock the barrel to and fro on its booge or bulge, until he had sufficient momentum to swing it up onto the end he wanted to work on (puncheons and hogsheads needed two men to execute this) then, with a 'driver' placed on a barrel hoop, he would force the hoop downwards with his 2lb hammer, drawing the staves closer together. This required some skill; hoops had to be kept horizontal and had to be worked from the centre of the cask out, each one though, driven towards the booge. Some of the older casks were already misshapen and working them with cam hooks would have done nothing to restore their symmetry. These could weep badly and sealing the gaps by whorling the hoops could take some fine judgement; in some cases, with the larger hogsheads and puncheons, extra bands might have to be added and the experienced coopers would come to the job armed with a supply of hoops, togger, reeding etc. ready for trouble. Particularly in the process of closing gaps between staves, some casks evolved over their lifetimes into very odd shapes accentuated during their travels by the apparently arbitrary addition of

181

extra hoops.

Sometimes it was the heads of casks that leaked and once again, they would have to be rocked onto their sound ends so that now, reeding or newspaper could be rammed into cracks to reinforce the original packing. And if both heads leaked? He had to work twice as fast. Both Joe and Jack were craftsmen who took their duties seriously out of deference to their craft and tradition – their standing lay in their competence. Incidentally they rejected tasters through the day because accidents were a real threat but at the end of the day there might be one or two reserved by way of celebration.

Once on the 'Gascony', in the confines of the hold so much rum had seeped out during the voyage that the downholders became light headed just working among the fumes. Inevitably with any shipment there would be some seepage, the gangs accepted it as one of the few perks of the job to be set against all the unwholesome smells they normally had to work through. This particular shipment was exceptional though and having downholders drunk as they worked the cargo made sure that supervisors earned their wages that afternoon. The pitch hands had to find their share by more traditional means.

Generally speaking, so long as you had committed coopers, barrels and casks were trouble free; they were too big to steal and too strong to damage seriously. The numbers needing cooperage varied considerably from about ten per thousand up to forty or more but casks had a long tradition, were well understood and survived rough handling; they were designed for the demands of the trade. It was bottles that caused the problems.

*   *   *

WATCHERS

If RML were discharging cargoes into PLA sheds RML had to employ a Customs 'watcher' whose job it was to make sure items were not stolen or interfered with on their way to a storage bay . He also had to check the belongings of fee paying passengers. At the end of a working day he would go round with the shed foreman watching him lock all the doors and adding his own Customs lock in case the foreman or others, had designs on the contents.

The significant feature of rum in bottles of course was its accessibility. To men who had already put up with ten years of austerity with no obvious end in sight, the appearance of thousands of bottles of alcohol was just an open invitation; they were even spared the forward planning of having to remember to bring their gimlets. In spite of their best efforts, Customs Officers and supervisors had little hope of restraining men hell bent on making the most of each rare and golden opportunity - the whole process of discharging, sorting and storing, was carried out in a general alcoholic haze. Unfortunately the same confusions took place: importers' marks on the side of cartons were just as hard to interpret as those on casks, colour, maturity and type were just as varied, causing delays which once again played directly into the hands of the epicureans. It was particularly awkward for tally clerks whose job was, of its nature, more cerebral requiring clear heads and accurate recording. The less focussed they became, the longer shipments sat on the quays, the rum more inviting.

There was one occasion when all the cartons had been off-loaded, sorted and stored in the shed. Two lighters arrived both to receive their allotted nine thousand cartons each. Work proceeded for the best part of the day, apparently smoothly, when suddenly they ran out of one of the consignments. The lighterman had monitored six thousand cartons into his barge, the Customs Officer agreed, and there were no more of his mark to be seen anywhere in the shed or on the quay. Three thousand cartons had vanished. They had all been tallied into the shed the day before so they must have gone somewhere and as the horrible possibility dawned, Customs, watchers and supervisors became very worried men – it appeared to be a masterly demonstration of smuggling from under their very noses. After the initial rush of panic they began to look around them and someone noticed that one of the other lighters, unrelated to this consignment, seemed to be sitting uncomfortably low in the water. As soon as they examined it and with a huge sigh of relief, it became clear what had happened: Ben Rylands who had the job of tallying very specific cartons into his lighter was far beyond distinguishing niceties of red or orange estate marks and he accepted whatever was offered. He had tallied fourteen thousand cartons into his lighter and still they kept coming. The next day was spent unloading the entire cargo and re-stowing it into the correct craft.

The very worst shipment was in 1947 when I was a newcomer and just a casual tally clerk. Jamaica was anxious to off-load some of its huge stockpile of rum and the 'Baranca' came in with three thousand barrels and a hundred thousand cartons - a huge shipment which heralded the new primacy of the bottle over the cask. All the top decks were full of rum, someone had thought it a good idea to send so much in one shipment, the gangs knew it was a good idea - and equally the supervisors knew it was madness. No 1

Shed, Royal Victoria Dock had been set aside for this shipment but they couldn't fit it all in. In theory and with Custom's permission, it should have been possible to go over side directly into the waiting lock-up barges but the confusion of types and marks meant that everything had first to be sorted on the quay then set out in the shed. It took a week to get all the rum off the ship all the while those cartons were proving irresistible to parched throats. Rum came over the side on set boards sixty to eighty cartons at a time, had then to be tallied and sorted before the quay gangs could either wheel them to the right shed bays or stack them on the quay. They were using porter's trolleys to move the cartons seven at a time - electric scooters being virtually unknown then. A private security firm had been hired to help maintain order but being unused to the talents of dockers, bottles quickly started to go missing. Right from the outset porters were getting drunk and they were incapable of placing the sorted cartons in the correct bay. They wheeled them everywhere, which was a nuisance but worse, whatever bay they took them to, right or wrong, they frequently crashed the metal foot of the trolley into the bottom of the standing rows of cartons. This was not realised as a problem until the following day when the leaking rum was found to have reduced the stiff cardboard cartons to an alcoholic pulp incapable of supporting the tiers above them. When the doors were unlocked next morning, swathes of tiers were seen crumpled and smashed across the shed floor creating an atmosphere of about 90% proof. Shore gangs had to be brought in to clear up the mess and naturally joined the party while quay gangs were still collecting fresh sets.

Customs men and supervisors found themselves engaged in an exercise of damage limitation, salvaging every bottle still intact, each one having to be given clearance individually. The quay was overflowing with barrels and cartons as yet more were off-loaded. Lighters filled the dock around the 'Baranca' patiently waiting their turn to be called in to receive a couple more packages as they were identified. Customs men were inspecting damaged cartons to see what could be saved, perhaps tying two or three bottles together wrapped up in a soggy, scrap of cardboard with a smeared mark on it somewhere. Sherrif & Co in Ireland were expecting fifty thousand cases delivered by two lighterage companies, each taking twenty five thousand but in the event they would have been lucky to have ended up with forty thousand fairly random bundles.

And still the drinking continued in spite of watchers, supervisors, Customs and police. Many of the men had to be taken to hospital with alcohol poisoning and one man died: it was the worst rum shipment anyone could remember. The only slight compensation was that for a short period afterwards, rum arrived in much smaller quantities with casks once more predominating.

Rum wasn't the only consumable to arrive in casks as they were also used as containers for a range of syrups and juices. When barrels were stored in the upper holds of a ship, irrespective of contents, they were stored 'on the run' in one of two ways:

The easiest to work were when rows of barrels were separated by boards. In this case the lowest row would have been stowed on the ceiling with chocks holding each barrel in place, then planks were placed across them so that the row above it could be rolled up a plank to sit on boards with more chocks to hold them secure. In this way four rows of barrels could be laid on the run, each separated by boarding from rows above and below. A substantial quantity of timber work would normally have to be included to brace the stack but once this was removed on arrival in the docks, it was an easy matter to place a ramp in position and roll the barrels, one at a time down to the hatchway. Better still, if the barrels extended out so as to nearly reach the hatchway, a four foot square table would be erected at a convenient height so that each row of barrels could be rolled down a gentle slope onto the table for the crane to lift. The table height could be adjusted for each row and a very comfortable and controlled discharging could take place with no fear of damage. The big disadvantage in this method was that it required each barrel to have its own chocks, or scotches, to keep it in place and more importantly for the shippers, on most upper decks only four rows could be fitted in.

A second method came in during the fifties and this was to stack each row of barrels directly on the ones below. Only the bottom row needed scotches and so long as a substantial partition was built to contain the shipment, this had the advantage of being able to squeeze in an extra row, making a stack of five interlocking tiers. The problem was off-loading, for once the hatchway had been cleared and the partition removed, the difficulty was to remove each barrel in a controlled way without causing an avalanche. Once again the solution was to construct a table and work two rows at a time but if the cam hooks from the crane were fixed to the top barrel as it came free, it would pendulum violently across the hatchway smashing anything – including itself – and anyone in its path. Instead, by working a ship's winch, cam hooks could be placed into the ends of a lower barrel and very gently pulled out to the hatchway. The barrels above would also move but slowly and help act as dampeners to the overall movement. By working cautiously, barrels could be dragged across the lower levels or across the ceiling with no risk of swinging and with no uncontrolled collapsing of the pile. As an added safety feature, old sacks filled themselves with sacking were often placed so as to soften the fall of one barrel on another or onto the ceiling. None of this eliminated the possibility of barrels cascading or acting as hazardous pendulums but a good gang working with care usually had no serious problems.

For rum both systems worked well, the commodity was valuable with a high rate of pay attracting good gangs willing to take their time working methodically. The difficulties arose with fondants.

During the period of rationing sugar imports were strictly controlled to liberate hold space for more necessary items. Importers were always looking for ways of ducking these restrictions and one of the confectionery trade's methods was to import 'fondant' in barrels. This was a highly viscous paste like the inside of a soft centred chocolate composed mostly of sugar and water; so long as it stayed inside the barrels it was fine. Unfortunately this commodity had a poor rate of pay which meant men worked fast to get a reasonable return and it would often be more careless gangs who worked it. The normal practice for dockers rolling casks was for two men, each with their docker's hook set in the rim at opposite ends of the cask to pull it with the rim running past the hook, something like a child with a hoop. The hook could be used, if necessary, to pull out barrels and set them rolling which, with care, had little ill effects. The whole operation though was vulnerable to poorer gangs hacking and tumbling casks indiscriminately causing the fondant to seep out and this quickly coated the hold, the gang and then the quay in a viscous sludge. From a benign looking little job fondant quickly descended into a very unpleasant, sticky mess.

The worst example of this was not exactly the gang's fault. In No 3 hold of an ex-Liberty ship, three hundred barrels of fondant had been brought in from Jamaica. Now No 3 hold being at the centre of the ship was close to the engines, it was summer and the combination of these two factors, we assumed, caused the barrels to dry out: the staves shrank, the hoops became loose and fondant seeped through cracks on almost every barrel. The gangs started discharging but it was quickly realised that this amount of seepage was excessive and some drastic measures would be needed. The two coopers were called in and they waded through the goo trying to close the seams by hammering down the hoops. They did their best but when the gang returned they were still faced with lifting out three hundred barrels of fondant while standing in six to eight inches of the mess. When the barrels were finally cleared, with relief the gang by-passed the residue and work was begun on the contents of the lower hold. This was emptied in due course and the discharging gang happily left the shore gang to clean up using steam hoses to wash the contaminant into the bilges of the upper hold.

At that moment, a Ministry of Food Inspector arrived and as it was his job to maximise shipments of food for a hungry nation, he decided the fondant was fit for human consumption. The discharge gang was recalled, fresh barrels were obtained and for days the men tried to get the fondant into barrels. They were issued with shovels and the fondant glued itself to the shovels, they tried to scrape the fondant off the shovels into the barrels with pieces of wood and the fondant stuck to the wood – and to their hands and boots, to the coamings and to their clothes. After days of wretched endeavour, they eventually managed to fill between thirty and forty barrels of reclaimed fondant which was finally off-loaded onto the quay. The Ministry of Food's Inspector was notified; he came down examined the barrels and condemned the lot. They were promptly taken away by the rubbish barge.

Fruit juice was also imported in barrels during this period, mainly orange and grapefruit and was subject to similar problems of leakage. Later on the problem was made worse because barrels of juice from the United States were first lined on the inside with wax. The wax sealed the cracks between the staves and thus held the juice more securely - to start with. Unfortunately it also meant that, as the juice was no longer in contact with the wood, the staves could dry out and shrink in transit leaving the wax liner as the only effective seal. As the barrels were being unloaded the wax inevitably cracked and the juice poured out. Up to two thousand casks of fruit juice might be arranged on the quay in long lines according to their marks, and most of them would be leaking, no attempt was made to store the juice in sheds as the PLA didn't want their sheds contaminated.

Two thousand barrels were too many for two coopers to usefully impact; in any case there had been a shipment of rum somewhere in the docks and that had to be their priority. The only answer was to get a couple of needlemen to spend their days hosing down the barrels, first to wash off the tacky, seeping juice but also to wet the staves and hopefully cause them to expand and tighten. This was a very pleasant little job and as the barrels remained standing on the quay over a hot summer's weekend, there was substantial overtime for the lucky pair.

On about two occasions only, a ship arrived with a consignment of raspberry purée in barrels. The quantities were small and should have presented no problems but unfortunately a couple of the barrels on each shipment had damaged heads and were leaking badly. The barrels were placed on the quay and on both occasions in no time at all they were almost hidden beneath swarms of wasps. Where they came from was a mystery and the East End outside the docks must suddenly have become a wasp-free zone - but for the quay gangs their jobs immediately became both unpleasant and painful. Keeping the juice off their hands and face and out of their hair and clothing suddenly became imperative. How much the 'wasp factor' came into the decision making I couldn't say but after these couple of deliveries, raspberry purée shipments disappeared from RML ships.

*   *   *

TURN ROUND TIME

Typically a ship would take five to seven days to discharge and as long or longer to load. Two to two and a half weeks would be assumed for the total time needed to turn a ship round.

On the north side of Victoria Dock behind 'E' and 'F' sheds and along from Royal Mail Lines' Main Office, lay the Tobacco Sheds. Backing onto the great mass of railway tracks and close by the Customs Offices, these solid, brick built sheds were really warehouses in which importers stored their leaf tobacco until it had reached the required state of maturity. Different docks had particular storage and processing facilities, famously for example, the London Dock had its Brandy Vaults and somehow the Victoria Dock had gained grain mills on its south side and tobacco sheds on its north. We clerks had nothing to do with them and so whatever we heard was hearsay, such as the belief that so tight was the security on the movement and bonding of tobacco that far more was lost to the weather because of bomb damage than was ever lost through theft.

Royal Mail Lines occasionally had a consignment of tobacco; a 'Loch' boat from North America sometimes carried one so also did ships of the Holland America Line but the overall throughput for us was low. When it came, leaf tobacco arrived in containers confusingly called 'hogsheads' but which had nothing in common with rum casks; these boxes were constructed out of thin slats of softwood with spaces in between and held together by withies. The overall shape was of a flat truncated cone and they were designed so that when they were stacked by gantry cranes in the sheds, there was good air circulation. Hogsheads were stored like vintage wine, carefully labelled and left to achieve their own type of maturation according to the arts and sciences of the trade. Again this was received information, RML had no direct dealings with these sheds and once a consignment of tobacco was off a ship and being trundled across the quay accompanied by a Customs Officer, responsibility passed to the PLA , we were just pleased to see the last of it

Some of our tobacco imports went straight to WD & HO Wills in Bristol but most went into the sheds and were the property of the many small specialist tobacco companies around London who supplied their own discerning customers. Very occasionally there was a shipment of West Indian leaf tobacco bound into tight, heavy bales held with a tough hessian cloth and these, it was believed, went to the manufacture of local, hand rolled cigars.

Tobacco was not allowed to be discharged onto the quay or to be moved from the quay unless a Customs Officer was present, it was too valuable. If an Officer were delayed, perhaps after lunch, gangs had to fill in working something else, or even just wait if nothing was available, until he arrived. Very occasionally RML had a consignment of made up tobacco, cigarettes, cigars or pipe tobacco and this, of course, was highly desirable for those who wanted to make easy money. In this case Customs did their best, born of many years experience, to get these imports through the docks as quickly as possible and into the Cutler Street bonded warehouse. As a result, most of these deliveries were tightly guarded and incident free but there was one occasion which stood out:

When tobacco arrived made up it was always of a very specialist range, connoisseurs' items you might say – fat Churchillian type, hand made cigars or fancy exotic cigarettes, often in distinctive packaging or presentation cases. No two boxes were ever the same and this had the advantage for those whose job it was to know the consignment, to see immediately if one went missing. This occasion proved to be one such exotic order of perhaps a dozen cases.

With hindsight it did seem as if events were working towards a specific conclusion: destiny appeared to be taking a hand. The ship had been cleared, the holds emptied and although there were normally a few items left over at the end of a voyage, on this occasion there were so many – personal effects, unclaimed parcels of coffee and ginger, a whole miscellaneous assortment - that when they put them into the shed's secure lock up, as was customary, they filled the entire cage. The cage was locked and Customs added their own additional lock as they always did if there were items of interest to them, which ensured that the cage could only be re-opened if a Customs Officer were present. At the same time it was discovered that paperwork for the tobacco shipment was incomplete and Customs refused to take it up to Cutler Street. It was clear that the paperwork would take days to unravel and with no space in the shed's lock-up, it was obvious from the outset that they had a major security problem. The solution was to place the cigars by the side of the cage and employ an experienced security guard to watch the goods constantly while the shed was open and working. No one was happy about the situation but the guard was good and vigilant and it was hard to see what could go wrong. Whenever the sheds were locked, as an additional safety measure, a Customs Officer added his own extra lock, effectively turning the whole shed into a security cage. The goods were obviously vulnerable but the consignment was small and easily overseen by a guard; all eventualities seemed to have been covered.

The guard or 'watcher' knowing that he was going to be there for some time decided to make himself comfortable and put the largest package hard up against the side of the cage so that he could sit on it and use the lock-up as a back rest. All the other packages he gathered around himself close by and there he sat surveying his kingdom of responsibility while not entirely disinterested gangers worked through the shed's other items.

Thus the days passed without incident and at last the paperwork was completed. With considerable relief a group of RML clerks, the shed foreman, PLA and Customs Officers all finally descended on the secure items. Because the watcher was clearly having no problems, they decided first to work their way meticulously through the goods in the lock-up as these had to be made over to the PLA for long term storage. With this out of the way they turned their attention to the tobacco: each box was listed, opened, their contents checked then loaded on the electric scooter ready to be

dispatched to Cutler Street without further delay. Finally they came to the last box, the security guard got off his throne and the Customs Officer
opened it – only to find that it was nearly empty. The poor watcher nearly died on the spot. A case measuring about four feet by three feet by two feet, once full of the highest quality cigars had been successfully eviscerated. Someone had neatly taken the base off the case, emptied it then carefully replaced it. You could have cut the incredulity with a knife. The miserable security guard began apologising, saying he couldn't understand it and so on, but no one suspected him.

   How it was accomplished remained a mystery but on reflection what they assumed happened was that someone hid in the shed as it was locked at lunch time when the watcher was away and spent his hour carefully opening and emptying this largest case. The contents presumably were hidden somewhere else in the shed, to be collected in small batches as they worked other goods. If they had taken the contents of other cases, the guard might have noticed that they had changed position or been tampered with, the alarm would have been raised and getting the items through the dock gates would have been far more difficult. By taking cigars from the case he was sitting on, any disturbance he would have assumed due to himself, giving the thieves plenty of time to get their hoard out. Probably the cigars were all away before anyone knew they were missing. The guard was seen at various warehouses in the area after that but he was never seen working inside the docks again. The cleverness of that job was a considerable embarrassment to the security system.

*   *   *

BOUNDARIES
   Local council boundaries were interesting. The Queen Victoria Dock was securely within West Ham while the Royal Albert was divided unequally between West Ham and East Ham. The King George V though was a patchwork produced by these two boroughs and sections of North Woolwich reaching in from the south which didn't help the situation as Woolwich was part of the LCC whereas East Ham was a county borough. On a day to day basis of course, this was an irrelevance but the word was, maybe apocryphal, that during a sudden emergency, someone with a clear head would be needed to consult a map and decide precisely which fire brigade to call out.

*   *   *

EAST INDIA DOCK
The East India Dock was a very old and small dock suitable for sailing ships but not modern (1950s) vessels. They were mostly used by coastal steamers at this date but our partner company, PSNC, had three ships, 'Somer Isle', 'Cien Fuegos' and 'Eluthera' that could use the facilities, mainly to work sugar consignments. The dock had many cranes that were hydraulic and could only lift 30cwts. In winter they regularly froze requiring the ships to go over to using their derricks.

190

Because meat ships to South America had a real, if declining, secondary role as passenger liners, these vessels had to keep to strict timetables. If ships were to compete still with improving airline schedules, they had to maintain departure times, even if arrivals were more uncertain. Passengers were important to the Company's image and their welfare was a priority.

Twenty year old vessels were subjected to increased insurance premiums and they had to be maintained to a very high standard of fitness. Every two years a ship would have to go into dry dock for a complete overhaul where everything from engine repairs to the removal of barnacles took place. This was an expensive business and if Captain Spinks or his successors had booked a ship into dry dock, it had to be there no matter what other considerations there might be. This was a long term plan and passenger timetables would be arranged to include this contingency. Meat importers though, beyond the intimidation of a Marine Superintendent, were sometimes more casual about working to these deadlines. As the wartime dislocations to trade diminished through the 1950's, pressure for meat, especially frozen meat, declined and importers began to remove their shipments only as they could sell them: lorries suddenly became 'unavailable' and in effect the ships were used as free cold store. On most occasions this was an inconvenience rather than a problem; Scruttons could vary their work pattern to allow for sporadic delays from importers. Trouble began when importers' delaying tactics interfered with the passenger timetable and even more seriously when they coincided with a dry dock commitment. There were excruciating times when uncooperative importers caused a ship to go for its service still with meat on board.

As a rule, RML used the Harland and Wolff dry dock in King George V because its facilities were less restrictive than those of Green and Siley Wier's in the Royal Albert and there was the added advantage that Harland and Wolff had a huge factory just outside the docks, so that even major engineering problems could be dealt with. As part of their dry dock equipment, they had a giant twenty five ton crane, a specialist piece of machinery, used for lifting large engine parts. When meat was still left in the holds of a vessel in dry dock and when this crane was not being used for ship repairs, it could be enlisted to off-load meat; it was all that was available there. Being geared to lift twenty five tons, its mode of operation was always slow and stately and could not be speeded up to raise one and a half tons of beef. Working meat at this majestic slowness was very time consuming and besides, to see this small blip of cargo suspended from such an almighty machine, looked pretty silly. In such circumstances it seemed expedient not to let on to onlookers that you were part of Royal Mail Lines.

The problems did not end there: at the normal meat berth, 'Z' shed, derricks lowered meat directly onto a trestle table from which (by this time) quay gangers ran it straight to the backs of lorries by electric scooters. In the dry docks though the quays were too cluttered with old anchors, chains, hawsers, life rafts, planks and so on, to allow lorries to get anywhere near the ship. Room for manoeuvre was still further restricted by a scattering of workshops, of varying permanence, on and around the quay. Under these conditions any meat still left on a ship had to be discharged onto standard electric trolleys which then wriggled their way in and out of the clutter to get to the nearest approach for lorries. On one occasion it took a day and a half to discharge seventy five tons of beef; the ship was behind schedule anyway, it had to leave immediately on the next high tide and to watch this off-loading in desperately slow, slow motion did nothing for blood pressure levels. The passengers waiting down river at the Tilbury landing stage were taken by train to the docks so as to avoid a second stop for the vessel. Boarding the ship at No 3 King George V berth may have been an added inconvenience for them but they remained blissfully unaware of the days of frustration caused by the machinations of a few meat importers. This was one of those rare occasions when passengers and cargo handlers rubbed shoulders but for RML what was worse was the knowledge that one of their ships was sailing on full ballast tanks and empty holds, while exporters were desperate for hold space. Odd, looking back, what Head Office let the importers get away with.

Meat was also a problem in another important way, its susceptibility to contamination. More commonly it was the fear of contamination that caused problems, so that a small unconsidered incident at another port could bring the full force of the British Health Authority to bear on a single shipment. There was an instance when a small parcel of beef from Argentina, bound for Portugal caused us considerable dislocation. It was at a time during the sixties, when working conditions were just beginning to improve so, for example, protective clothes, still very much a novelty, were becoming available for particular situations. The dock environment was becoming cleaner, smog was a thing of the past and there was a new awareness in standards of hygiene. Science was being used to seriously enhance the health of the docks but it sometimes took major efforts of re-appraisal for a traditionally minded work force to come to terms with this new circumstance.

On this occasion, the 'Durango' made a scheduled visit to Lisbon on its return voyage to London. Meat was off-loaded onto the quay there but unfortunately at the time, Portugal and Argentina were in the middle of a political spat and Portugal refused to accept the carcasses which had to be re-loaded back onto the 'Durango'. The ship came straight to London and berthed at 'B' shed, Royal Victoria but as soon as the Health Authorities heard of the Lisbon incident, they refused permission for this meat to be landed. The fear was that it might have been contaminated with foot and mouth disease - but it took some while for people to realise they were serious. When the meat had been reloaded onto the ship it had just been dropped into the refrigerated hatchway of No 1 hold, which meant that all the other meat destined for Smithfield in the hold's compartments was locked in. Any risk of contact between the suspect load and the rest of the hold's contents would have been to condemn the entire shipment. The docks were capable of working hard and well so long as they worked within a clearly understood framework; new standards lead to new situations which could bring work to an abrupt standstill. Health Officers had the rules and RML had the problem, no one had the solution. The remaining holds worked normally and after three days most of the ship was ready to depart. Serious money was beginning to be lost by RML, importers, exporters and the gangs; now it was imperative the Health Authorities came up with a way out. They offered a compromise solution, under strict supervision the offending meat could be taken out by gangs dressed in fancy, new protective clothing and put into the hatchway of No 5 hold at the other end of the ship. The uniform would just go with the job nowadays but at the time having to wear white overalls, gloves and hats with wellies on their feet was hugely embarrassing for the ship and quay gangs. No one wanted to be seen wearing such pansy kit. No 5 hold had already been re-loaded with machinery exports and the meat would not contaminate anything there, so this offer was quickly accepted. Old wooden bogies were found and brought up alongside No 1 hold and sheets thrown over them. All other work in the area had to stop as the beef was lowered onto its transport. The sheets were quickly wrapped over each set and it was trundled along the quay for reloading aft.

A shore gang had to remove the contaminated hatch covers, disinfect them and then the hatchway itself before work could begin emptying the locker compartments. Everything proceeded smoothly, the lockers were cleared, the holds re-loaded and once the ship had been given cautious permission to sail, she made straight for Rotterdam where the carcasses were disposed of somehow but without incident. This very expensive crisis was finally defused - and all over six hundred quarters of beef.

Not all meat products were so precisely controlled and FW's general cargo gangs had to deal with various by-products from the River Plate abattoirs from time to time. As these shipments were not intended for human consumption – I assumed they were destined for dog food - they could not be carried in the refrigerated holds of meat ships, so a general cargo vessel had to make an occasional detour to the Plate Estuary. Whether pickled or raw, whatever was being collected had not needed refrigeration in Argentina and additional weeks spent in the enclosed space of unrefrigerated stores ensured that these leftovers from the meat industry were not pleasant things to work among, just opening the hatches made you retch. An afternoon spent working through stinking carcasses hardened the heart of even the most well-disposed bus conductor at home time.

Cow hides arrived sporadically for use in the wide range of leather trades in Britain, from flying jackets to bookbinding. There were two ways of preparing hides for their voyage to London, one tolerable, the other less so.

The less nauseous hides were known among the gangers as 'Bibles'; they were skins dried stiff with their neck and leg sections folded in, to form a neat rectangle. This had been further curved round in half and tied with a string giving the overall appearance of a large leather bound book. The nick name chose itself.

For some reason known only to the leather trade, hides were also needed in a wet form, semi-pickled in an evil smelling chemical. These would have been laid out well enough across the hold ceiling, each hide overlapping its neighbour like a row of toppled dominoes – meticulously neat but an orderliness lost I'm afraid on the discharge gangs. Perhaps the loaders in Argentina had particularly strong stomachs or maybe the smell and condition matured in travelling across the Atlantic but by the time they reached the Royal Docks they were stomach churning. Not only did they give off an overwhelmingly unpleasant, decaying odour but they also oozed a clammy slime which bonded the limp skins into one congealed mass: the idea was for the downholders to carefully peel off hides, one at a time and carry them to the net waiting in the hatchway. In practice with these 'stinkers' buried deep in the confines of the lower hold, the atmosphere overpowering, downholders just rushed in, grabbed what came away in their hands, ran it to the nets and gulped the marginally fresher hatchway air. What couldn't be discarded so easily was the reek of the slime contaminating men's clothes.

Deep in the bowels of the foremost hold far away from all the more wholesome commodities, a general cargo ship returning from the River Plate would sometimes bring in a shipment of 'tankies'. These were the bits of Argentine cattle left over once the meat and hides had been removed; they were collected and stored in huge tanks - hence their name - and arrived in varying degrees of putrefaction. Their ultimate destination was to end up as glue or animal fertilizer but these fairly innocuous end products gave little indication of their noisome origins. Bundles of bones, heads, hooves - who knows, no one examined them too closely – had been wrapped hygienically in paper parcels originally but as they could only be extracted by downholders clambering over piles of them, the bags tore and everything from the dockers' boots to their hair absorbed the foul stench of rotting carcasses. Ship surveyors inspecting the parcels stayed for not a moment longer than was necessary to fulfil their contracts but still went home reeking. Once again gangers might dip their faces under the cold water tap and smile affably at their bus conductor but the chances were that they would be walking home.

Once these holds were emptied, a shore gang would diligently hose them down and disinfect them under the direction of a Health and Safety Officer - even so, the reek impregnated the fabric of the hold for months and considerable care had to be taken when deciding what goods could be stowed there on future voyages.

Passengers as I've already said were rare in the Royal Docks but as there were two distinct categories I ought perhaps to mention them for completeness. The passengers that RML wanted to cultivate and who raised the Company's image above freight carriers were of course the rich who steamed out of Southampton (mostly) on ocean going liners. These were exotic creatures with whom we had no dealing except unexpectedly in the late sixties when it was discovered that dock staff too were able to take advantage of the policy of allowing employees to travel on luxury cruises at seriously discounted rates if there were unfilled cabins. My wife and I had some excellent voyages on the *'Andes'* and it was nice to see what our work in the docks had been underpinning all those years.

Less edifying was the transporting of poor Portuguese to South America, usually on the *Highland* boats. Apparently it had been a long standing operation which was renewed after the War; ships would leave London and go to Portugal where immigrant families, travelling steerage, would board for a fairly comfortless journey to Brazil to pick coffee beans during the season. Entire families went, many of them to emigrate. The No. 5 Shelter Deck, just an open space with no partitions, lockers or privacy, was made over to them and family groups spread themselves across it surrounded by their meagre possessions. Emigrants supplied their own blankets, RML provided food. The Highland vessels could take 200-300 regular passengers so were equipped for looking after travellers. It was not a service that RML City staff took much cheer from, preferring to focus on the rich and glamorous gracing their cruise ships but the trouble was that these customers by the 'Fifties preferred to fly. For me the situation was remote except that *The Alcantara,* a RML passenger ships was on charter to the Government to take emigrants out to new lives in Australia – I was tempted.

In spite of Fred Waterman's self belief - and his first-hand knowledge of rampaging bulls - no one had much experience in handling animals. With strict quarantine laws operating it was always a bigger problem than just animal welfare.

A PSNC ship had been down south on the wool run and it so happened that an Antarctic expedition had finished its project at about that time. The team had been taken to the wool port of Punta Arenas on mainland Tierra del Fuego where they were in the process of disbanding and disposing of their equipment. One member of the party who acted as dog handler during the expedition, felt unable to leave the huskies behind to face an uncertain future so when he heard that this ship was due, he arranged their passage back to Britain. Six ring bolts were welded to the open deck and each dog was given enough chain to permit it to move around during the voyage but not enough for them to make contact with each other. .

The dog handler was a quiet university student who had very efficiently taken care of the paperwork associated with organising the quarantine arrangements for arrival back in London. Although he had built up a close relationship with the huskies over the duration of the expedition, there was one area in which his knowledge was deficient – one of his huskies was pregnant. During the voyage the bitch gave birth to a single pup and both mother and baby prospered. Six huskies had left Chile, six had been cleared for arrival at the docks and seven dogs were brought in. There is something about officialdom that always required the world to fit the paperwork: if there were discrepancies then it was reality that needed to make the adjustments. Customs were adamant: any six could enter the country but not the seventh. The student could not just abandon one and while discharging went on all around them, the dogs and their handler stayed put. Not being very pleasant animals as far as the dockers could see they had to be given plenty of distance as men worked the wool. Quite what the Customs were expecting to happen was unclear, perhaps they were hoping that one of the huskies would conveniently meet with an accident but the dogs remained stubbornly healthy and for days the handler stayed with them, feeding and cleaning up after them. So long as a problem did not directly affect the working of a ship or its sailing times, it could be ignored, decisions postponed but ultimately there came a time when this one piece of red tape threatened huge financial losses: either the dog had to be sent back on its own to a most uncertain future or it had to be let through to quarantine.

Whether the Customs Officers fell in love with the huskies during the period that they were deliberating their fate, or whether they just got cold feet over the implications of their stand I don't know but at the eleventh hour, all seven were allowed through.

Animals from the Americas destined for Australia spent a period of quarantine in Britain before continuing on their journey. One consignment of quarter horses arrived from the United States on a Loch boat which carried a small quantity of cargo bound for France. The ship berthed at Le Havre, off-loaded its cargo then came on to King George V Dock. It was discovered by the Port Health Authority that horse fever was present in that area of France and they immediately boarded the ship and put a restriction order on the movement of animals. Vehicles arrived to collect the horses and were told to wait while it was hoped that something could be worked out. The problem with these complicated situations was to find someone with sufficient authority and interest to pester their way to a solution. The importers, concerned about the welfare of their horses, knew nothing of shipping regulations, while the dock staff had to hope that the Health Officers would work at finding a way round their own regulations; RML had dozens of other commodities to deal with so clerks, like everyone else as it happened, tried to ignore the horses. The Health Authorities though, sat tight offering no solution. The horses stayed on board and were fed, watered and exercised while the main business of the docks carried on around them. In the end the ship's clerk reckoned that, although not necessarily at the sharp end when questions were asked as to why nothing had been done, he was very adjacent. He spent the best part of a day making contacts with the Australian owners, the quarantine stables, Health Officers, anyone who had an interest, to find out what was possible.

The final solution was to arrange for a three month quarantine period in a Belgium stables to satisfy the British Authorities, then a further three months were to be spent in British quarantine to comply with Australian regulations. RML got nothing out of the exercise except an unscheduled trip to Belgium for one of its Loch boats but it was the nature of maritime trade that if a problem cargo was refused entry into a country, it was the ship and the shippers that were inconvenienced. The onus fell on them to come up with a solution. The cargo handlers did not escape the consequences altogether for it was part of the Health Authority requirements that all the horse manure collected, both on the ship and on its journey to Belgium, be bagged and under strict surveillance, taken to an approved tip and be buried.

One interesting conundrum occurred during the off-loading of a shipment of melons. The fruit was in the top deck of No 5 hold, right at the stern of a PSNC ship. After the hold itself had been cleared, a locker at the rear of the hold was opened where it was known a small remainder of a consignment had been stowed. As the men opened the locker door, a South American staggered out. He had managed to stow away as the ship was loaded and had lived on melons for the thirty days of the voyage. After he had been fed and rested he was handed over to the dock police who in fact wanted nothing to do with him preferring him simply to be returned to his country of origin. He was put in a cell for a while then when the ship was due to sail; he was returned on board to be repatriated. The problem was, to where? The police questioning him had discovered that he claimed to be a Panamanian student studying in Chile but had no passport for either country. Panama refused to accept him and so did Chile. When I left the docks seven years later, he was still onboard the same ship, Britain had also refused him a passport and he was permanently stateless. Being a PSNC ship, its home port was Liverpool and whenever she arrived there, this young man had either to stay on board, go ashore for essentials in the charge of a ship's officer or go to prison until it was time for the ship to sail again.

Fortunately, this stowaway turned out to be a bright, accommodating man who in time was found to be entirely trustworthy. Eventually he became a valued member of the ship's company, working on general duties during the voyage, with the special advantage of being able to act as interpreter in South America, particularly at trade fairs and presentations by British industry. The Liverpool police eventually came to know him and relaxed their regulations so that he could go ashore while the ship was in port, knowing that he would return in time to sail. There seemed no solution but the student apparently accepted his rather odd way of life; what happened to him was anybody's guess, we had more to think about than Panamanian stowaways - perhaps he was broken up with the ship.

In the forties and fifties dust was seen as a nuisance rather than a hazard, something to be worked through rather than avoided. If the items themselves were not definitely toxic then breathing in the dust from them was regarded as no more than working in a localised fog - and they were common enough. The problem for the downholders was compounded by the confined spaces in which they had to work for however slight the escape of a particular powder, and often it was very considerable, it could only hover and swirl around the working men, fed continuously by every new disturbance. Most cargoes capable of producing a dust were taken out of the docks by barge so quay gangs were largely spared the discomfort; the brunt of these problems was borne once again by import gangs working general cargoes. Working in clouds of dust became a fact of life for these gangs - the priority was always the rate of pay over inconvenience. Whatever the actual health hazards, different items produced their own specific aggravations, the worst in terms of blackening power being carbon black. Mercifully it was only a very occasional import and the quantities were always small. Carbon black was a close relation to soot but in a very fine particle form. Although it arrived in multi-wrapped paper parcels weighing perhaps a half hundredweight each, powder always seemed to get out. As the packets were easy to handle the gangers could afford to treat them with extreme care as though they were handling some delicate antique but however daintily they were lifted, the contents gently puffed and spread their way into the atmosphere. So intrusive was the blackening power of this substance that it was never carried in ship's holds but relegated to lockers on the top deck which were normally reserved for general items such as mops and buckets. It was imperative that carbon black came nowhere near regular cargo spaces, the contamination would have been permanent. It is a pity that no such scruples extended to the handlers. The men had to squeeze their way into and out of the locker then simply walk the parcel across the deck to a set board ready for the crane to lift off - but from the very first disturbance puffs of black dust started to appear and just hover. These wisps were slight at first but getting thicker with every movement. Incidentally this was one of the few commodities that were discharged onto the quay so that ship gangs had the not very consoling knowledge that, however black they got, they had colleagues equally contaminated over on the quay. The quantities were always small and as far as possible, work was arranged so that a gang could move carbon black as their last job of the day. Normally the amount of work involved occupied no more than an hour so fitting it into a day's routine was not a problem; what the work did highlight once more was the totally inadequate washing facilities in the docks and the lack of protective clothing or face masks. By the end of that hour the locker was pouring thick, dense smoke - it looked as if it were on fire - with black dust clouds billowing around the doorway. Men had to gasp for air then plunge in the locker space to collect a parcel before having to breathe in again. Back home, however hard they scrubbed that evening the evidence of this hour's work could be seen days after; carbon black ingrained itself deep into their pores. Mercifully there was no overpowering smell associated with carbon black so getting on a bus was not a problem and, deemed amusing by some, they got used to having 'That Coal Black Mammy of Mine' sung at them. In case it needs saying here, not a racial slur but an Al Jolson impersonation – uncomfortable for us, acceptable then. The world moves on.

By contrast, perhaps the whitest powder that the RML ships very occasionally carried was refined flour from the United States. This was something of an oddity since grain handling was the exclusive preserve of the PLA cornporters using grain machines, whereas flour in bags was worked as a general cargo by FW gangs. The cargo was easy, the sacks strong and manageable. Problems were slight but insidious, they crept up on you - especially they crept up on the uninitiated. Although the sacks were strong they were regularly pierced by dockers' hooks as they manipulated them to the hatchway to make up twenty sack sets. As they rose out of the hold, a fine almost imperceptible dusting of flour gently floated back into the hold and onto everything and everyone down there.

One of my first jobs in the docks was tallying one of these flour shipments and as luck would have it, I was wearing a new, smart and costly raincoat. I was on deck watching the sets swing out and over my head, aware of the hazy atmosphere building up around us but not making the mental connection. Work continued throughout the day, each set sending down its own fine sprinkling on everything lying under its path. Then it rained.

Washing helped get some of the dough out of my hair and the rest gradually grew out but that coat was forever starched with that stale, crusty batter mix. It didn't go down too well back home either with ration coupons squandered. Welcome to the docks.

Although most dusty conditions fell to general cargo gangs there were times when, to their disgust, toerags found that 'grain' too could sometimes pulverise. In the early sixties there was a bulk shipment of alfalfa pellets which turned out to be re-constituted pea sized granules intended for animal fodder. The consignment was labelled 'grain' on the ship's manifest so, with nothing else to go on, it was handed over to the PLA cornporters with their grain machines to extract. By this date the big machines had taken over, there were new levels of efficiency and expectation; the gangers knew fairly predictably, how long off-loading would take and what their pay would be: but not for alfalfa pellets.

As soon as the men started working, everyone immediately realised that something was amiss: the manifest might say 'grain', but the clattering noise these pellets made as they were sucked up the pipes was telling a different story. Normal grain working wasn't exactly quiet but this was deafening and the downholders suddenly had a very good reason to finish the job as quickly as possible, presumably ear protectors would be compulsory now. This cacophony was telling the supervisors, as they gradually realised, that the power of this machine was flinging the pellets against the sides of the suction pipes and reducing them back to powder.

The lighterman with an order to collect pellets found his craft filling up with dust; at first he assumed it was a quirk of the cargo's top layer but as the clouds increased, as if he were laying a smoke screen, he like everyone else realised that whole pellets were never going to arrive. Hasty discussions confirmed that, no, the machine could not be modified to reduce this pounding and, no, the importers could not make do with alfalfa dust. Work had to stop while out of mothballs, they brought one of the old, small floaters which although slow, preserved the pellets more or less intact. The noise in the pipes was still bad but the results in the lighter were improved marginally. This slight success though was at the expense of a plummeting work rate: nostalgic but unrewarding. Schedules for the ship's movements between berths for reloading had to be put back, then further delayed as supervisors rediscovered how agonisingly slow these machines were. No one was happy; the importers were not satisfied with the best the docks could offer and management was irate that this one cargo took a day and a half to extract when exporters were expecting to get their goods moving. The situation was bad but at least the managers were spared the conditions down in the hold. The downholders missed the dust cloud accumulating over the lighter but soon, as the pellets rolled towards the suction pipes and more particularly as men waded through them, pellets disintegrated and the atmosphere thickened. Here there was nowhere for the dust to go, the conditions became unbearable and all involved with supervising - RML and PLA - were embarrassed to require the men to be there. For a day and a half, men were deafened, blinded and gasping for breath as the suction pipes, at their own leisurely pace extracted the collapsing pellets. By way of recompense the gangs were offered the unprecedented allowance of a full week's wages and RML never bought alfalfa pellets into the docks again.

Going over to new, more powerful grain machines also caused problems for Colman's who regularly imported mustard seed to be taken round to Norwich by sailing craft or small motor barge. For some reason cornporters walking through the seed did not crush it or send up clouds of dust, so from their point of view mustard was straightforward; the difficulty for Colman's was that the newer machines hammered the grain to dust in the same way that alfalfa pellets disintegrated and although they wanted their mustard seed milled, they preferred, thank you, to do it for themselves.

Unhappy with recent results from the new grain machines Colman's, at one point demanded their seed to be worked by an older machine. They were told initially that this was no longer an option but they insisted - an old machine was duly disinterred. Everyone realised how slow the work was likely to be but then they discovered a new difficulty; Coleman's had changed from sail to large motor barges and the old floaters had delivery pipes designed for small craft, they simply couldn't get the pipes up and into these new vessels. A lot of time was wasted trying to reconcile the irreconcilable with the ultimate solution being to tell the motor barge to stand off while the cornporters discharged into a number of small dumb barges. This at least cleared the ship's hold and allowed the general cargo gangs to get the vessel turned round, the mustard seed still as whole as Colman's wanted it, but in the wrong craft. The flotilla was sent on its way for the PLA to sort out, possibly transferring the seed to the coastal barge through their granary at Millwall or even via their grain solos but it must have been an expensive operation and a costly consignment of mustard. What effect this extra process, whatever it was, had on the quality of the seed whether or not it pounded mustard to dust like the new grain machines, I never learnt but this special request turned out to be, in effect, a last chance for the Royal Docks; whatever it was that happened to the seed, Colman's were not impressed and from then on they transferred to Rotterdam.

But it was the general gangs who dealt with the great majority of dusty cargoes, the worst of which was undoubtedly fishmeal. Everything about it was loathsome: the smell, the heat, the stowing and packaging. Everything. It seems that this was only a post-War import for in earlier years it was guano that had been shipped. There used to be a company in Silvertown called 'The Peruvian Guano Works' which after World War II became 'Peruvian Warf'. The change may have been significant. Anyway the story goes that labourers were increasingly unhappy about chipping the accumulated droppings of seabirds from rocky islands off the Pacific coast of Peru; the demand for fertilizer was still there but the workforce was becoming less enthusiastic. Someone hit upon the idea of by-passing the sea birds' biochemical processing and going directly for the fish which could be vacuumed out of the sea then dried and ground to dust. Whatever the consequences for the ecology of the area, the product proved a financial success and the venture prospered. That was the story we were told.

By the time the imported fishmeal reached the Royal Docks there were problems, not the least of which fell to the import clerks: perhaps as a quaint gesture to continuity with the old guano trade, exporters used 'pelican marks' to identify batches. Pelicans, it appeared, were the birds which had created the guano and exporters stamped their image, followed by a Roman numeral on the outer paper wrapping as a means of identification. Inside the paper wrapping was a hessian sack which contained half a hundredweight of fishmeal but unfortunately one of the main problems with the substance was its propensity to heat up. Sustained warming during the voyage caused the hessian and paper to become brittle and disintegrate taking the pelican mark with it. As soon as men tried to carry the bags out to canvas spreads the integrity of the packaging collapsed. The unfortunate ship's clerk would be grubbing around for odd scraps of evidence to discover if it was 'Pelican V' or 'Pelican VI' that was being worked and he would find himself brushing away fishmeal from intact bags to try to work out loading patterns as sacks were being worked around him. As they were trodden on they collapsed, sending clouds of dust billowing into the confined space to settle on other cargoes, hair, clothing, ears, eyes and lungs - the smell was overwhelming. And somewhere in the background would be one of the 'Forty Thieves' waiting for an opportunity to claim light measure for his clients.

The dangers of overheating were apparently well known and efforts were constantly made to try and minimise this risk. Lloyds' Certificates issued in Peru required a moisture content of between seven and fourteen per cent; a higher moisture content made fishmeal a highly unstable cargo, we were told. The trouble was, according to the ships' officers of the time, that most of the sacks were stored outdoors in Callao and establishing the moisture content of each sack was quite impossible, so some sort of improvised monitoring during the voyage seemed in order. Ships' masters, it seems, used to fill glass jars with samples of each consignment and place them conspicuously on the bridge, the belief being that if they saw the contents darkening, then the fishmeal was heating up and they had a potential problem. What degree of darkening signalled abandon ship, I was never privy to.

Those who were employed to find a solution seemed to think adequate ventilation was the key; gaps of perhaps eighteen inches were left between the rows so that there might be, for example, three solid rows, a gap, then three more and so on down the length of the hold. To keep the mass stable in rough seas, various braces were added between the tiers but as timber was apparently scarce in Peru anything might be used from pieces of rusty metal, broken tools or old dunnage from other voyages. Whatever combinations were tried, some overheating always seemed to occur, so experimenting with different gap patterns continued with different shipments.

For gangs trying to off-load, this situation was inherently treacherous: without protective clothing, men had to wrap old pieces of hessian round their hands if the bags got too hot. They had to carefully carry each bag in the hope that it would survive at least until it was out of the hold, knowing that as they clambered their way across, bags were failing under their boots. Not only were they having to contend with clouds of evil smelling, blinding dust while carrying decaying, half-hundredweight loads but they also had to contend with whatever latest ideas on ventilation patterns were being tried, a sort of hop scotch on a collapsing surface. Men would slide into chasms as bags broke, step backwards into them, unused to a new, innovative layout or just lose their footing in the billowing dust clouds. Broken legs and arms, serious gashes and impalements were everyday occurrences with this cargo.

In the early nineteen fifties a charter vessel for PSNC berthed with fishmeal aboard. For my sins I was the ship's clerk on this job and as the gangs were arriving I noticed puffs of smoke coming from the ventilators. I warned the relieving officer, got the PLA involved and sent a message back to Head Office – with the hatch covers still in place the fishmeal seemed to be only smouldering but it was anybody's guess what would happen once they were removed. While I was trying to sort things out around the hatches, a meeting was hastily convened between representatives of the TGWU, RML and FW; with Captain Chamberlain then RML's Marine Super offering £4 an hour for twenty four hours. Some thought the gangs would not take such risks for the money; others thought that the gangs would string the work out to get as much as possible. In the event the gang involved, 'Ory Mantelow's, simply accepted the offer and got on with opening up the hatches. Personally, I believe it was the bonds of loyalty to his shipworker Bill Holland that carried most weight; loyalty was always underestimated by the management.

With the hatches cautiously removed, the cargo continued only to smoke – it didn't seem to be getting worse – but as it was, it was bad. Discharging began. The conditions were awful; smouldering fishmeal smelt and smarted more sharply than raw and there was no escape in the confines of the hold. The fire brigade waited alongside on the quay in case a full scale inferno erupted while the gang, who had thoughtfully been issued with shovels, carried the smoking bags to spreads. Once again no protective kit was supplied to these men who worked continuously for twenty four hours in this stinking oven. I came to realise how bad conditions were down there as I had drawn a second short straw, I was given the night shift and responsibility for tracing the source of the fire.

At eight in the morning after discharging three hundred tons, 'Ory's gang stood down while a second team took over for the next session. They had to return home, of course, in the clothes they had worked in for twenty four hours. The fishmeal was landed onto electric scooters on the quay and was rushed to waiting 'accommodation barges' hastily made available by Thames Steam Tug and Lighterage. The weather was not kind, it rained intermittently which did nothing to help the moisture content and which may have accounted for the fact that the mass of sacking and fishmeal continued to smoulder in the lighters. Tarpaulins were brought in and thrown over the heaps between scooter loads but whether this helped to diminish or incubate the existing heat nobody was analysing.

Mantelow's gang returned on Saturday morning after a day's respite – but still reeking – and continued to work a further twenty four hours, leaving the second gang with just a clearing up job to do on Sunday. A true fire never did develop fortunately, so the fire brigade were never directly involved but the heat had been sufficient to blister paint both in the hold and the barges. The lasting problem was that however much they cleared, fumigated and repainted the damaged metal work, the acrid smell remained, risking the contamination of all later cargoes. It proved a very expensive operation.

Those of us who had been down in the hold found that we couldn't sleep at night so overpowering was the smell – and that for men not exactly unused to penetrating odours. Wives could not bear to have our clothing in the house - even after several rinses in the copper, mine remained permanently on the line in all weathers for weeks. The only good to come out of that incident was that at last some thought was given to the need for protective clothing.

For me the saddest part of the whole affair was the lack of gratitude shown by the various managements. Once the stinking cargo was on its way to the dump, it was back to business as usual; as I recall, none of the newspapers reporting the incident seemed interested in the Herculean efforts of the gangs involved and the docks once more settled back into their traditional attitudes of confrontation.

*   *   *

RML CHANGES
In 1926 RML (RMSPC) moved from Moorgate to Fenchurch Street. Most shipping lines had their offices in this area because the direct railway line from there to the docks allowed runners to maintain the flow of information and packages between City and ships.

When the PLA eventually got rid of the jetties in Victoria Dock, RML moved from its base at 'I' jetty to the various wooden sheds clustered around the Tidal Basin end of that dock. Long established staff members used to look back with considerable nostalgia to the days of 'I' jetty.

I spent the last eight years of my working life first at Royal Mail House then, when it was sold, at Furness, Withy House by which time us three clerks sat round a desk were effectively all that remained of Royal Mail Lines. My job had become one of trying to match importers with abandoned imports scattered around various sheds. As one of the few people left who knew the old working geography of the Royals and, particularly useful this, knew Custom's duty classifications on our more established imports, I still had a role to play.

As an aside and as a reminder of how partial this account of dock life is, it might be useful to indicate some of the differences between the import and export working environments within our Company. I was never a RML export clerk but for every ship I supervised off-loading there was a corresponding infrastructure dealing with her reloading. This is how I saw it.

An incoming general cargo ship had to berth where it could in the crowded life of the Royal Docks in the 1940s and '50s. For a large company like RML getting berths was a constant preoccupation; there was always another ship waiting at Gravesend or heading up the Channel. For Head Office in the City, a ship moored down River was wasting Company resources and any berth was deemed acceptable. For the import ship's clerk this meant supervising the off-loading through the conditions he and the FW gangs were given: bomb damage and under investment meant that the facilities available to him were very uneven at different berths. Improvisation was frequently necessary and the use of tight, experienced gangs was invaluable in minimising the berth's shortcomings. Each ship, each berth and each range of cargoes, in themselves were enough variables to work with – knowing the shipworker and his teams made a huge difference.

Import clerks working in the remoter areas – remote to RML facilities that is – often had to improvise 'offices' for themselves (usually a cubby hole on the top deck and open to the elements) to keep track of the flow of paperwork. Each barge load or lorry load had to be documented and dock passes issued to reflect the change of responsibility and this record keeping had to run alongside the actual movement of goods.

Exports, on the other hand, were delivered to a PLA shed over a period of weeks. The shed would usually be on an annual rent to RML – the same sheds were occupied by RML over decades (1, 2, 3 Sheds, South Side, Victoria Dock) - so that the shed foreman, although a PLA employee, would be familiar with the way the Company operated by working continuously within a RML operation. The foreman would collect the paperwork from lorry drivers, issue passes and only as the exports were being loaded would the documents transfer to RML administration, for only then did the shippers take responsibility for the goods. Thus for exports, the ship's clerk had the benefit of knowing the berths, equipment and facilities on a day to day basis. In the era before mobile phones he also had the knowledge that, should a major incident arise, the RML offices and infrastructure (eg telephones to Head Office) were a short walk away at the main dock office near Gate No. 6. An export clerk worked within a limited area close to the centre of RML operations so whatever the cargo, the context for its loading was more ordered - and incidentally, the export clerk had somewhere comfortable to eat his sandwich and, crucially, access to toilets.

Exports that arrived by lorry or train became the responsibility of the PLA inside the docks. Items were stored in a shed – usually, and obviously, one of our an annual rent sheds – according to their port of destination ready for Customs clearance and loading. Permanent or casual labour employed by the PLA off-loaded from the vehicles with the cost eventually going to RML. Customs then examined the exports in the shed and put a blue or white circle on each to show they had been cleared. Once a ship had discharged all its imports somewhere in the Royal Docks it was brought round for loading. An assistant shipworker for FW was in the shed and he liaised with the shipworker on the ship to decide upon the order in which goods left the shed for loading. Thus the two supervisors working with Customs, knowing the layout of each hold and knowing in which order goods were to be off-loaded at future ports, decided on what the PLA dockworkers could take to the quay. Royal Mail's export clerk had to make sure that all the goods listed came on board and that they were securely and safely stowed ready for the next voyage. The FW assistant shipworker always had to be one step ahead of the shed gangs, clearing items with Customs and working with the shed foreman who would know where every item was stored, and also with his clearance clerk who was responsible for the current safe storage of the exports, to make sure goods were delivered when the ship gangs needed them. On the quay would be the two stevedores from the FW ship gang who arranged the goods for loading and at this point responsibility passed from the PLA to Furness, Withy. The export cargo superintendents for FW were often ex-ship's masters with a sound knowledge of ship stability, cargoes to be loaded and the cruise itinerary. Once stowed to the export clerk's satisfaction, responsibility for the cargoes safe keeping passed to RML.

Royal Mail kept imports and exports financially separate so if a ship were discharging and the only berth available had been one of their annual rent sheds then imports would hire the berth from exports and perhaps a third of the shed for import storage while exports were accumulating in the rest of the shed. It was up to the shed foreman to judge what was possible.

If exports were delivered by barge, this was much cheaper for the shipping company and the customer as there were no storage fees. Customs would ask for each lighter to be brought up to the quay for inspection and the shipworker would call for the craft when it was needed for loading. In this case four members of the ship gang would be needed to build the sets for delivery by crane to the hold.

One situation we import clerks were relieved to miss out on was the fashion for late delivery. Word had got around amongst exporters that the last goods to be loaded onto a ship would be the first to be off-loaded so exporters got into the habit of sending their goods as the ship was in the process of taking on cargoes in the belief that theirs would sit on top of the pile. Lorries would be queuing the length of the dock and for a mile outside with drivers waiting hours, or even days, to get their delivery up to the ship. Police had to deal with the queues, ship's clerks with the ultimate stowing pattern.

Let us suppose you were importing a case of samples from a Latin American country on a RML ship during the fifties. Agents in the exporting country would have checked that the samples had been paid for and that they had received Customs clearance there. You would then be sent a Bill of Lading itemising your goods in detail with you as importer, to reach you while the ship was still at sea. If the transport costs had not yet been paid and if you wanted your imports quickly, you would go or send a runner to Royal Mail House, settle the account, have your Bill of Lading stamped and be issued with a Release Note specifying the type and quantity of the goods you were expecting. Incidentally, it was boasted that Royal Mail Lines had the longest counter in the City - a huge length of polished mahogany - such was the number of daily transactions. Its only claim to fame now is having been on the site which became the Lloyds building.

For large traders, this Release Note would be passed to their hauliers or Lighterage Company for their collectors to present in the docks. In practice most importers called or sent runners to complete these Head Office formalities, giving some idea of how local most imports to the docks were. In your case let us assume you chose to collect the samples yourself. An estimate of when the ship was expected would be given at this time but it was not until she berthed that more precise timescales could be offered. As the ship began working and the range of commodities appeared, the ship's clerk would be in contact by telephone and runner, with both dock and Head Office, who in turn contacted importers with the news of when their goods were expected to be discharged.

Your case of samples would be sent to the transit shed for less urgent collection, while other importers were collecting directly their fruit, meat, sugar or whatever. To help locate items which passed at a more leisurely pace through a shed, RML employed a shed clerk who was a casually employed tally clerk taken on for this single job. Like many clerical jobs, the work of a shed clerk was really one aspect of tallying; some men spent their lives simply recording cargoes into (called an export tally clerk) or out of (import clerk) ships' holds but more able men were taken on for more demanding tasks which included this post of shed clerk. All these functions monitored or planned the flow of goods through the docks and this variety of employments constituted the army of casual clerical employees.

Our shed clerk would have been given a copy of the ship's manifest, to consider which items were likely to be going into store and therefore might be his concern (but not his responsibility, for that lay with the PLA shed foreman in charge of the entire shed and its contents). Shed clerks were employed by the shipping company to smooth the way for importers to collect their goods and let it be seen that there was a continuing interest in those goods - but they did it under sufferance from the shed foreman. As goods came into the shed, the clerk would measure them, note the mark and importer and watch where they were being stored. Any anomalies would have to be sorted out at this stage so as to forewarn the importer but in practice these were rare.

You would arrive to collect your case, show your Release Note to the gate policeman who would direct you to the Port of London Authority main clearing office. Here you would be told what storage fees were owing to the PLA and you would pay your dues, collecting a receipt in the process. Now you would be directed down the dock system to where the shed with your items was located, maybe in sight, maybe a mile away. Once you had tracked it down, you would search out the shed foreman, show him the Release Note and he would send you up to his office where his writer would take your PLA receipt and Release Note, check that they had your goods then issue you with a Black Order. From here you would be sent round to the nearest RML office, again it might be a mile away, Black Order in hand, to find the inside clerk dealing with this ship; he would check the manifest, Bill of Lading and Black Order then issue you with a Tick Note to confirm that you were empowered to collect the items indicated.

If you were lucky, the shed clerk would also be in the RML office and he would accompany you back to the shed or perhaps you'd already met him there. In any case you needed to find him so that he could tell the shed foreman exactly where your item was stored - a single case might take some finding amongst the hundreds of tons of cargoes. As your goods were being retrieved and put on a trolley, you would be sent round to a convenient Customs Office where an officer would be detailed to examine your items. You would go back with him, in his time, to the shed by which time your case would have been placed in the 'lock up' to provide some privacy while the officer removed the lid and carefully inspected the contents. Once satisfied, you would go back to his office, pay any necessary duty and get a clearance certificate. Back at the shed once more, you would see the writer again to collect a dock pass to let you and your package through the gate, sign to say that you had received the goods, load them up then bid a cheery farewell to the shed clerk, the foreman, the writer and anyone else in the neighbourhood who might have played a part in this exercise. You would leave the docks, mission accomplished – say, the best part of the morning.

That was for straightforward items. Sometimes there were hiccups in the paperwork which might for example lead to the shed's writer issuing a Red Order, instead of its Black near relation. Perhaps a regular importer with Royal Mail Lines might not have been able to get to Head Office to pay his shipping fees or there might be a dispute about whether they were being paid on the other side of the Atlantic, which circumstances would mean that there had been no Release Note. The PLA writer would recognise this but as far as the dock authority was concerned, so long as he had paid his shed storage charges, he could take the goods. The Red Order arriving at an inside clerk's desk was a warning to RML that they should make sure that they were happy to let the goods go, confident that eventually their dues would be met.

Most imports were in large consignments and many importers would be bringing in similar commodities on a regular basis. This had the advantage that importers knew the system and the dock staff knew the cargoes but regular shipments increased the profusion of types, marks and qualities as much as quantities, to be recorded meticulously in case of later disputes. In these days before computers, safety checks were built into the system by increasing the paperwork and employing extra clerks to deal with it - the docks still seemed at heart a deeply Victorian institution.

*   *   *

WATER GUARDS

Water Guards, somewhat oddly, were concerned with ships. They were responsible for clearing each ship as it entered 'locking in' through the lock gates. As each ship entered the lock its River Pilot left to be replaced by a Dock Pilot who was to guide the ship to her berth. At the same time the Water Guard went on board to deal with issues of quarantine or dangerous cargoes. If there were quarantine problems the ship would be flying a yellow flag until the health issues were resolved. The Water Guard had no interest in the cargoes in the five holds but in illicit or dangerous goods in the bonded stores. Items in these stores were the responsibility of the Chief Steward during the voyage and the Water Guard needed to know from the Bonded Notes how much alcohol and how many cigarettes, for example, had been brought on board and how many had been consumed during the voyage. He also concerned himself with watches, perfumes and other gifts held in these stores and once he was satisfied that everything was accounted for, he sealed the Bond Store Room and preparations for the main work of off-loading could begin. At this stage at the locking in, once the Water Guard was happy, RML shore gang could then go on board to prepare the hatches in readiness for berthing and discharging. For routine shipments though the procedure tended to be more relaxed and as the Water Guard was clearing the ship, frequently some of the shore gang were allowed on deck while others guided the ship through the lock.

Port Health Officer. We might include here in this mixed list the MOH officers who worked for the PLA inspecting empty holds once the gangs had finished off-loading. Usually, of course, clearing up was the work of the FW ship gangs and only if cargoes had decayed to the point of worthless rubbish would the RML shore gang become responsible for a hold's hygiene. Either way, holds had to be spotless. Each empty hold had to be inspected by the Health Officer for each working ship and each hold issued with a separate Certificate of Health and de-ratting certificate before reloading could begin.

Interest in the defunct paperwork of a vanished shipping line is likely to be limited at best and yet for many souls who spent their working lives in the docks, these pieces of paper and card were their experience of dock life - just as much as cargoes were for the handling gangs. The downholders had the task of dealing with whatever cargoes were imported, the clerks had to visualise and monitor their throughput.

Planning clerks had to construct an order and timescale in which shipments could be off-loaded safely and advise importers when they should get their transport ready. This ordering had to be done before and while the ship was being brought up from Gravesend. The planning was systemised by an army of clerks and their array of documents.

But there is a second and more self-indulgent reason for me including this section. When I was getting acquainted with the way RML did things, documents were stored, as I have already noted, in wooden huts that passed for offices. All the paperwork associated with a shipment was wrapped up into a parcel and stored in the loft space above a working office - and this for every ship and every shipment, just in case there was a later claim. These sheds had suffered bomb damage and some of the pre-war parcels were decomposing so that when, during RML's building initiative of the fifties, the Company's new factory was built just outside Victoria Dock, all the old, current and ultimately future parcels were carefully stored there as precious records. Thus a considerable compilation of information on Royal Mail Lines' presence in the Royal Docks accumulated in that factory, all meticulously completed and catalogued. Ten years or so later, the Company was in decline and the accumulated contents of our factory were disposed of so the question for me was: was this hoard of documents stored somewhere else or were they all destroyed? For those of us who had taken it all so seriously over many decades, that demolition wiped out a way of life. I hope I'm wrong but now there may be no examples of these parcels in existence, in which case this little chapter alone, bears witness to the commitment and attention to detail of so many clerks over so many years:

SHIP'S PLANS were essential for planning the whole operation. As a ship completed its loading in America, an officer would set out the position of all the cargoes as sketched bricks in the five holds, on a schematic outline print of the ship's profile. These would be copied in triplicate and airmailed back to RM House to arrive a week or so before the ship. At worst, the plans could be landed at a South Coast port and rushed to London as the ship made its way up the Channel to allow some preparation time. One copy was retained by Head Office so they could advise importers when their goods would be likely to emerge, the other two were sent to the docks where RML's Chief Superintendent passed one immediately to the clerk he wanted to supervise discharging. The first duty of that ship's clerk was to get himself an inside clerk from the Call next morning, someone to deal with the office work while he was watching the ship; Jack Banfield was the sort of clerk to look out for. In spite of frequent requests for him to join the permanent staff, Jack preferred to keep his independence and remain casual but his knowledge of procedures was extensive and any ship's clerk would be more than happy to engage him. At the same time a planning clerk would also be taken on, to spend time quietly examining the plans just to acquaint himself with the reality of what cargoes were arriving and to search out potential problems. He tried to read how the cargoes would come out of the holds and what would be the best order, taking into account the need for general and cornporter gangs, overside and barge work, shed work, cargoes which might contaminate others, and so on. The ship's clerk would be working an earlier ship, the inside clerk occupied with making out forms, someone was needed to pour over the ship's plans to arrange the future off-loading sequence for the ship now making its way towards the docks.

The types of cargo listed on a ship's manifest would give an idea of the way the ship would be worked, the manifest and plan together should have given a good idea how long the off-loading might take, while the plan itself, by showing where different cargoes were stowed gave an indication when each might appear for hauliers to collect.

WORKING BOOK: Ship's plans and manifests were big things, large flapping sheets of paper, unsuitable for working from the top deck of a discharging ship. Before the ship made her berth, the ship's clerk had to copy out the manifest, with advice from his planning clerk, into a long thin Working Book used sideways. The Working Book combined information from both plans and manifest, by listing items according to hold and deck, starting with the top deck, each hold being set out on a different page. Thus the contents of a ship could be read in the order in which they were expected to be worked from each hold by turning to a different page, allowing the clerk at any time to see what items of cargo each gang in each hold would be working and roughly, when they might appear. This was important, not only in discussions with the shipworker and top hands over equipment, problems and rates of pay but also to forewarn importers when their transport might be needed.

EXHAUST BOOK: Also before the ship arrived, the ship's clerk made out another book, to be completed as work progressed and this was the Exhaust Book. Before the ship started working, the total tonnages were listed for each hold, set out on separate pages according to the manifest, so that the amount of cargo moved by each gang could be set down at the end of each day and subtracted from the total. After three to five days work therefore, with all the holds empty, the Exhaust Book should have shown a neat series of zeros and the pay owing to the gangs could be easily established. Thus the Working Book dealt with commodities, importers and transport while the Exhaust Book dealt with tonnages, rates of working and rates of pay. The Working Book might list a consignment of grain for a particular mill and the total tonnage, while the Exhaust Book would show how much of that grain had been worked through a morning or day. The Exhaust Book showed a clerk and his Superintendent how well each cargo and hold were working and how much longer each might take to finish before the ship was ready for reloading. The book was also an effective reminder for the ship's clerk of how much cargo was worked through periods when bickering started over allowances and off-loading slowed. This should have been clear from the tally clerk's independent records of course, but this was not always so, even if he were conscientious and accurate; for example, each lighterman would say when his lighter was full if taking on bulk cargoes. A hopper would theoretically measure two ton sets of grain, a grab, one or two tons of sugar and the tally clerk would record these. Any commodities that were spoilt were the work of the shore gangs and by subtracting this from what was in the hold originally, the total should have agreed exactly (in an ideal world) with what the tally clerk saw swinging over the deck and what each lighterman estimated was in his lighter: and this for each hold. With such tangled interests, an Exhaust Book was invaluable. There was also the point that a few days later a bill would arrive from the stevedoring company and various additional allowances or tonnages might unaccountably find their way onto the list – one stevedoring clerk added imaginary expenses as a matter of course, in the hope that the shipping company would not pick them up. He was known to be a crook and an Exhaust Book carefully compiled by the ship's clerk set the record straight.

These then were the main operational books for a ship's clerk but before the ship started working, back at the dock office his inside clerk's first job was to make out all the tally cards. For each item of cargo on the manifest, for each hold, each importer, mark or destination, a separate card had to be made up; a consignment for one importer might be spread across two or more holds, or he may have wanted different parts to go to different places – even leave by different forms of transport. A tally clerk merely recorded sets as they came over, so that he had to be given a card sufficiently precise that each separate item could be monitored on its way, and that was a knotty little job for the inside clerk to organise. For something like bulk sugar, only one card would be made out for hundreds of tons of cargo, all bound for Tate and Lyle, but on top of it might sit rum casks where every two or three barrels might be bound for a different importer or be of a different quality, each needing its own card. A single case of samples like the one you went to the docks to pick up would need its own card; two hundred for one ship would not be unusual, though often there were less. These cards were then handed out to the tally clerks one at a time by the inside clerk who maintained overall control of them. Once the ship's clerk and shipworker had decided which cargoes would be first to be worked from each hold, each tally clerk collected his card, filled it in for as long as the consignment lasted then, finding out from the ship's clerk what was the next out, he returned to the RML office, handed in one and took the next. A good tally clerk, for long runs, tried to get the same number of items on each line to help with the totals later; it was usually easy to achieve this with good gangs working bags and crates of a standard size when downholders would send over the same number in each set. Things got more difficult if there were a variety of marks or if containers were broken and goods ullaged, or if some sort of fiddle was going on. The Golden Rule for tally clerks was that they should mark down what they saw. If a long run of goods were being loaded into lighters, a tally clerk also changed cards with each barge so that one card recorded what went into one barge and the name of that craft was also noted on the card. They did try to make things watertight.

GREY BOOK: The independent records of the inside clerk were kept in the Grey Book, a large alphabetically indexed book into which he had copied out the ship's manifest in alphabetical order, according to commodity. As tally clerks returned their cards, he noted down next to the Grey Book listing, what quantities had come out of the holds. This was important because the inside clerk also had to deal with clients' transport out of the docks; a lighterman or lorry driver would arrive with his importer's release note and the inside clerk had to know immediately if that cargo had already been off-loaded and was ready for collection. A quick reference system through alphabetical listing of commodities made life easier.

Thus a lighterman might shout up "Have you got three parcels of timber for me there, Bert?" I would have to check the lighterman's release note against my working book to confirm importer, quantity and destination then, while the lighter was being loaded, the lighterman would go to the office, hand the note over to the inside clerk, who entered the details against the listing, got the lighterman to sign next to the entry, then issued him with a receipt. That receipt was RML's document to say that as far as the Company was concerned the barge and its load were free to pass out of the dock and were beyond their responsibility.

Goods which were stored in one of the transit sheds, it should be noted, became the responsibility of the Port of London Authority and RML made over these commodities, with suitable documentation of course. It was then the shed writer who collected the release notes from the lorry drivers, made sure the additional storage dues had been paid and issued the Black Order and dock pass. When there was extensive shed work with apples, say, constantly flowing through it, then the ship's clerk left the ship for much of the time, the inside clerk left his office, and they both worked from the shed using whatever facilities they could muster – see 'Apples' earlier.

RETURNS: From this mass of paperwork, a regular flow of information was sent up to RM House by runner, letting them know the movement of goods out of holds, and out of the docks, and these were known as the Returns. Throughout the day, at convenient moments, when lighters were being manoeuvred, when gangs were changing from general cargo to cornporters or equipment was being redeployed, the ship's clerk would send a Return to say what had left the ship and the inside clerk would send corresponding information to say what had already left the dock. The last Return left the docks at 5pm and would usually be a complete summary of the work that day, with the inside clerk and ship's clerk working together.

Fred Dennison was the runner for all this paperwork round the docks. He was not up to being a clerk but was conscientious enough and pleased to have the regular overtime which came from visiting those ships still working after 5 o'clock, collecting their Returns to dispatch the next morning. He had been injured at some time, was weak and partially deaf and would have been unable to take on the hard physical labour of moving cargoes. He spent his time running miles each day to where the ships were working, collecting Returns and swapping tally cards with those who were working too far from the office to be able to get back. At the end of each working day though, all the tally clerks had to go back to the dock office to check their cards, check quantities and marks, and also make sure that they had signed them all. The inside clerk then issued each tally clerk with a 'Tick Note' to fill out and sign, as being the entire quantity of goods he had seen out that day. The inside clerk checked the completed Note against his Grey Book entries, then countersigned it, agreeing with the recorded movements. These Tick Notes were important as they went to Furness, Withy as a record of what work they should pay their gangs, or in other words, what RML was prepared to pay FW for cargoes handled. FW of course had its own tally clerks and their records ought to have agreed completely with RML's but as might be imagined, this was frequently not the case. There was the need for diligence when finalising these records at the end of the day.

Once a ship had stopped working with all the holds cleared, the goods collected or stored, the associated paperwork completed, two other large document were made out:

DAMAGE REPORT: The first of these was the Damage Report on which was listed all the commodities which had suffered damage before they got to their transport. Damage had to be listed accurately as this report would form the basis of any legal proceedings brought by a dissatisfied importer against the condition of his goods. Items might have decayed or been poorly stowed or been subjected to adverse weather conditions – 'rolling and pitching of the vessel' – and damaged goods from these sources could not be attributed to the gangs. Ship surveyors had the function of distinguishing these types of damage for importers and the Damage Report was RML's assessment of the situation. Because of the importance of this document, it had to be signed by a senior officer from the ship who also had the duty to note down any particular points of damage he had seen.

RUMMAGE REPORT: The second large document was the Rummage Report, which effectively stated that a senior officer of the ship had gone round to all the 'London Spaces' on the ship and found them to be empty. This would mean inspecting, not only the holds which had had London bound cargoes but also any lockers or cupboards which had held items for London. Two items which spring to mind were juice essence and yeast.

Both were strong smelling and although placed in cans, they could not be risked in the main holds in case of contamination. The orange and grapefruit essence was usually held in deck lockers and were easy enough for the gangs to off-load. The yeast could have been stored anywhere away from the holds and could easily be overlooked particularly if it had been placed in one of the more obscure cupboards. In practice this cargo was never forgotten in my experience, mainly because of its associations; the yeast extract was stored in transit sheds for trans-shipment by other lines to Burma and India to help build up ex-prisoners from Japanese labour camps. No one forgot the yeast.

Some items would not have been touched by gangs at all: for example, the ship's mail was kept in one of the secure cabins and the senior officer acted as his own tally clerk when he personally made it over to the GPO delivery van which was sent down for each working ship. Like the Damage Report, the Rummage Report also had to be signed by the ship's officer, as it was he who had had to do the rummaging. Sometimes he forgot to go to more obscure 'spaces' and on one famous occasion actually forgot the mail, the reason for the Company's existence, which continued with the ship back to sea.

Finally there was a small Discrepancy sheet which noted shortfalls in items for different importers or goods left over or uncollected. These three documents were sent up to Head Office to RML's Claims Department for them to deal with. With the paperwork complete and the next ship on its way, all the locally held documents, tally cards and half completed books were put together to form that shipment's parcel. This was what was stored in the new Royal Mail Lines' factory; nothing was ever thrown away until, I am assuming, RML itself ceased to have a presence in the Royal Docks. Perhaps these records went back to Victorian times, perhaps only more recent but without the ships or the personnel this paperwork would now be the only expression of the Company's one hundred year presence in the Royal Docks. It would be nice to learn that at least some of these parcels had been preserved somewhere.

*   *   *

CABBAGE

If you had spent any length of time working in the docks it wouldn't be long before you heard the call of 'cabbage' barked out then echoed and re-echoed down the quays or through the sheds. Everyone's favourite over stewed vegetable, 'Cabbage' meant Customs Officer and when the cry went up it warned those within earshot that an officer was on the prowl. Suddenly everyone looked as if butter wouldn't melt.....

In 1946 my mother met her sister-in-law in the Barking Road while both were out shopping. Although they lived in neighbouring streets, since my father's death and my mother's remarriage, the families had grown apart. Now they shared a common tragedy for both had lost sons during the War and as they sympathised with each other's distress the idea of holding a joint memorial service in a local church seemed a sad but positive way to bring the families back closer together. At the time I was just back in Civvy Street and had a temporary job as a clerk at a local Tax Office but with a young family to support I urgently needed something more permanent. After the church service, at the reception, I fell into conversation with Uncle Ned - I hardly knew him – and he suggested working in the docks. My grandfather had run the stevedoring company of Charltons which had the Brocklebank Wells trade and with my father's early death and his later retirement, Uncle Ned now had control of the business. It was clear that he was managing the company quite well without input from our branch of the family but he suggested, he could get me more general work as an employer's nominee; perhaps as I knew about clerking and knew nothing of how the docks ran, offering my services as a tally clerk might be suitable. With most men still in the Forces, the docks were acutely short of personnel, getting in would be assured and I would find no shortage of work although I would only be casually employed. I can't say that I leapt at the idea but in those bleak post-War years with alternatives hard to find, I decided to give it a try.

There was an interview in the Minories where I was reminded that the work was casual but that 'dabbing on' was now in force during periods of unemployment I would be eligible for 'fall back' pay. Next I visited the Poplar branch of the TGWU to get my card, then the National Dock Labour Board to collect my brief permitting me to be an Ocean Steam Ship Tally Clerk. Not long after a letter arrived telling me to present myself for the first Call at 7-45am one Tuesday morning in February 1947. No particular dock was indicated, so I decided to 'present myself' at the nearest, the Royal Group, where after all our family connections lay.

From the 'Ferndale' I walked through No 9 Gate past the solid round faced policeman known, I later discovered, as 'Country Boy'. He was well known for his simple rustic manner but more significantly for being incorruptible. Many a seaman, fresh off a ship, would try to slip him half a crown to let them through – and no questions asked. Country Boy would just smile his bemused smile, direct his new acquaintance to the end of the queue and continue dealing with everyone in his slow, deliberate, imperturbable way.

Through the gate at 7-30, I was pointed in the direction of Barclay's Bank outside of which the tally clerks had their Call. Along from where I stood hundreds of men were milling about huddled against the cold and it was a shock to see how old they all looked. Youth of course was still in the Forces, where I had been for six years and I had rather forgotten about the rest of the populace. I was also shocked to see how poorly dressed they all were: ideas of City smartness and Naval correctness were rudely replaced by an array of ill fitting greatcoats – old Army, old Navy, old nondescript. This was the bitter winter of 1947 and for men who spent their days labouring outdoors keeping warm was imperative, with scant choice in what to wear. This unprepossessing crowd I was to discover were substantially the last generation of dockers who knew how to work according to the old disciplines.

At 7-45 I was outside the Bank and was surprised to discover that there were only six of us looking for work. We had just had time to learn that we were all new when we became aware of the presence of Dan Dunn of RML, the only representative that morning wanting clerks. We seemed to form an incongruous little band compared with the dockers along the road who, by this time had separated out, with gangs on the pavement grouped round their top hand and the ship workers and quay foremen taking up their pitches in the middle of the road where they began to call off their gangs.

Dan Dunn clearly hated the Call; the whole exercise of selecting men, he found an embarrassment and demeaning to both himself and the casual clerks. As he seemed unable to decide who he wanted or even how to go about it, I explained that we were all new and pretty clueless and were hoping for a lead from him. This seemed to concentrate his thinking and he promptly engaged me and the man standing next to me (George Coker), telling us to report to No7 Shed, then he hurried away to a more congenial environment. And that was it. Not sure what to do next I happened to glance again up the road and was surprised to see that the crowd had all but disbursed, each gang on their way to their place of work; within little more than five minutes, the apparent shambles of down and outs had been transformed into a clearly directed workforce. Following their lead George and I set off to find No 7 Shed. The nearest sheds to us were 31 and 33 and with them as our guide we walked down the length of the Royal Albert Dock, trying to come to terms with our new surroundings, until we found No 7. It had all proved fairly straightforward except the ship Dan Dunn had told us we would be working at was not there, nor in fact was anything remotely RML nearby. If we had misheard him there was the real prospect of us spending our first day wandering the vast complex that formed the Royal Group of Docks in the hope of stumbling across our ship by a process of elimination. Fortunately I had spotted a familiar face somewhere back along our route and in these unfamiliar surroundings all I could think to do was to track down my Uncle to see if he might know where our ship had gone. We found him without too much trouble, explained with some embarrassment our predicament and he suggested trying King George V - there was more than one No. 7 Shed it transpired - sending us back down past our place of Call and round to the next dock where eventually, at 9 o'clock we made contact with No 7 Shed KGV. To our relief the RML's

'*Gascony*' was berthed alongside. Ernie May, the ship's clerk told us to 'check the shed'.

The task of a tally clerk I knew was to count and record but such a job description took no account of what was being counted and where the counting took place. This first day I learnt that both factors were crucial in determining the nature of the work – unimaginable to someone late of Guthrie Chalmers, the Navy and the Tax Office. The basic rule for tallying, as for cargo handling, was that exports were measured by volume, imports by weight and as the '*Gascony*' was taking on cargo I was given a standard four foot rule to measure with.

'Checking the shed' turned out to mean measuring the volume of everything in it. Now if you are given a measuring stick you assume a greater level of accuracy than is perhaps warranted especially if you are a smartly dressed newcomer looking to make a good impression. The learning experience that day and for a while after was trying to understand the level of accuracy needed – and the reason for needing it. Ship's clerks and ship-workers tried to load according to the ship's itinerary with the first port to be visited having the most accessible cargo, the second, the next most accessible and so on. They also tried to cram items into every nook and cranny of a hold, while ensuring the ship was balanced and consignments not too widely dispersed. There were five holds already working when we arrived and goods were moving out – had been moving out – before George and I could see them never mind measure them. In most of the shed bays there were huge piles of jumble, each bay signifying a different port of call and men were snatching disparate items as the ship's clerk called for them. Most vividly from that first day I remember thousands of sheets of glass and tens of thousands of galvanised buckets. The glass was easy to measure from junior school maths but the buckets, for conscientious new arrivals, were a nightmare; all this equipment was desperately needed, we were told for re-stocking the garrisons in the West Indies. The buckets were originally in sets of eight, probably with an exporter's mark, though no one had explained this but as they were held together by particularly feeble twine, loose buckets were clattering all around us. As the shed gangs handled them the strings broke and men were grubbing around for any odd lengths to hold a few of them together; sets of two or three were as likely as eight. Most of that day we spent up high clambering over the jumble, just to find out what was there before it was raced away from our outstretched rulers. As a career move it wasn't looking too promising; the options were to go back to the labour exchange or keep counting. I counted.

The reason for tally clerks was to provide a disinterested record of cargo movements: import ship's clerks were far more skilled than I was at judging volumes of goods in a shed and hold spaces to stow them in. Shippers and stevedoring companies arranged their own teams of tally clerks and as only one collection of items made its way into one hold each day, in theory all records should agree, the situation clear cut. In practice records were frequently used to try to extract extra monies for the gangs and tally clerks could not help but become involved in disputes; this first job was a useful

218

introduction to the nature and priorities of dock work. I was tallying groups of buckets, nominally eight to a set out of the shed, many of which would have come apart by the time they got onto the quay. At the ship's side someone else was recording the items into the hold using his own laws of approximation and was arriving at an entirely different total. Future haggling was unavoidable.

Later I learnt to my satisfaction that what we two clerks had been asked to do was to attempt the impossible. In less chaotic circumstances additional shed tally clerks would have been taken on – maybe Dan Dunn didn't realise how many were wanted or perhaps he didn't like the look of the other newcomers. Whatever the reason George and I were trying to do the work of ten or twelve men; we had been engaged as port clerks and the normal procedure we discovered was that for each port on a ship's itinerary, two tally clerks would be employed to cover the items for that destination. So a ship travelling to six ports would need twelve port clerks in the shed to adequately monitor the goods out, which roughly balanced the number of clerks on the quay watching whatever goods went into their hold. Assuming that our failure to keep up with the loading was somehow down to our inexperience, we stayed on voluntarily that raw winter's evening working at last in relative quiet after the ship had finished for the day. We were able to spend our time clambering over heaps of exports to make some sort of sense of what we were dealing with. At nine o' clock, after twelve hours getting to know that unheated shed, we went home with lists of items, marks and volumes ready for the next morning's onslaught.

So, a quarter of a century earlier this, broadly, was the world my father had known.

*   *   *

ST MARY MAGDALENE'S

At lunch times as a restorative, I often used to cycle back to St. Mary's churchyard. In the peace and over a marmalade sandwich I would spend half an hour hoping to discover my father's grave. In truth that never was likely as it was a pauper's grave and the records it seems had been destroyed in the Blitz. Now it's a nature reserve.

A tally clerk taken on at the Call got work where he could and in my six years as a casual clerk I worked for companies both large, like Royal Mail Lines, and relatively small like my Uncle Ned's, Charltons. Old hands like Ernie Monk were quick to show us new arrivals how to make the most of our engagement whatever the company. It meant being prepared to stay on after six thirty when the sheds shut, to complete our day's returns using the cubby hole at No 4 hold as an office. These were cold, comfortless mast housings rarely bigger than a broom cupboard but they did have the virtue of a flat surface to work off. The two hours spent here brought the week's pay from around £6 to £9-4s-6d. It meant a twelve hour day, mostly spent out in the elements but the take home pay was better than many permanent staff received and this was reason enough for many tally clerks to reject offers of full time posts. In working these extra hours it also had the incidental advantage of demonstrating to ship's clerks that you weren't frightened of paperwork.

I have already mentioned that my first office work for RML when still casually employed, was as an export planning clerk. The work was fiddly involving filling up an outline schematic elevation of a ship's hold with little coloured boxes, a job that permanent staff were keen to pass on to a casual worker. For the stevedore loading a ship there was always an element of thinking on one's feet and it was not always the case that the proposal of where an item would be stowed when still in the shed, was in fact where it ended up. People on the other side of the Atlantic needed to know precisely where to go to get their imports and a planning clerk had to balance a methodical, detailed administrative role with the more energetic commitment to visiting each hold and noting where goods had actually been stowed. Errors could waste a lot of time and prove very expensive for shippers. The advantage though for a tally clerk was that he could get indoors away from the weather and if he could find a space in one of RML's offices somewhere, he'd have access to a toilet - usually at the annual rent shed.

Like all casual employees tally clerks tended to follow one firm, shipper or stevedoring company and from my first office engagement I found myself on Ernie May's list. Permanent staff that regularly had to engage men at the Call used to make their own informal list of clerks whose work in the past they had found satisfactory. I was already on various lists as a tally clerk but taking on a casual employee to handle some of the more meticulous work for a company needed careful consideration; with Ernie May's recommendation office work became more frequent. I got to know people, the paperwork and the way Royal Mail Lines did things; it made sense to take work from them when it was offered and I naturally got to know other casual clerks who regularly worked for the Company.

As men left the forces the number of tally clerks gradually outgrew our place of Call in front of Barclay's Bank and we moved to the railway tracks behind the meat shed along from the police station and the mortuary – unedifying but serviceable. By this time the Call had become more organised with union stewards mustering men away from the place of engagement and only at 8:15 when they blew their whistles were we allowed to cross over to vie for work with us on the tracks, engagers on the platform. At times when work was scarce, those more desperate for money would run to get a job, I never did but then I didn't experience the dark days before 'fall back' pay. As times became easier there were also men who deliberately held back so that if all the work was taken they could 'dab on' at the Box to entitle them to fall back pay then if they were more enterprising go off to their market stall or painting and decorating jobs. Officially men had to return to the Box during the afternoon to get a second stamp but in practice if it was obvious that no more work was going to come along, they could get two stamps in the morning then spend the whole day on their second income.

It became apparent fairly quickly just what a mixed bag tally clerks were, there seemed to be 'ex' of every other trade or profession: ex-teachers, ex-insurance salesmen, ex-civil servants as well as old or incapacitated dockers, all restless souls unable to settle to the routine of regular employment. In fact during the time of the Barkley's Bank Call, anyone turning up was offered work, such were the labour shortages at the time, and this simply added to an already diverse mix.

One of the very best tally clerks was Les Bradshaw who was a formidable number cruncher, whether at converting between American short tons and Imperial Measure or at cards. He was too bright to be a tally clerk and too restless to be anything else, he liked the variety and the freedom the job gave. He worked regularly for RML and as a consequence I got to know him and his endless series of hobbies, very well: when clothes rationing ended he took up dress making and as the period coincided with the 'New Look', he made a costume for his wife on a newly purchased sewing machine. It was the first 'New Look' in Rotherhithe. He took up gardening for a while but lost interest once he learnt the Latin names, then there was photography, classical music, fishing and wine making. Each time he bought all the equipment, studied it until he felt he understood the subject then dropped it. He couldn't be anything other than a tally clerk.

George Darkin was an ex-labourer in his seventies, too old for manual labour, deaf and pig-headed. He was always chewing something and had a mouth full of rotten teeth. He was already at retirement age when the War started but kept working and had the misfortune to be in 3/5 Shed King George V when it was bombed. He was patched up but was found to be profoundly deaf but this didn't stop him being sent around the country for the rest of the War tallying whatever made it back to Britain. Post-War employment appeared to be more of a rest cure for him and it seems as if he was only kept on out of deference to his age and service to the docks. He only worked exports and if you had to work with him as a port clerk, as I occasionally did, it was an awkward experience. He would say at two o'clock "Right, we're off home now, we'll do the rest tomorrow", and you couldn't argue with him, he was too deaf and cantankerous. If you went home the goods that you were supposed to be monitoring in the shed would be down holds by the following morning and you had an impossible task trying to trace them and to tally the rest of the shed's contents. It was easier to agree with him, put your coat on, shout and point that you were going out by a different gate, wave him goodbye then get back to work. If anyone asked where George was, the stock answer was to say he was taking a nap. One of the disadvantages of being a casual employee was that you had no choice in deciding who you were going to work with.

But George wasn't the oldest, there was one tally clerk known as 'Tom' who was in his eighties and he had been sixty years or more in the docks by the early fifties. He had had a formidable reputation as a gang leader and seemed to get by still on the strength of it. He was recognised as a significant link in the tradition of the docks – and tradition, community and loyalty were important then. He would be sat down by a hatchway, a pencil and docket would be put in his hands and he was told to tally the goods as they came over. At the end of the day he would be told "Right that's the last one, Tom" and what happened in between was anyone's guess.

Wally Stride was at the opposite end to the intellectual spectrum to Les Bradshaw. He was extremely conscientious and tried hard but he could not understand importers' marks, which unfortunately was largely what tallying was all about. If an importer had his own device, normally it was noted down on the sheet with the types and quantities off-loaded under that mark. They didn't mean a thing to him. On a tally sheet he would get four listings to everyone else's twenty or thirty and he would have to draw the mark huge, covering the whole sheet of paper and then add everything else written on the case: 'Fragile', 'This way up', 'Del Monte', etc. "Well you said put it all down and that's what I'm doing". He could not be told it wasn't necessary, it just confused him. Needless to say he was kept off general cargo as much as possible. He would hold up the off-loading as he slowly counted everything that appeared on the set board, gangs could threaten him but he was too simple to understand and all they could do was complain to their office. He lived with his mum until she died then he lived on his own. He wore the same mac everyday whatever the weather all the time he worked in the docks, he never changed it. He had a brother in the docks but poor Wally, through no fault of his own, was an embarrassment to him and he tried to keep his distance. Actually, shipping companies came to like Wally because no matter what the cargo, he could not be bribed, he wasn't bright enough to fiddle and shippers knew that his records were meticulously correct if laboriously constructed.

When I was offered permanent employment as a ship's clerk, the allure of a secure, pensioned post proved too strong and I left the free-wheeling world of the tally clerks. The work moved from monitoring cargoes to monitoring men and needed a much broader appreciation of what was happening as a ship was off-loaded. In this new role I needed time to consider how the ship was discharging and I would frequently stay late, pleased to have an office, of sorts – actually a decrepit wooden shed - to work in. Once manual work had stopped for the day and the transit sheds were locked, the clamorous activity of the docks died away. I would often have the place to myself and by the half light of our single bulb, would spend a couple of hours making sure that I understood the next day's work: times and sequencing, gangs and cargoes, lighters and grain machines. As the docks grew quieter and a dingy silence settled over the room, the rats would appear crawling through holes and broken panes and over the stick furniture. I was able to work with them at a distance but as they grew bolder I needed a deterrent, more to bolster my spirits than to seriously trouble their activities. There was an old sabre which permanently occupied a corner of the shed - I suppose it would be called an antique these days - left by someone unknown perhaps decades before and I kept it by me on these night watches. When the rats became too confident, I would clatter it against the newly installed Canadian stove and watch them scurry back into the darkness. For a brief moment there would be a stillness to take on another day's docks at work.

*   *   *

OMELETTES

For a while after the Second World War one thing you didn't want was a stranger bumping into you, tapping you on the side and saying something like "Oh, sorry mate, how're yer doin' ?" It meant three things: eggs were becoming more commonplace, there was a shipment of them somewhere in the docks and in your pocket there were the ready scrambled makings of an omelette.

The following images are taken from miscellaneous documents left by my father. For the most part they are incidental to the text but may be of interest.

The first group are standard Royal Mail Lines publicity material and a menu from one of the (Company subsidised) *Andes* cruises available to employees.

The photographs of the working docks are taken from a series of publicity cards distributed by the Port of London Authority and these particular examples were used to brighten RML's main dock office. My father saved them when the office closed and my thanks to Martin Garside and the PLA for kind permission to include them here.

The extracts from the working book are something of a mystery as the book does not appear to fit the list of documents discussed in the main text and the hand writing is not my father's. There are details however which may be of interest. This is the only direct evidence I have that RML ever imported goods into the Royal Docks – the rest is just memory.

Finally there is an expanded image of Jack Blackman's 'Blue' Union Minute Book referred to on p39.   MES

From an undated leaflet (1960?) listing the fleet and ports visited by RML

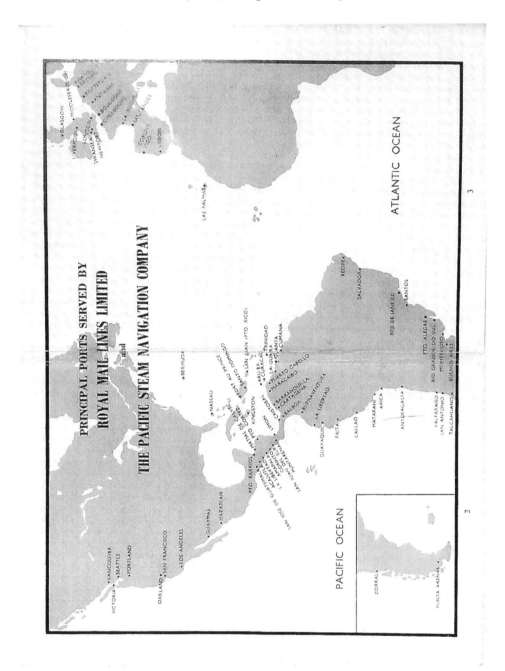

The preferred image of RML as seen from Royal Mail House

R.M.S. "HIGHLAND BRIGADE" 14,500 TONS GROSS. Royal Mail Lines passenger service from United Kingdom to Spain, Portugal, Canary Islands, Brazil, Uruguay and Argentina.

R.M.S. "DURANGO" 9,800 TONS GROSS
Royal Mail Lines' Cargo/Passenger Service between United Kingdom and Brazil and River Plate.

From a series of PLA publicity photographs, probably late 1950s/early '60s

'Z' Shed centre bottom with the three RML annual rent sheds opposite

Potentially self-powered cranes in practice were usually towed to site by tug

The 'London Mammoth' floating crane in King George V Dock

The 'Glenorchy' locking in from the Thames to King George V Dock

233

Bulk sugar being worked by grabs into Tate & Lyle barges

235

Floating grain machine discharging bulk grain into lighters

Note pallet hooks correctly placed! (See page 87, MR WARWICK)

239

'Brothers' loading crated car parts for export to New Zealand

241

Two Tugs bringing a South African vessel up stream to the Royal Docks

243

64 h.   "TWEED"   @ R. PLATE.

Berthed 4.13 a.m. 11th July, 1955. (Monday).
No. 2 Shed, Royal Victoria Dock.

Draft F. 21' 6"
        A. 23' 6"   Om. 645.
        M. 22' 6"

                Meat   General
Tonnage   902   4696.

Commenced 8 a.m. 12th July, 1955.
Final 5.15 pm. 25d July 1955

1 OFFICER	18th July				
1 WATCHER.	to 21st July.	6/4	4	8L 3/6	0 - 9 - 4
					0 - 8 - 9
1 OFFICER	24th July.	8a.m. to		9/-	1 - 18- 3.
1 WATCHER		7 p.m.	.11	4/6	1 - 0 - 3.

all port charges except 5-7 p.m. 24th officer.
Watcher " " " 21st

CUSTOMS AND EXCISE ACCOUNTS (OVERTIME).

1 OFFICERS 1 WATCHER	12th JULY	6/4	1	8/- 3/6	0 - 2 - 0 0 - 1 - 2
1 OFFICER	13th JULY 22nd JULY	6/4	2.	8/-	0 - 1 - 8 0 - 2 - 0.
1 OFFICER 1 WATCHER.	14th JULY 15th JULY.	6/4	2.	8/- 3/6	0 - 3 - 4 0 - 3 - 6.
1 OFFICER 1 WATCHER	17th JULY.	6 a.m. to 5 p.m.	9	9/- 4/6	2 - 0 - 6 1 - 0 - 3.

DECK CARGO TONNAGE.

REGISTERED TONNAGE.

~~QUAY AND SHED SPACE AGREEMENT.~~

~~No. 22 SHED TILBURY DOCK. 17th 7/9 1940 @~~
~~4/-.~~

QUAY AND SHED SPACE AGREEMENT.

Nos. 1 & 2 Sheds, Roy. Vic. Dock. 5424 sqs. yds @ 3/-

3 weeks = £46 - 16 - 9.   £15 · 12 " 3.

HIRE OF CRANES   ~~£46 · 16 · 9~~ 324-18-10

WATCHMANS ATTENDANCE   £10 - 4 - 0

OVERTIME   7 - 5 - 7.

CANTEEN FACILITIES   20 · 0 - 0

1024

"HIGHLAND BRIGADE" R. PLATE.

Berthed 2-19 p.m. 19ᵈ October 1955. (Wednesday)
@ 25/27 Shed Royal Albert Dock.
Draft. F. 25' 0"
      A. 26' 0"   Cil. 368 Tons
      M. 25' 6"

Tonnage. 3303 Meat.   368 Fruit   112 Gen

Commenced. 8-0 am. 20ᵈ October, 1955.
           5-10
Final. 7-0 pm. 2ⁿ November 1955

Shifted from 25/27 Shed   07-35 · 20/10/55
All fast 29 Shed. R.A.D. 07-55 · 20/10/55.

Shifted from 29 Shed.   6·54pm - 21/10/55.
All fast 'Z' Shed. R. Vic: Dk. 8·07pm · 21/10/55 ·

Customs & Excise Accounts (overtime)

1 OFFICER -					8/-	8 - 0	
1 WATCHER	20/10/55	8am - 7pm	1		3/6	3 - 6	
1 OFFICER	21-25 Oct.	6 ~ 7	3		8/-	12 - 0	P.C
1 WATCHER	2 Nov				3/6	5 - 3	P.C
1 OFFICER			6		9/-	1 - 7 - 0	P.C
1 WATCHER	23/10/55	8am - 2pm	6		7/6	9 - 0	
1 OFFICER	25/10/55	5/6	1		8/-	8 - 0	

Certificate of 1 Deck cargo Tonnage

Registered Tonnage   8554·78

Deck cargo   137·54

OPEN DK 106·15 TONS   8692·32

D/Bs 30·80 "

B470. A. 755. 5880.	Overtime	12 - 1 - 10
" " " 5881.	Hire of cranes	18 - 9 - 7
B420. A. 755. 2341.	Overtime	14 - 10 - 3
	Canteen	10 - 0 - 0

1094.

"DURANGO"   R. Plate.

Berthed 5-52pm. 4ᵈ November 1955 (Friday)
@ 'A' Shed. Royal Victoria Dock.
DRAFT. F. 23' 4"
         A. 24' 0"   Oil. 659·85.
         M. 23' 8"

TONNAGE   5002 Meat.   143 GEN.

Commenced 8·0 A.M. 5ᵈ November, 1955.
Final ~~11·30 A.M.~~ NOON November, 1955

Left 'A' Shed. Royal Victoria Dock. 6-30pm 15/11/55
All fast No. 29 Shed. R. Albert Dock. 7-30p~ 15/11/55

Customs & Excise Accounts (overtime)

1 OFFICER —				8/-	8 - 0 .	
1 WATCHER.	20/10/55	8am - 7pm	1	3/6	3 - 6 .	
1 OFFICER	21 - 25 Oct.	6 "" 7	3	8/-	12 - 0 .	P.C
1 WATCHER	2 Nov			3/6	5 - 3 .	P.C
1 OFFICER	23/10/55	8am - 2pm.	6	9/-	1 - 7 - 0	P.C
1 WATCHER.			6	1/6	9 - 0	P.C
1 OFFICER.	25/10/55	5/6.	1	8/-	8 - 0	

Certificate of Deck Cargo Tonnage.

Registered Tonnage   8554 · 78

Deck Cargo   137 · 64

OPEN DK 106·75 TONS   8692 · 32
D/Bs   30·50 ""

B470. A. 755. 5880.	Overtime	£2 - 1 - 10.
" " " 5881.	Hire of cranes.	18 - 9 - 9.
B420. A. 755. 2341.	Overtime.	14 - 10 - 3.
	Canteen.	10 - 0 - 0

249

103

"EBRO"   Jamaica & Bermuda

Berthed 4-33 p.m. 23rd October, 1955 (Sunday)
@ No. 2 Shed. Royal Victoria Dock.
Draft.   F. 23' 9"
         A. 25' 10"   Oil. 488 Boiler
         M. 24' 8½"   91 Diesel.

Tonnage.   6632 Wt.   8233 Mst.

        Commenced 8.0 am. 24ᵈ October 1955.
        Final 3-15 pm. 31st October 1955

Customs & Excise Accounts. (OVERTIME)

1 OFFICER	25/10/55	6/7 p~	1	8/-	4 - 0	P.C
3 WATCHERS	25-28/10/55	6/7 pm.	3	3/6	10 - 6	
1 OPPACER		6/7 pm	3	5/-	7 - 7	P.C
1 WATCHMNR	26-27/11/55	6/7 p~	2	3/6	7 - 0	
1 OFFICER	23/10/55	5/6 pm.	1	9/-	9 - 0	

Certificate of Deck Cargo Tonnage.

Registered Tonnage.   8554 · 98

Deck Cargo.   137 · 54

OPEN D/G. 106·74 Ton.   8692 · 32
D/G.   00·00 "

Registered Tonnage.   3250 · 37

Deck Cargo (TWEEN DECKS)   213 · 00
                                     3463 · 37

Quay and Shed Space Agreement.

No. 2 Shed. Royal Victoria Dock 3345 q yd @

2 weeks   3/- per q yd - £ 9 - 12 - 5 per week.

B420.V.476.3939.   Hire of cranes. £172 - 3 - 0

                    Electric Lights   4 - 4 - 10

                    Watchman   2 - 8 · 0

                    Overtime   18 · 10 ·

251

105.T.

"SAMANCO"   W.C.S.A.

Berthed 5.36 p.m. 24ᵈ October, 1955. (Monday).
@ No.15 Shed. Royal Albert Dock.
DRAFT. F.
        A.   Oil.
        M.

TONNAGE. 5590 Wt.   4996 Msr.

Commenced: 8·0 a.m. 25ᵈ October, 1955.
          Final. 2-30pm. 1ˢᵗ November 1955
Left No.15. 7·0 pm. 27/10/55. All fast No.13 Shed. 8·30 pm.
Left No.13 Shed. 6-50 a.m. 28/10/55. All fast No.20 Shed. 7-30 a.m. 28/10/55.
Left No.20 Shed. R.A.D. 6-30 pm 31/10/55
All fast 'D' Shed. R.V.D. 7·45 pm. 31/10/55.

| 1 OFFICER | 24/31 - 13-55 | 6/7 ·pm | 3 | 8/- 2/6 | - 5 - 2 | P.C |
| 1 WATCHER | " 1/11/55 | | | | 2 - 4 | P.C |

252

Customs & Excise Accounts (OVERTIME).

1 OFFICER	25/10/55.	6pm - 7pm	1	8/-	4 - 0	P.C.
1 WATCHER				3/6	1 - 9	P.C.
1 OFFICER	26/10/55	6pm - 7pm	1	8/-	4 - 0	P.C.
1 WATCHER				3/6	3 - 6	
1 OFFICER	27/10/55	6pm - 7pm	1	8/-	4 - 0	P.C.
1 WATCHER				3/6	3 - 6	
1 OFFICER	30/10/55	8am to 7pm	11	9/-	1 - 16 - 0	P.C.
1 WATCHER.				4/6	18 - 0	P.C.

CERTIFICATE OF DECK CARGO TONNAGE

REGISTER TONNAGE.	3758 · 92 .
DECK CARGO	196 · 76
	3955 · 68

D B TANKS 19·54.

S/ DECKS 176·76.

B.470. A. 767. 5885.	Hire of Cranes.	£73 - 3 - 0.
" "	6 - 5 - 5
B 520. A. 767. 1387	Hire of Cranes.	62 - 7 - 5
Canteen	10 - 0 - 0 .
B.420. A. 767. 2342	Hire of Cranes.	6 - 3 - 2

80~

"LOCH RYAN"   @ NORTH   R. 4008.

Berthed 1846 hrs 17th August 195

No. 28 Shed, Royal Albert Dock.   T. 2988.6.0.4.

DRAFT. F. 27' 10"

A. 28' 2"   OIL.   5"

M. 28' 0"   11

	Lt	Mar	Gr
Tonnage	3356	4394	300

24.8.55.	Hold.
25.8.55.	"
26.8.55.	"
24.8.55.	"
26.8.55.	"
25.8.55.	"

Commenced 8 a.m. 18th August, 1955
Final 1.0 p.m. 28th August, 1955

24.8.55.	Hold.
"	"
"	"
25.8.55.	Hold.
"	"
26.8.55.	"
"	"
"	"
"	"
25.8.55.	"
26.8.55.	"

COPY

407. 13. 475. 1587.
1618.

"LOCH RYAN"

TRIMMING ACCOUNT.

@ 1/4d per ton	199 - 4 - 5
increase 10%	19 - 18 - 5

OVERTIME TRIMMING

4.	1 min meal hr @ 153/6d per min	7 - 13 - 6
3.) 5)	1390 meal qrs @ 64/6d per 100 qrs	44 - 16 - 7
4.) 5)))	2 ord O/time min hrs @ 76/9 per min	7 - 13 - 6
3	641 ord O/T qrs @ 32/3d per 100 qrs	10 - 6 - 9
	increase	7 - 1 - 0

ALLOWANCES TO CORNPORTERS.

4. " " "	Working overhead(8 men each 1£) loss of output(12 men ea 10/-) Dunnage (8 men each 1 hr) 2 Tanks No grids (8 men ea 2 hrs) (8men ea 1 hr)	15 - 16 -5 5 1 - 11 - 1 3 - 2 - 2 1 - 11 - 1
3. " " " "	Caked grain on boards.Working over lead(8 men each 2£)Loss of output (6 men each £1) Caked grain on boards(8 men ea 1 hr) Working over lead(8 men each £1) Loss of output (6 men each 10/-)	24 - 17 - 3 1 - 11 - 1 12 - 8 - 7
5.	Dunnage on seperation cloth (8 men each 1 hr)	1 - 11 - 1
"	Working over lead(8 men each £2) Loss of output (6 men each £1)	24 - 17 - 3
3. "	Shifting pipes to facilitate dis- charge Lighterage Gratuities	2 - 12 - 10 1 - 7 - 0
		£388 - 0 - 0

"LOCH RYAN" @ NORTH PACIFIC.

Berthed 1846 hrs 17th August 1955. (Wednesday)
No. 28 Shed, Royal Albert Dock.

DRAFT. F. 24' 10"
       A. 28' 2"   OIL. 577 Boiler.
       M. 28' 0"   110 Diesel.

	Wt	Msr	Grain.
Tonnage	3356	4394	3000

Commenced 8 a.m. 18th August, 1955.
Trial 1.0 p.m. 28th August, 1955.

April 9ᵗʰ 1948

Bro Mott could Bro Rutter tell him when and Were
was it agreed By the Two Unions that men should
Work Perkins and Homers Barges with Fixed Beam
on Butter. firm Port Line No 4 Hatch
Bro Rutter Junior said that agreement was a
Gentleman agreement
Resolution in future No firm should work any
Barge with a fixe Beam this is Refered to all
Lighterage firm Moved By Bro Fadden Second by Bro Rutter
            Put to a Vote Carried

Bro Mott asked Question can he Branch Bro
Griffiths of No 5 Branch Now Port Manager
Case He ordered men to Work when his own
Society was out on Strike Bro Troy Second Resolution
            Put to a Vote Carried

Bro Rutter said the Strike was caused By Mr
Platt of the White Union, Platt was called By
White Union official at Transport House to state
his Case Why he cause a General Stoppage

      Branch   Closed   9 30

BIBLIOGRAPHY

London Docks: 1800 – 1980 A civil engineering history   I. Greeves

London Docks   John Pudney

Twelve Decades of Maritime History 1839 – 1961 from 'The Journal of Commerce' October 7th 1960

Atlantic and Pacific Breezes..Royal Mail 125 Years   ed. B.P. Shaw

By Royal Charter: The Steam Conquistadores   John E. Lingwood

London's Lost Riverscape: A Photographic Panorama   Chris Ellmers and Alex Werner

Printed in Great Britain
by Amazon